TRIALS & TRIUMPHS

BY LEE BENSON
AND DOUG ROBINSON

RESEARCH AND APPENDIX
BY BOB WOOD

Deseret Book Company
Salt Lake City, Utah

"If you can meet with triumph and disaster,
And treat those two impostors just the same ... "
— "If," by Rudyard Kipling

Library of Congress Cataloging-in-Publication Data

Benson, Lee, 1948–
    Trials and Triumphs : Mormons in the Olympic Games / Lee Benson
    and Doug Robinson.
       p.   cm.
    Includes index.
    ISBN 0-87579-628-1
    1. Mormon athletes—United States—Biography. 2. Olympics—
History. 3. Winter Olympics—History. I. Robinson, Doug, 1955–
II. Title.
GV697.A1B46 1992
796.08'8283—dc20
[B]   92-9066
                                           CIP

Printed in the United States of America

10   9   8   7   6   5   4   3   2   1

CONTENTS

FOREWORD

For me, the apex of my athletic career came on two late January evenings when I reveled in the accomplishments of my teams — the Oakland and Los Angeles Raiders — as the world champions of professional football. Yet even as I admire my Super Bowl rings, I can't help but think of the words of Duane Thomas. The enigmatic running back of the Dallas Cowboys was questioned as to the magnitude of such a contest. His simple yet profound reply was, "If this game is so big, how come they're playing it again next year?" John McKay, the former University of Southern California football mentor, once told his very nervous team prior to heading out for the Rose Bowl: "Hey, remember there are a billion Chinese who couldn't care less!"

I mention these anecdotes only because, in my opinion, they are *not* applicable to the Olympic Games. Every four years the entire world comes together to witness a sporting spectacle unrivaled since it began back in ancient Greece. A few years ago I was at a luncheon featuring Bill Toomey, the 1968 gold medalist in the decathlon, and tears came to my eyes as I spoke regarding the accomplishments of this man. There is something about the Olympic experience that transcends the normal "sports-thought" we incur every night watching ESPN.

This book is not simply an anthology of victors, a "golly-gee-whiz" look at champions in an effort to make us feel "warm and fuzzy" inside. In fact, it includes very few gold medalists. In this day and age of voluminous media access, we flip the

remote control from contest to contest, viewing the partici-
pants in a somewhat dehumanizing vein, almost like the stiff
characters that move across the screen in a Nintendo game.
Lee Benson and Doug Robinson succeed in personalizing the
struggles inherent in the quest for athletic success—the hours
of preparation and the sacrifices required, not to mention the
gamut of emotions experienced.

This is an edifying look at the athletes who have achieved
the distinction of being Olympians, true to the credo espoused
in Doctrine and Covenants 104:13 about being stewards over
their earthly blessings.

Walter Pater once stated: "Not the fruit of experience, but
the experience itself is the end. A counted number of pulses
only is given to us of a variegated, dramatic life. How shall we
pass most swiftly from point to point, and be present always
at the focus where the greatest number of vital forces unite in
their purest energy? To burn always with this hard, gemlike
flame, to maintain this ecstasy, is success in life."

May you be uplifted and inspired by the people in this
book who understood and acted upon Pater's words.

TODD J. CHRISTENSEN

PREFACE

Ever since Alma Wilford Richards boarded the USS *United States* in New York Harbor in the summer of 1912 bound for the Games of the IVth Olympiad in Stockholm, Sweden, Mormon athletes have been chasing Olympic dreams. To date, more than 60 have participated in the Summer Olympics, in any number of sports. This book is about them. It details who they are, what dreams they chased, and when, where, and how they chased them.

The stories of a dozen of these Olympians are presented as separate chapters. They reflect the values of sacrifice, hard work, dedication, persistence, and self-discipline common to them all — just as they illustrate the fine line between triumph and disaster, between winning and losing, between a gold medal and no medal at all, that every Olympian has to walk.

Every effort was made to chronicle all Mormons who have participated in the Summer Games since the beginning of the modern Olympiads in 1896, including those who became converts after their Olympic competitions were over. If there are omissions, they are unintentional and regretted.

ACKNOWLEDGMENTS

There is no way this book could have been written without the considerable help of many people. Of course, there were the featured athletes themselves—L. Jay Silvester, Paula Jean Pope, Henry Marsh, Jay Lambert, Paul Cummings, Ed Eyestone, Clarence Robison, Doug Padilla, Robert Detweiler, Peter Vidmar, and Karl Tilleman. They graciously interrupted their busy schedules to endure long hours of questions, and they did so with patience and thoughtfulness. Their material was greatly enhanced by the reflections of numerous family members, friends, and coaches. Also, thanks to the Deseret News for use of its photographs and its library, which provided a wealth of background information. Further thanks to the Brigham Young University library archives; to Randi Greene, who assisted our efforts in locating Mormon Olympians; to Jude King; and to Todd Christensen. Finally, thanks to the people at Deseret Book—Sheri Dew, Richard Erickson, Jack M. Lyon, and Patricia J. Parkinson.

ALMA RICHARDS

BY LEE BENSON

The grave sits on a bluff overlooking the town. To all outward appearances it is indistinguishable from the graves around it, another testament to a person's life. But beyond that, it is a testament that even if you were the strongest, the fastest, the biggest, and the quickest; even if your athleticism did take you all over the world, where you taught kings to say Parowan correctly ("Pair-a-one," not "Pair-a-wahn"); even if Jim Thorpe himself was thankful you were a late-bloomer — still, in the end, the best finish is also where you started.

It was his last request: to be buried in his hometown, in Parowan, Utah. They held a funeral in Orange, California, where he lived the better part of his life, where he was a one-man gang for the Los Angeles Athletic Club, where he got his law degree, where he taught school, where he retired. But they buried him in Parowan, Utah, not far from the fields where he chased the rabbits that kept him humble and first got him in shape.

Say this about Alma Wilford Richards: He never forgot where he came from.

★   ★   ★

He stood in the middle of the Olympic Stadium in Stockholm feeling as alone as you can feel in front of 22,000 people. These were the Olympic Games of 1912, and Alma Richards was competing for the United States in the running high jump. He looked around at the other contestants, 57 in all, representing some 20 countries, and wondered where he stood with them. He had never competed overseas before. He had competed only twice outside of his native Utah, and then only in the competitions to earn a spot on the United States Olympic Team.

It was hot, close to 90 degrees, and he wore a floppy felt cap, partly to keep the sun away from a case of red-eye he had picked up on the voyage over the Atlantic Ocean on the *Finland,* and partly because he believed it brought him luck. On his first jump, at five feet nine inches, he cleared the height with the cap on — and it stayed.

As the bar moved up, going past six feet, fewer and fewer of the original 57 competitors moved with it. And still Richards was alive. He tried not to think, just to act and react, as both the pressure and the bar went up.

The entire Olympic movement, for that matter, was on the rise in July of 1912 in Stockholm, Sweden. More athletes (2,547) from more nations (28) than ever before had congregated for only the fifth Summer Games of the modern era. The revival of the Olympic Games had begun 16 years earlier, in Athens, Greece, after a 1,503-year layoff. In 1896 the motto of Citius, Altius, Fortius (Faster, Higher, Braver) was reinstated, and the youth of the world were called to reassemble for the first time since A.D. 393. The hosting Greeks proceeded to live a personal nightmare of sorts as they failed to approximate any of the athletic dominance they had once exercised over the rest of the world. Much had changed in 15 centuries.

But when Spyridon Louis, a postal messenger from Athens, won the marathon, the final event of the Games, face was saved, and, for all intents and purposes, the Olympics were born again.

The Games of the 2nd Olympiad in 1900, the Games of the 3rd Olympiad in 1904, and, especially, the Games of the 4th Olympiad in 1908, held in London, slowly but surely gained momentum for the concept — a showcase and showdown of the world's best amateur athletes. By the time King Gustav V of Sweden secured the 1912 Games for Stockholm, the Olympics had the world's attention.

The United States, while still exercising political isolationism at home, nonetheless embraced the Olympic movement enthusiastically. The team the U.S. sent to Stockholm in 1912 was the biggest of all the nations' teams, bigger even than Sweden's.

So it was no surprise when the high jump bar was raised to 189 centimeters, about six feet, two inches, that Alma Richards looked around and saw that of the six jumpers left, five were Americans. They were joined by one German.

Richards looked at his teammates — George Horine, H.J. Grumpelt, Jim Thorpe, and E.R. Erickson. He knew barely more about them than he did about the German, Hans Liesche.

Of the six, Horine stood out as a high jumper. The American collegiate champion from Stanford was the reigning world record-holder. At the U.S. Olympic Trials four weeks earlier at the track of Stanford University in Palo Alto, California, using the scissors style of the time (high jump rules in 1912 dictated that the head had to follow the body over the bar), he set a world record of six feet, seven inches.

As for Thorpe, the full-blooded American Indian had already won the pentathlon in these Olympics and was on his way to another gold medal in the decathlon. He was destined to be hailed as the World's Greatest Athlete no matter how he fared in these high jump finals.

As for Grumpelt, Erickson, and Liesche, Richards knew little more than that the four of them had this in common: They were yet to clear the bar standing at 189 centimeters.

Then Liesche went over, on his first try.

Horine, no surprise, followed.

Thorpe, Grumpelt, Erickson, and Richards all jumped, and all failed. A second time they jumped, with the same result. Suddenly it was getting even warmer in Stockholm.

For their third and final tries, Thorpe, Grumpelt, and Erickson all again bumped the bar and retired from the competition. It remained for Richards to either join them, or — as had been his habit at every height so far all day — come through on his last try.

He took a deep breath, remembered that he had jumped higher — his six-foot, three-inch jump at the U.S. Trials in Evanston, Illinois, for one good example — and, legs kicking high, gave it his best leap.

Now it was the German, the world record-holder, and Richards. The bar was raised to 191 centimeters, a fifth of an inch over six foot, three inches.

Almost before it had stopped vibrating, Liesche cleared it.

Horine and Richards missed twice each, then Horine, nursing a cold and wishing for all the world that he was back at Stanford, his alma mater, jumping in comfort, missed his final try.

Again Richards faced a third jump that meant either elimination or a new height for him and Liesche — in his case, a height he'd never cleared before. He tugged at his cap and sprinted down the runway . . . and now it was just he and the German. And he wasn't at all confident.

Since the start of the competition, Liesche had made it a habit to clear the bar at every height on his first jump; with

Richards it had been just the opposite. Leische was obviously an experienced jumper; Richards wasn't. And if you wanted to get technical, Berlin, Liesche's hometown, was a lot closer to Stockholm than was Parowan.

The officials moved the bar to 193 centimeters, an even six feet, four inches, and signaled for the two remaining jumpers to continue. The American was to jump first.

Seated next to the high jump pit were Horine, Thorpe, Erickson, and Grumpelt — Richards's competitors of a minute earlier, his rooting section now. "Go Dick," they implored, using a nickname they derived from Richards's last name.

But instead of jumping, Richards did a curious thing. Two curious things, really. First, he removed his cap for the first time all day. Next, he walked to the side of the field and, in full view of the 22,000 spectators, knelt down, bowed his head, and prayed.

"God," he said — and he recounted these words often in later years — "give me strength. And if it's right that I should win, give me strength to do my best to set a good example all the days of my life."

He got up, put his cap on, and returned to the runway. Horine, it was said, had tears in his eyes. Liesche was by now getting interested.

★　　★　　★

The road to Stockholm hadn't exactly been a straight one for Alma W. Richards of Parowan, Utah. Go back four years from the high jump finals in Stockholm and he didn't even know what a track meet was, or a track for that matter. Parowan didn't have one. Go back four years before that and he was an eighth grade grammar school dropout, resolved to ride the range forevermore on the back of his favorite horse.

Born in Parowan on February 20, 1890, to Morgan and Margaret Richards, Alma Wilford Richards was the ninth of

10 children. His father was 44 years old at the time of his birth, his mother 37. Morgan Richards met Margaret Adams when he was sent, upon direction from Brigham Young, in a covered wagon to Southern Utah after emigrating from Wales to Utah in 1854. A convert to the Church, Morgan Richards was, at various times, an Indian fighter, a Minuteman, a bishop, the manager of the Parowan Cooperative Mercantile & Manufacturing Company, and, in 1896, the first auditor of the State of Utah. Alma was six when the family moved to Salt Lake City so Morgan could begin his life in government.

The Richardses returned to Parowan in 1900. Morgan was anxious for the rural life, and Alma was with him on that score. He went through the motions of public schooling through eighth grade and then, at 14 and already approaching 6-foot-2 and 200 pounds, left school, a not uncommon occurrence in 1904.

While riding the range four years later, Alma returned to the path that would lead to formal education. One cold night he found himself in the railroad town of Lund, Utah. Bunks being at a premium in the town's only shelter, he was assigned to double up with a train passenger named Thomas Trueblood—Professor Thomas Trueblood, to be exact, from Michigan State University.

Trueblood and Alma found an immediate rapport, and instead of sleeping they talked long into the night, the young cowboy of his yearning for freedom, and the professor encouraging the 18-year-old to resume his studies so he could be genuinely free. "Get your education, and you can travel like me," he said as the train pulled out for California the next morning.

The impact thus made, Alma moved in with his sister, Margaret Anna, and her husband, Alfred Durham, in Beaver, Utah, and enrolled for the ninth grade at Murdock Academy, a boarding and college preparatory school 30 miles north of his hometown.

When the coaches at Murdock asked the 19-year-old Richards if he would like to come out for the track team in the spring of 1909, they had no idea they had just clinched the school's first-ever state championship—just as Alma Richards had no idea he was on his way to the Olympic Games.

In the state meet, held at the University of Utah on May 14, 1909, Murdock Academy shocked the Salt Lake High School, a perennial sports powerhouse and the premeet favorite, by outscoring Salt Lake 32–22. In winning the high jump and shot put and finishing second in the broad jump and pole vault—events he'd barely been introduced to—Richards scored enough points to claim the state championship all by himself. He was awarded the gold medal as the meet's most outstanding performer.

Richards moved on the next year to Provo to attend 10th grade at the Brigham Young High School, a program that was run in conjunction with Brigham Young University. There he came to the attention of Eugene L. "Timpanogos" Roberts, the head track and field coach at BYU.

After watching Richards attempt, and make, a high jump of 5 foot, 11 and one-half inches at BYU in the fall of 1911, Roberts composed himself enough to say that Richards, who was wearing his basketball uniform when he jumped, was the most gifted natural jumper he ever laid eyes upon, and with a little work on his technique he could be one of the top high jumpers in the world.

Richards took that as a compliment.

Roberts took it as a crusade.

He worked with the raw athlete all through the winter, encouraging him to set his sights on making the United States track team that would compete the next summer in the Stockholm Olympics—the Olympics was yet another new concept for Richards—and, when Roberts wasn't working on Richards's high jumping technique, he was going around town trying to drum up funds to send himself and his protégé to Northwestern University in Evanston, Illinois, to compete in the U.S. Olympic Trials the following May.

Roberts went to the banks, the feed stores, the businesses on Main Street, and they all turned him down. Finally, he was able to talk the BYU administration into a $150 donation, but that was barely enough money for one person to make the trip, not two.

When he put Alma on the train for Chicago, "Timpanogos" Roberts gave him a copy of his favorite poem, Rudyard Kipling's "If." If the coach couldn't go with him, Kipling could. On the two-day trip, Richards, away from home for the first time (if you didn't count wandering the range on his horse) memorized the poem—especially the part about "If you can fill each unforgiving minute/With sixty seconds worth of distance run,/Yours is the earth and everything that's in it,/And which is more, you'll be a man, my son."

At Northwestern, he knew no one. And no one knew him. But no sooner did he arrive than he went to the track and jumped six feet, two inches, just to shake off the train lag. Luckily, Amos Alonzo Stagg, the revered football coach at Chicago University and a member of the U.S. Olympic Selection Committee, was watching. Luckily, because after Richards won the competition the next day, with a jump of six feet, three inches, the sentiment in New York, where a handful of Olympic administrators were sifting through Trials results from three separate Trials competitions held concurrently at Stanford, Cambridge, and Northwestern, was that the jump by the unknown Richards was a "freak" and that he shouldn't be included on the Olympic team.

Stagg set them straight, said Richards was the most gifted natural jumper he'd ever seen, and told them they'd leave him off the team over his and his football team's dead bodies. A diplomatic compromise was reached when Richards was named as a "supplemental" member of the U.S. Team.

Supplemental or not, the sophomore from Brigham Young, *the high school sophomore,* was on his way to Stockholm.

★   ★   ★

His prayer over, Richards's mood changed. It changed considerably. "I felt as if the whole world was lifted off my shoulders," he wrote later. "My confidence returned completely. I thought of my folks, the BYU, Utah, my people, that I was representing our country against a fine athlete from another country."

He looked at the bar at the end of the runway, set now at an Olympic record height of six feet, four inches. He sensed the crowd, straining with its collective body English to help him to the height. He strode off confidently . . . and cleared the bar with a good inch to spare.

Now it was Hans Liesche's turn. The German took his mark, inhaled a deep breath, was about to take off . . . and stopped cold. He was distracted by a crowd that was suddenly on its feet, stomping and screaming.

The stretch run of the 800-meter final was underway, and on the far turn Tad Meredith, an American teenager, had sprinted past the pre-race favorite, Hans Braun of Germany. Liesche watched as Meredith, with his two teammates, Mel Shepherd and Ira Davenport, in tow, carried the United States to a gold-silver-bronze medal sweep. All three runners bettered the previous world record, held by Braun, who finished fourth.

After witnessing this upset of his countryman and teammate, Liesche turned his attention back to the business of the high jump. Or tried to. He ran down the runway and

Above: In 1919 in Paris, General John "Blackjack" Pershing awarded four medals to Lieutenant Alma Richards

Far left: Prior to the high-jump competition in Stockholm, Richards poses for the camera in his USA uniform

Left: Richards leaps over the bar during a dual for the world record with Clint Larson at BYU

leaped . . . and for the first time all day failed to clear the bar
on his first pass. He was doomed.

As Richards watched silently from the side of the runway,
Liesche missed on his next two attempts. When the bar clanged
off the standards on the last of the two, the jumper from
Parowan, Utah, who only two years earlier was jumping in the
Utah high school championships, who only three years earlier
had been chasing rabbits among the cedar trees in the red hills
surrounding his hometown, had claimed the first Olympic gold
medal ever won by a Utahn, a Mormon, and a Parowanian.
From Liesche, a gracious loser, he got two kisses — one on each
cheek.

After watching the tall American with the strange hat win
the Olympic gold medal, King Gustav of Sweden went to the
winner's podium. He stood at attention as the Star Spangled
Banner was played, then gave the bronze medal to Horine,
the silver medal to Leische, and, to Richards, the gold medal
and an olive wreath, which he draped around his neck.

The king, as it turned out, had a son, Gustaf Adolf, who
was an aspiring high jumper himself. After the medal ceremony, the king invited the American champion to his palace,
where he was introduced to the prince, and they circumvented
the language barrier by talking high jumping. For years, their
correspondence would continue across the oceans.

Upon his return to America, Richards and the American
team were accorded a rousing welcome. Their showing in Sweden had been a dominant one. The U.S. won more medals,
and more gold medals, than any other country. In New York
City, a ticker-tape parade in the team's honor was held along
Fifth Avenue and along Broadway, and a banquet was held
that night.

When Richards arrived at the Union Pacific railroad station in Provo, Utah, on August 22, he was greeted with a more
intimate welcome. As the *Provo Post* relayed in the next morn-

ing's edition: "Over a thousand people gathered at the Union
Passenger station shortly after 6 o'clock last night to welcome
Alma W. Richards, the world's champion high jumper, on his
return from the Olympic Games held at Stockholm, Sweden.
The Provo City Band was out and practically every auto owner
in the city took his machine to the station to join in the auto
parade scheduled to take place upon the arrival of the hero
of the hour."

In his speech at BYU, Richards thanked the town and the
school, and he dedicated his gold medal to his coach, "Timpanogos" Roberts. In conclusion, he said that for his next goal,
he was going to finish high school.

★   ★   ★

If ever there's been an example of success in one area
having a contagious effect on all other aspects of life, consider
what happened to Alma Richards, once an eighth grade dropout, in the wake of his Olympic gold medal performance in
Stockholm: First, he graduated with honors from Brigham
Young prep school, leaving with his degree in 1913. Next, he
was awarded a scholarship to Cornell University in Ithaca, New
York — not an athletic scholarship but an *academic* scholarship.

Cornell did say Richards could join the track team just the
same, which he did. And if there were any suspicions that his
competing days were over, now that he was 24 years old and
working toward a degree at one of America's most demanding
academic institutions, they were soon dashed. In the summer
of 1913 he won the national AAU Championship high jump;
in the International Intercollegiates (while still wearing BYU's
colors), he won the high jump and placed second in the broad
jump and discus; and by the spring of 1915, now fully uniformed
at Cornell, he won the high jump at the Penn Relays, setting
a national collegiate record of six feet, five inches.

By now, Richards was becoming something of a track and

field dynamo, not content with specializing in the high jump only — an event that he wasn't even entirely sure was his strongest.

When the National AAU Championships rolled around in the summer of 1915, held in San Francisco in conjunction with the World's Fair, he entered the 10-event decathlon. If Jim Thorpe, his roommate in international competitions immediately following the Olympics, could manage the 10-event, two-day grind, Richards thought he could too. He couldn't compete head-to-head against Thorpe, because he had become a professional football player, where he not only dominated the gridiron but got paid for it as well. The strict amateur rules of the day forbade the mixing of amateurs and professionals, and Thorpe's track and field days were long over.

Still, there were plenty of heirs anxious to become the next Jim Thorpe, chief of whom was C. Avery Brundage of the Chicago Athletic Association, an all-around athlete whose legacy in later years, as it would turn out, would be to crusade — as the head of the International Olympic Committee — against any form of professionalism in the Olympic Games.

In San Francisco, Brundage had no argument with Richards's amateurism. He was 25 years old, still in college, and had paid his own way to the meet. And, like Brundage, Richards had strong principles. Upon returning from Stockholm Richards had turned down a number of endorsement offers, including a $1,000 deal from a tobacco company. An avowed opponent of smoking (while his church attendance often waned, his dedication to the Word of Wisdom never did), Richards declined, saying, "I hope I never need money that badly."

After the two days of the decathlon were over, Brundage found himself a distant second, some 500 points behind Richards's 6,858 total.

"Alma Richards Wins Distinction of Being Best Athlete

in U.S." said the headline in the August 13 edition of the *San Francisco Chronicle.*

Of additional significance was the post-meet research done by track and field purists, who compared the caliber of the decathlon performances in San Francisco with the decathlon competition at the Stockholm Olympics. With the exception of the 100-meter dash and the high hurdles, which times were identical in both meets, the performances in San Francisco far exceeded those in Stockholm—where, by winning the decathlon gold medal, Jim Thorpe had been established as the finest athlete in the world.

In a comparison of Richards's and Thorpe's decathlons, Richards exceeded Thorpe's Olympic performance by nearly 1,000 points.

★   ★   ★

Thus the stage was set for Alma Richards to enthrone himself as the World's Greatest Athlete at the Olympic Games in 1916—except for one hitch: there was no Olympic Games of 1916. Instead, there was World War I. And instead of challenging Jim Thorpe's legacy, Richards challenged the Germans, reporting to General Pershing's Eighth Division in Europe.

It was a better time to be a soldier than an athlete, although Richards managed to find a track meet anyway. On June 1, 1919, as the war was winding down and the Huns were in retreat, the Army convened the American Expeditionary Force Track and Field Championships at Colombes Stadium in Paris.

Hundreds of the Army's best athletes entered the competition, including Lieutenant Richards, by now 29 years old. The meet lasted two days, and Richards, clearly happy to be back in his element, entered as many events as possible. He qualified for the finals in each of the events he entered—the high jump; the standing broad jump; the hop, step, and jump;

the broad jump; the shot put; and the discus. Due to conflicts in the schedule for the finals, he had to scratch from the shot put and discus, but he placed first in the high jump and standing broad jump; second in the hop, step, and jump; and third in the broad jump. The 14 points he scored exceeded the next highest score by four points.

Amid Army-style pomp and ceremony, the meet's medal winners were presented their awards by General John J. Pershing himself. By the time Richards walked up for his fourth medal, Pershing said, "Whose medal are you coming for now, Richards?"

"Mine, sir," answered Richards as the troops laughed.

"Good to see old-timers still making good," rejoined the General.

★   ★   ★

In 1947, the state of Utah, celebrating 100 years since the Mormon Pioneers first settled the Salt Lake Valley, was in a centennial mood. Among other things, there was the question as to who was Utah's track and field athlete of the century. Eugene L. Roberts, the former BYU coach, was commissioned to come up with a system for making the right choice. Roberts said he didn't need a system.

"I feel honored to be made a member of the 'jury' selected to agree, if possible, upon what Utah athletes should be considered as the greatest performers of the century," he wrote to the *Deseret News*. "However, in this letter of acceptance I cannot refrain from saying that the one most outstanding track and field star of the century was Alma Richards, who could have failed to score points in the Olympic Games, the National AAU decathlon, and the American Expeditionary Forces Meet at France, and he still would easily qualify as the Athlete of the Century of Utah."

They awarded Richards his trophy at the Centennial Track

Meet in Salt Lake City in the spring of 1947. Appropriately, the meet was held at the University of Utah, near Cummings' Field, where 37 years earlier Alma Richards, then a ninth grader, led the Murdock Academy to the state track championship.

There was some surprise when Richards didn't compete in that 1947 meet — even if he was 57 years old. As it was, his competitive career had lasted until he was 42 years old. He won the 56-pound weight throw (his favorite event as he got older) in the 1932 Southern Pacific AAU Championships in his last competition.

★   ★   ★

After World War I, he migrated from Cornell to Stanford for graduate studies. After a year of graduate school, he enrolled in law school at the University of Southern California, emerging in 1924 with a law degree. All the while he continued to compete in track and field, wearing the livery of the Los Angeles Athletic Club. In one particularly memorable meet held at Occidental College in 1922, Richards, at the age of 32, won the discus, the 56-pound weight throw, and the high jump — and placed third in the shot put and fourth in the hammer throw. In the process, he defeated the top college performers from USC, Occidental, UCLA, Harvard, and a dozen other universities.

He never did use his law degree, at least not for formal practice. Teaching intrigued him more. He got a job at Venice High School in Los Angeles, teaching ROTC at first, then science, which would become his specialty for the next 32 years. He encouraged his students to excercise their brains, to become knowledgeable and free. The influence of Professor Trueblood lingered.

★   ★   ★

Although Alma Richards competed almost continuously for 24 years, he and Hans Liesche never met again. The two best high jumpers in the 1912 Olympic Games failed to have a rematch.

They were geared for it in the next Olympiad, in 1916, when the Olympics were scheduled for Berlin, Liesche's home city. The German was rather looking forward to that. But Germany's invasion of Belgium and part of France in August of 1914 escalated, by 1916, into a full-scale world conflict, and that was that. Instead of facing off in the Olympic high jump, their countries faced off in a world war.

The two athletes lost complete track of each other until 1954, when Richards was inducted into the Helms National Hall of Fame in Los Angeles — an event that came to the attention of a German sports writer and acquaintance of Liesche. Remembering the Olympics of 1912, the writer arranged for Richards, now 64, and Liesche, 63, to trade addresses. A correspondence ensued. Richards wrote: *"Dear Friend Hans Liesche: Much has happened in the world and to us since we competed together in the Olympic Games in Stockholm, Sweden in 1912. After your fine spirit of sportsmanship in this championship, I have always had a sincere feeling of friendship for you and the German people. When I went to Europe as a Lieutenant in the United States Army in 1918, I prayed that I wouldn't meet you on the field of battle.*

"George Horine died a few years ago. Jim Thorpe passed away last year. They were both great athletes and good men.

"I have always felt that you should have won the 1912 high jump. I made the best jump of my life up to that time. As I remember, you were interrupted a great deal. First, the gun sounded for the start of a race; second, the band started playing; third, the officials hurried you somewhat. At that moment and as time has passed, I have respected you as a great jumper and most of all, as a fine representative of your country.

"Enclosed is a picture of my lovely wife and myself. I have been well all my life. Hope that you are well and happy."

And Liesche wrote: *"Dear Sportsfriend Richards: I am very much delighted to hear after so many years of my victorious opponent at Stockholm 1912. I have thought often of A. Richards and wondered whether he is still alive. I heard that Horine passed away. Of Thorpe I heard that he was in financial difficulties.*

"Having heard what you said about me, I was deeply touched. But the best high jumper on that particular day in Stockholm was not Hans Liesche or Horine but certainly Alma Richards, USA, who mastered the winning height of 1.93 meters as nobody else did. Even if I took all the heights up to 1.91 meters at the first try and apparently effortless I could not master the 1.93 meters.

"In October 1912 I became a soldier through our conscription laws and served right on until 1919 when World War I was over. I am married since 1928 and through being active so long I have kept my slim figure. The photo enclosed is two weeks old. The same as I recognize you after 42 years, so will you probably still recognize tall and lanky Hans."

And so their Olympic bond held. Through two World Wars. Through a dozen Olympiads. Through half a century. And in the end, both insisting the other was the best.

CLARENCE ROBISON

BY DOUG ROBINSON

By the time he finally retired from the world of running and track meets, the hair was white and the face wrinkled and tired looking, but the stride was still long and strong. Clarence Robison was out-hiking and out-hunting men half his age, those long legs still eating up the mountainside. Was it any wonder that he went the distance on the job? For four full decades he served as head track coach at Brigham Young University. Forty years. He was coaching the children of his former athletes. But then, he always has had uncanny endurance, they say.

Robison began coaching in 1949, and the day he officially retired in 1989, at the age of 65, hundreds of his former athletes gathered from around the country to honor the man who had coached more than 100 All-Americans, 20 Olympians, countless world and American record holders, and future executives, lawyers, doctors, dentists, coaches, physical therapists and journalists. The athletes honored him the only way they could: they sent him on an expense-paid fishing trip to Alaska with his sons. He never could get enough of the outdoors.

By then he was known simply as Coach or Robbie. He had

been coaching so long that few could remember he had done anything else in his life. It was nearly forgotten that Robison had been an athlete himself, an Olympic distance runner, no less. Undertrained and unheard of, he went to the 1948 Olympics in London and competed in the 5,000-meter run against, among others, the legendary Zatopek. He can still remember pulling up to the shoulder of the great Czech runner in the middle of the race and looking into his face. That smile. He would never forget that smile.

Robison's career was short, too short, lasting a few abbreviated seasons, only two of them at the international level. At the peak of his career, just when he was becoming a force, he gave it all up to become a collegiate head coach. Who could pass up such a rare opportunity at the age of 25? He brought the lessons of Europe home with him. He dismissed all the old tales about overtraining, about running too much — all of which he had learned at his own expense — and put his runners through some real training, the kind he had never had, and the Cougars became one of the nation's collegiate track powers.

But even all these years later he wonders what might have been if he had had such training, if he had continued his running career just a little longer.

★   ★   ★

Each spring Clarence and his father Archie hitched the horses to the wagon and headed for the mountains to cut wood for the family sawmill. They set up base camp at the same spring each year, and every morning they rose with the sun and hiked to a plateau where the timber was full and thick. Clarence, a young boy, ran ahead of his father up through the switchback trails until he was out of sight, then ran back to find him before running ahead again, and so on, back and forth. His energy and legs knew no bounds and never would;

the only thing that could slow him was a child's imagination. In the evening, fearing wild animals lurking in the dark, he clutched his father's hand as they made their way back down the mountain, comforted by the sight of Archie's head and shoulders framed in silhouette against the evening sky.

Clarence, the youngest of three children, spent most of his waking hours working side by side with Archie on or near the family farm. He always knew what it was to work. He knew what it was to milk cows and feed the livestock before the sun climbed over the mountains. He knew what it was to pitch the loose, unbailed hay onto a wagon from dawn to dusk. When he was a teenager he could pitch hay with any grown man in the valley, which is why he was always able to find work on neighboring farms.

The Robison farm was near Fillmore, Utah, backed up against the eastern side of the Wasatch Mountains. The family had little money—this was the time of the Great Depression— but Clarence didn't know it at the time. Only years later did he learn how close his folks, Archie and Charlottie, had come to losing the farm. They didn't have indoor plumbing until Clarence went away to college, and for years they had no car; they drove a horse and buggy to church on Sundays. They lived in a small frame house, which Archie had built with his own hands, and heated it with the wood they cut on the mountain. It was a meager existence, but there was always plenty of love and kindness and food in the house.

The family owned 200 acres, most of it planted in orchards—apples, peaches, pears—and watermelons. It was Clarence's job to chase the deer out of the orchards and the neighboring kids out of the melons. It became an annual rite of autumn, a sport, Clarence versus the neighbor kids. They came in packs at night to swipe the melons. Clarence ran down so many of them that when court was held at the end of the month, 15 to 20 kids were there to be tried for attempting to heist melons at the Robison place. They'd try to outrun him, but it didn't do any good. How were they to know they were trying to outrun a future Olympian? He toyed with them. He'd catch up with them and then run alongside them, smiling.

For Clarence, nothing was finer than being in the mountains, and nothing ever would be. He didn't even cross the state boundary until he went to war; there was never any need to. He had all he needed in the mountains next to his home. He hunted and fished and hiked whenever he could get away from chores and school. When Clarence and his boyhood pal, John Mitchell, went to the mountains, they didn't bother with horses. As far as they were concerned, horses were too slow. They preferred to jog and walk up the mountain on their own, taking shortcuts where no horse could go. They jogged the high rim trails, looking in the various canyons for trophy bucks at sundown. They learned that by running they could see more canyons and more deer.

As a teenager Robison worked for the forest service, building fence and maintaining trails during the summer. At the end of the day the other forest service employees rode a truck for 90 minutes from the top of the mountain back to town, but Robison didn't bother. He found that by running down the mountain he could get home in half the time and enjoy the scenery to boot.

Clarence was still too young to carry a gun when he began hunting with the men. The hunters used the boy as a bird dog. He ran ahead of them to flush bucks out of the various canyons. The only complaint the men had was that he was too fast; he chased the deer out of the canyons before they could get there.

It was a sad day for the local deer population when Robison could finally carry a gun. On more than one occasion, from the top of a mountain he spotted a deer walking below him, making his way to a saddle in a distant ridge, and Clarence reached the saddle before his quarry did.

Above: Growing up on the Robison farm in Millard County

Right: The great Emil Zatopek (203) merely smiled when Clarence Robison (230) challenged him later in this Olympic race

Left: Clarence Robison winning a collegiate
race in typical fashion—no contest
(photo courtesy *Deseret News*)

Below: Robison (18) on sabbatical with the
New Mexico basketball team during World War II

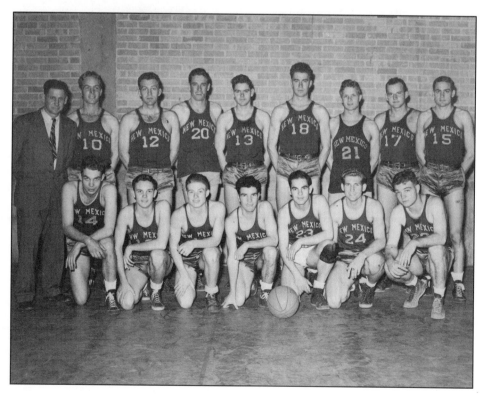

"I got a lot of deer just because I could run without resting," he says. "It made hunting more fun. It was great to have that energy."

One day Robison was hunting in a foot of snow in the mountains when he spotted a five-point buck working his way up the canyon. He took a shot but only wounded the animal, and the buck wheeled and ran back down the canyon. Robison dashed down the mountain and gave chase, following a trail of blood in the snow. The deer raced past four other hunters. They all took shots but missed, then followed on foot. Robison passed them all, running for nearly a mile up over a ridge, struggling to keep his footing in the snow. He caught up with the buck in a stand of oak and shot him, then collapsed face down in the snow, his lungs on fire. Minutes later another hunter arrived on the scene. He stood over Robison for a moment, looking down at him in the snow, before breaking the silence: "I wanted to meet the guy who outruns them."

Robison's endurance was natural; it was a gift. No one could outlast him, though they would try. The Navy tried. During World War II he was sent to training camp in Florida, where he and the other recruits were sent on 35-mile hikes with full packs—child's play for Robison. He marched for 2 1/2 days in the everglades once and thought it was *fun*. Robison's future father-in-law tried his endurance too. After returning from the Olympics, Robison visited his fiancée, Monita Turley, on her family ranch in Arizona. Her father, Fred, a stern, hard-working taskmaster, eyed the young man up and down. "I need to get hay in the barn," he said. "Would you help me?" The next morning Turley called Robison out of bed at five o'clock, and they pitched hay from dawn to dusk. For three straight days they did this, with Robison collapsing in bed exhausted each night. His hands were blistered—they had grown soft while he'd been in Europe—but he kept working, knowing well what the old man was up to. "He was just trying to see if I could work," recalls Robison. "I thought, *You old codger, if you think you can get me to quit...* " They worked on opposite sides of the wagon, and Robison always made sure he stayed ahead of Turley. After three days of nonstop work, Turley's parting words to Robison were, "Thanks. I think you can teach my grandkids to work."

Even as Robison advanced in years and his exercise was limited to racquetball and handball, his energy never failed him. Friends tell endless stories of his endurance, most of them of the hunting variety. On one hunting trip Robison gave his horse to Floyd Millet, his former college coach, and then proceded to walk up and down mountains and in and out of gullies and canyons without slowing for an entire day. "I had a hard time keeping up with him even on a horse," recalls Millet with a laugh.

Robison seemed to delight in seeing people try to keep pace with him. When his athletes asked to go hunting or fishing with him, he warned them: "Oh, I'm not sure you want to." The athlete invariably replied, "Coach, I can walk anywhere you can." By the end of the day Robison was carrying the kid's gun.

Sherald James, one of Robison's former milers, went hunting with him, and the younger man never forgot it. "He had us going up one mountain after another, and he never faltered," says James. "Those long legs were eating up the ground. I had to jog alongside to stay up with him. I don't think he missed a mountain, and I was wringing wet with sweat. He knew what he was doing to me."

Then there's this story: After hunting and hiking up and down mountains all day for eight hours, Robison returned to his car and found that it was broken down. He walked 35 miles back to town, in the dark, on dirt roads. He was 66 years old.

Even then he was serving as a hunting guide. Hunters would eye the thin, white-haired man and wonder how he was going to help them find a bull elk. But he earned a reputation. "Oh, you're the guy who walks forever," they'd say.

They all discovered what the kids in Fillmore already knew: you couldn't outwalk, outrun, or outhike Robison. When he was in grade school, the older kids locked him out of their tag games because he simply couldn't be caught. No one was surprised the day they lined up the Millard High boys for a half-mile race, and a freshman named Robison won. The tallest kid in the school, he was a star in basketball and track. As a senior he won the 880-yard run at the state track and field championships, and then he moved on to BYU.

★ ★ ★

For the first time in the history of the college sport, Robison won three firsts in the distance and middle-distance events. The smooth-steppin' running machine won the mile in good time, then stepped off a fast 1:59.3 in the 880 and topped off the day by winning the two-mile event. That was 3 1/2 miles of competitive running, but the big-bounding BYU star never faltered as he again proved himself one of the greatest tracksters. (Salt Lake Tribune, May 1, 1948.)

There was no more dominating figure on the distance-running scene in the Rocky Mountains than Clarence Robison in the late 1940s. On the track, Robison was beaten once in three years of conference competition. In cross country races, Robison was never beaten and rarely even challenged. He smashed a course record so badly in one race that race officials decided he must have taken the wrong course. He described the route he had taken, and the officials agreed it was the right one, but they never did give him the record.

Long-striding Clarence Robison of BYU again stamped himself the state's outstanding distance runner as he showed his heels to a select field of gallopers Saturday afternoon in the senior *division Intermountain AAU Cross Country Championships. (*Salt Lake Tribune, *June 1, 1947.)*

For Robison, footraces were just another day in the mountains chasing bucks out of the canyons. Running came easily to him. At 6-foot-3, he was never difficult to find in a pack of runners. He was exceptionally tall by any standard of the day, let alone among the tiny men who usually were distance runners. He towered over his rivals, those long, smooth strides swallowing up so much of the track that it hardly seemed fair.

When the team needed the extra points, sometimes Robison was asked to compete in three events — the half-mile, the mile, and the two-mile — and won them all handily. There was no competition for Robison, so he rarely had to push his body to its limits, never learned race strategies and pacing, rarely ran fast times. He ran just hard enough to win so that he would be rested for winning another race later in the meet. All of this put him at a disadvantage when he went to national-class meets, where the competition was considerably better.

*In the two-mile test it was Robbie all alone. Ira Hill took an early lead, but weakened in the heat and dropped out. The crowd rose and gave Robison a tremendous ovation as he sped his second win of the day with the pack 50 yards behind. (*Salt Lake Tribune, *May 22, 1948, at the Mountain States Conference Championships in Denver.)*

Robison came to BYU in 1940 and ran for the freshman track team, but then the war began and he spent the next three years in the Navy. While attending officers training school in Albuquerque for a year, he attended classes at the University of New Mexico and played for the school's basketball team, leading the Lobo guards in scoring. He returned from the war in 1946 and made the BYU basketball team, but Millet, who coached both the basketball and track teams, saw his potential elsewhere. "You can become great in track and get national recognition," he told Robison. "In basketball you may spend a lot of the season on the bench." Robison agreed. He played in a couple of games and quit to concentrate on track—whatever that meant.

At the time, there was really no such thing as a full-time runner. Nowadays any collegiate runner's routine includes year-round training, running 50 to 70 or more miles a week, hard interval work on the track two or three times a week, and seasons that last from January to June. In Robison's era, runners began training when the mud on the cinder track dried in the spring, which in Provo meant early April. The track season lasted two months and consisted of six meets. The cross country season consisted of two meets. Nobody ever thought of running during the off-season, and running in the snow was out of the question.

"We thought if you ran in the snow, you'd burn your lungs," recalls Robison. "We kind of played basketball in the winter and waited for spring."

At the time, it was widely believed that running long distances harmed the body. When Robison was in high school, his father forbade him to run anything longer than 220 yards. Later, he confessed to his father that he had tried the 880 and won. His father never said anything after that and rarely missed a meet, but his attitude toward running reflected the times. Distance running was considered dangerous. Robison's workouts in college were silly by today's standards: six laps for time on Monday, three laps for time on Tuesday, three laps for time on Wednesday, six laps for time on Thursday, rest on Friday, compete on Saturday, and rest on Sunday. Interval training and speed workouts were unheard of. So were over-distance training runs. Runners never ran farther than the distance they raced. Robison ran less than 10 miles a week. The belief that distance running was unhealthy was so pervasive that even as Robison warmed up with several laps before a track meet, members of the BYU faculty shouted cautions to him: *"Be careful. You're going to hurt yourself. Don't overdo it."*

"It was thought that running too far or too long would result in physical damage — heart damage and that sort of thing," explains Robison. "Even the cross country races were only two or two and half miles. We didn't even talk about 10,000 meters in those days. We didn't even know how far that was. Our workouts were gauged in laps, not miles. The distances we trained weren't 1/20th of what they do now. It seems silly now. I used to jog 15 miles in the mountains in a day when I was a boy. I should have wondered why it would hurt me to train the same way. It just didn't dawn on me. Any book you got, or any coach you talked to, that was what they thought. Who was I to argue? I was a beginner. We just greatly underestimated what the body can do and should do. I don't know how we succeeded as well as we did."

Given his training, Robison's times are remarkable. He ran 880 yards in 1:52.6; the mile in 4:11.8 (this was several years before Roger Bannister broke the four-minute barrier); 1,500 meters in 3:53.5 (roughly equivalent to a 4:10 mile); and two miles in 9:17.0. And along with all that natural endurance, Robison discovered late in his career that he had speed. One day he was asked to run a leg on a 4 x 440-yard relay team in Europe. He clocked 48-flat.

"If only I had known what background work and interval training could do for you," says Robison. "I wonder what I could have done. I had natural ability. I had the speed to run middle distances, and I could have developed the endurance and done something on an international basis. I really believe I could have set world records."

★   ★   ★

At the sound of the gun for the start of the 5,000-meter run, Robison broke for the pole position and settled into the pack, close behind the leaders. It was a clear, sunny Chicago day, with a light, cool breeze blowing in off Lake Michigan — perfect conditions for the 1948 U.S. Olympic Track and Field Trials. The top three finishers in each event would make the U.S. Olympic Team. Robison, cheered by a small group of Mormon missionaries in the stands, held his position in the pack, careful to stay within striking distance of the frontrunners. After each lap, as the field moved past the grandstand, the public address announcer read off the names of each runner. Every time he came to Robison, however, he paused, then skipped him altogether and went on to the next runners: *"Curtis Stone, Jerry Thompson, Horace Ashenfelter, Don Black . . . Fred Wilt."* He never said Robison's name until the race was finished. He simply didn't know who he was. And who did?

Robison was virtually unknown outside of the Rocky Mountains, and he was a newcomer to the distance events. He had been a half-miler and miler throughout his entire career, but in 1948, with the Olympics coming up, he and his coach decided he had a better chance to make the U.S. team in the 5,000. He had been beaten in the mile in national meets, and in conference competition he seemed to win the longer two-mile races more easily than the shorter races. Still, he had run only one race farther than two miles when he tried the 5,000 (3.1 miles) for the first time in the 1948 NCAA championships. He finished fourth with a time of 15:37.7. Later in the summer he finished fourth again in the 5,000 at the national AAU championships. Entering the Olympic Trials, he had run the 5,000 just twice in his life.

Robison had moved to Ann Arbor, Michigan, in the summer of 1948 to pursue a master's degree in health science at the University of Michigan. While training with a handful of Michigan runners one day, he was spotted by Don Canham, the Michigan coach. Canham saw special talent in Robison, though the runner was inexperienced and unknown. He thought all Robison needed was more confidence and a strategy to make the Olympic team. A distance runner who lacks confidence, who doubts his ability to finish a race strongly, doesn't have the courage to stay with the leaders when the pace quickens.

"Robbie was a great runner," recalls Canham. "He just didn't know anything about pace. He always had a great kick at the end of the race, which meant he hadn't expended himself in the middle of the race. He just needed more confidence."

Canham conspired with Phil Diamond, a Detroit sports writer, to inspire confidence in Robison. Diamond would be interviewed on a local radio show about the upcoming Olympic Trials, and Canham would invent a reason to get Robison into his car so he would be certain to hear the show. All went according to plan. With Robison in his car, Canham turned on the radio just in time to hear Diamond say, "There's a dark horse working out here at Michigan. No one knows anything about him, but he'll make the Olympic team. He's Clarence Robison."

Robison was doubtful. The Olympic Trials field would be loaded. The war had ended, which meant a flood of past stars had returned to competition. The 5,000-meter race would include Wilt and Black, both former national champs; Stone, the reigning national champ; Thompson, the reigning NCAA champ; and Ashenfelter, a future Olympic steeplechase champ. Canham knew Robison's competition well, having seen them compete many times. He knew them all by name, and he knew their strengths and weaknesses. He produced a plan for Robison. "Run for the third spot; don't even worry about the first two places," he told him. Stone and Thompson were cinches to claim the first two spots, so Robison and Canham focused on the rest of the field. Canham believed that Black was the top contender for the third spot, and he believed he had a weakness.

"When he's under pressure late in a race, he quits," Canham told Robison. "Latch on to Black and don't let him go, and with two laps to go you challenge him, and I'll bet he quits."

Robison did just as he was instructed, and the race unfolded exactly as Canham had predicted. Late in the race, Black was in third place, with Robison close on his heels. With two laps to go, Robison pulled up on Black's shoulder. His rival responded and picked up the pace for the next 200 yards, but Robison kept pushing and finally Black dropped off the pace. *Hey, I'm going to be on the Olympic team,* he thought. Now he wanted more than a third-place finish. Setting his sights on Stone and Thompson, he decided he could beat them as well. With a lap to go he passed them and took the lead, but they passed him back on the homestretch. Stone was first in 14:40.7, Thompson second in 14:41.2, and Robison third in 14:44.07. Robison was going to the Olympics.

★   ★   ★

The U.S.S. *United States* was a floating athletic field on its voyage from New York to London in the summer of 1948. The U.S. Olympic Team was on board, bound for the Olympic Games. Robison ran laps around the deck, but it was more recreation than serious training. He and the other runners had to run around deck chairs, slow for the many sharp corners of the deck, and dodge passengers and other athletes. The deck was crowded with power lifters, gymnasts, and volleyball and basketball players. There was no clear path to run. Robison ran once a day, then spent the rest of his time performing calisthenics, playing games on deck, and relaxing. "It was more of an adventure than anything," he recalls.

For Robison the party stopped when the ship reached

London. He sobered quickly when he scanned the list of entries in the 5,000. Their times were stunning. The Europeans weren't merely faster, they were *much* faster, 45 to 50 seconds faster. After asking around, Robison discovered that the Europeans' training methods were vastly different from the Americans'. Czechoslovakia's great runner, Emil Zatopek, was running 11 or 12 miles a day—more than Robison did in a week. "I thought that was silly," says Robison. "I was naive."

He also was dumbfounded and demoralized. The Europeans were so far ahead of the Americans that it seemed ridiculous even to enter the Olympic race. "I had about the 40th fastest time there," says Robison. "These guys were just so much faster. I was way out of my element, and I hadn't run enough to know what confidence was. I didn't have the confidence to run with them. I couldn't even get excited, I just wanted to get it over. I knew I was going to get whipped."

Robison was overwhelmed again when he stepped into the Olympic stadium and saw thousands of people in the stands. He had never seen such a crowd. "I wondered more and more, 'What am I doing here?' " he recalls.

In the trials, Robison was stuck in the fast heat, and yet he found himself still close to the leaders in the late stages of the race. At two miles he moved to the shoulder of Zatopek, who was running in second place. Robison, who was struggling to hold the pace, turned and looked at Zatopek. Zatopek turned and looked at Robison—and smiled. Robison was shocked. Zatopek wasn't even breathing through his mouth.

"He was running that easily," says Robison. "He was out for a Sunday stroll."

Zatopek went on to win the silver medal in the 5,000-meter finals and the gold in the 10,000. In the 1952 Olympics, he won gold medals in the 5,000, 10,000, and marathon. Years later, when historians would note that Zatopek's face was always contorted in a painful expression during races, he replied,

"I was not talented enough to run and smile at the same time."
But he did on this occasion. Robison lasted two more laps and
then did something he had never done before and would never
do again: He quit.

"I realized I couldn't hold the pace," he recalls. "And when
I couldn't, I shut it down. Often fatigue is a strange thing. I
learned this later. You can run and hurt if you have the desire.
I wasn't exhausted afterward. I suppose that happens to many
young athletes: the greatest athletic opportunity of your life,
and you don't have the courage to accept it and run with it. I
look back now and think I could have done better had I known
a little more about athletics. I was not mentally prepared. The
other runners were so much better prepared, and I just didn't
feel like I belonged there. I was almost a beginner compared
to the others. I hadn't won national titles. I didn't have experience in big races. But if I had said to myself, I've got enough
raw talent that I'm going to get into the finals, I would have
made the finals. I just didn't fight when I should have."

Robison wasn't the only American runner to be humbled
in these Olympics. In the five distance-running events, ranging
from 1,500 meters to the marathon, only one American finished
in the top eight and none medaled. The Americans were simply
undertrained and behind the times.

Troubled by his Olympic performance, Robison decided
he would run with more courage next time. A week later he
went to France, where he was to run in a 3,000-meter race
against Frenchman Alex Guyodo, who had finished fourth in
the Olympic 3,000-meter steeplechase. For a time it appeared
that Robison might not race at all. American officials warned
their athletes not to drink the water, but the only other liquid
that was handy was champagne, so Robison, a non-drinker,
drank the water anyway and became ill. The day before the
race, Robison explained to French officials that he would not
be able to race because he was sick. They laughed at him.

"You just don't want to race the French champion," they told him. Robison decided right then that he would race and win. I don't have to run the way I did in the Olympics, he told himself. With two and a half laps to go, the race became a duel between Robison and Guyodo. They traded leads back and forth, neither of them able to shake the other. Guyodo entered the final homestretch with a slight lead, but Robison rallied and beat him by a foot. "That's the loudest groan I've ever heard in track and field," a coach told Robison as he looked at the disappointed hometown crowd. Robison was in no shape to care. Teammates helped him to the dressing room, stopping every few feet to let him throw up.

"I'll never forget how satisfying it was to lay everything on the line and run the way I should have run," recalls Robison. "It shows you what being mentally ready can do for you physically. I couldn't have medaled in London — the 5,000 was too far for me with my training — but I could have made the finals."

★   ★   ★

Robison returned to Europe with the U.S. national team in 1949 for his last hurrah. He arrived for a meet in Copenhagen a couple of days early, and on Sunday he attended church with the local Latter-day Saint congregation. He sat in the back of the chapel as the meeting began, but one of the missionaries recognized him from BYU, and he was asked to speak. Through an interpreter, Robison explained that he was in town to run the mile the next night in a big international meet. One of the many boys who were sitting on the front row raised his hand. "Do you think you can beat the Danish champion?" he asked.

Robison paused. He didn't know how to respond. "Yes" seemed arrogant, but "no" didn't seem right either. Robison had read about the Danish champ and knew that his rival had run the mile seven seconds faster than he had. While Robison hesitated, one of the missionaries blurted out, "Of course he can, because he lives the Word of Wisdom and the Danish champion doesn't."

"I didn't have a good answer, but any answer would have been better than that one," recalls Robison. "I thought of changing the subject, but the missionary proceeded to give these boys a brief discussion on what the Word of Wisdom would do for you."

Robison grew increasingly anxious as the missionary explained that the Word of Wisdom forbids the use of alcohol and tobacco. The last thing he needed was the added pressure of running for the truth of a religious principle. *Oh, well, they won't be at the meet anyway,* Robison told himself.

The next evening, as he was warming up for the race on a grassy area outside the stadium, Robison recognized two missionaries and 16 boys from church walking into the stadium. One of the missionaries walked over to Robison and whispered, "If you've ever run in your life, you'd better run tonight. These boys have come to see if the Word of Wisdom is really true."

Before leaving the hotel, Robison had offered his usual prayer, asking for protection and his best performance, but of course never for victory itself. But on this occasion he decided his best might not be good enough. He found an unused room under the stadium, knelt down, and prayed again: "I know the Word of Wisdom is true, and I have never broken it. This situation is not of my doing, and under the circumstances, bless me with victory. Nothing else will do."

The first three laps of the race were like any other mile race he had run. The pace was fast, and the Danish champion was running easily and strongly, six yards in front of Robison. They were just rounding into the homestretch of the third lap when, Robison recalls, "I had a most unusual feeling come over me. I was not tired anymore. Not believing at first, I began to increase the pace, and it didn't hurt. Going even a little faster, it still didn't hurt."

Robison passed the Dane going into the backstretch of the final lap and was still accelerating. As he came around the turn, his coach ran across the middle of the field to intercept him on the backstretch. "Slow down, you idiot!" he yelled. "You'll never make the finish line." Robison ignored him. He not only won the race, but he won by some 50 yards and was still pulling away.

"After the race, no one had to tell me who really won the mile," says Robison.

Robison's career was winding down now. He knew he could no longer continue. A year earlier he had been offered the head coaching job for the BYU track team. Millet, who was retiring from coaching, recommended him as a successor, even though Robison still had another year of school remaining. Robison accepted, and during the next year, while an interim coach served in his place, he completed his schooling, competed, and taught a full load of classes. It was a heavy load, but he managed to find time to run well anyway. He returned to the mile, which was more suited to his talents and his size, and placed fifth in both the NCAA championships and the AAU national championships. Thinking his career was finished, he stopped running for several weeks, but then he was asked to compete for the U.S. national team in Europe. Robison considered it another opportunity to learn more for his coaching career. While in Europe he quizzed athletes and coaches, looking for training and technical information, and he ran like he never had in his life. Robison ran 16 races that summer in Europe; he won 12 of them, including the one in Copenhagen.

Robison was tempted to continue his athletic career and perhaps return to the Olympics, but the amateur rules in those days prevented him from earning a living through sport. He couldn't even be paid to coach at BYU if he wanted to continue his running career. And so he really had no choice.

Robison ran his final race in Finland. He wanted to quit in style by breaking the stadium record. Teammates, knowing this was his final race, stood beside the track, yelling split times, but he missed the record by one-tenth of a second. Robison never ran another race, and he rarely ran even for exercise. From now on his running would be confined to chasing trophy bucks in his beloved mountains of Utah.

JAY LAMBERT

BY LEE BENSON

He is a doctor now. He has been a doctor for nearly four decades. You name it, he's sewed it up. Jay Lambert, M.D., has spent the best part of a lifetime getting people back on their feet, more than making up for that whirlwind summer of 1948 — when his specialty was knocking people off their feet.

When he had to choose between one or the other, between being a surgeon or doing surgery in the ring, he didn't fight the change. At medical school they told him he'd have to sign more than the Hippocratic Oath. He'd also have to sign a promise he wouldn't use his hands in the ring again. He smiled and asked for a pen. He never did want to be Joe Louis as much as he wanted to be Albert Schweitzer.

Not that there wasn't a void. You don't climb out of the ring after 10 years and just walk away — especially when it took almost the first seven years to get beat even once; you don't just turn your back cold on the sweet science if you have any feeling at all. So when the 18-hour days in medical school were over and the round-the-clock shifts in residency were completed, when he had established a practice, he found his way

41

back to the amateur fights, at ringside, along with his black bag. He was the doctor in the house.

Since the mid '50s he has been a fixture *outside* the ropes at the Fairgrounds Coliseum and other shrines for amateur boxing in and around Salt Lake City. Grimy, dimly lit, no-nonsense arenas, places where you find out if you can take a punch, places Lambert grew fond of as an aspiring young heavyweight and fonder of yet as the ringside doctor, attending to cuts, scrapes, bruises, and double vision.

"How many fingers am I holding up, son?"

"Eleven."

"Better sit the rest of this one out."

Several times the fight organizers wondered if they could compensate him for his services. Several times he told them no. Finally they gave him a plaque and let it go at that.

Attending the fights wasn't a chore anyway. They were usually competitive, often exhilarating, and always lively, and he had a terrific seat. And what better way to spend your Friday nights than assisting and encouraging young boxers to make themselves better? When you're young and formative and someone pushes you in the right direction, there's no telling how far you can go. Above everything else, Dr. Jay Lambert knew that.

★   ★   ★

Marv Jenson first saw Jay Lambert at the 1942 Inter-mountain AAU Boxing Championships, when Lambert was 16 years old and Marv wasn't much older. At the time, Jenson was an aspiring mink rancher and boxing manager. Mink ranching was going to make him rich and boxing was going to make him happy.

A passionate man, Jenson won an AAU boxing title as a welterweight, in 1937, and if it hadn't been for a bout with Rocky Mountain spotted fever he might have turned professional. As it was, in his hometown of West Jordan, Utah, a farming community split by the Jordan River 10 miles south of Salt Lake City, he became something of a neighborhood boxing authority — a lighthouse for kids being pushed around by other kids and a source of knowledge for aspiring boxers serious about getting an edge.

It was after Ted Atwood, a fledgling amateur fighter, asked him for a few pointers that Jenson started to think about forming a more formal boxing club. Atwood wanted some help in sparring sessions he was having with a friend named Ernie Hunick, who was getting the best of him. When Hunick, a couple of weeks later, came to Marv and said Atwood was starting to turn the tide and now *he* could use a few pointers, the idea turned to action.

The West Jordan Boxing Club operated first out of a building at West Jordan Junior High, next out of the basement of Marv and Margaret Jenson's home, and finally out of a shed on the mink ranch. As the country was coming out of the Great Depression, the West Jordan Boxing Club flourished. Both the boxing and the discipline were serious. To be a member in good standing, you had to train hard and fight harder. If you won five fights, you got a letter sweater with a felt WJ on it. Upon awarding it, Jenson, a faithful Latter-day Saint, would tell you that the sweater was yours as long as you didn't drink, didn't smoke, and went to church every Sunday. The only variable was that you got to choose which church.

When Jenson, who was watching the progress of several of his fighters in the 1942 Intermountain AAU championships at the Elks Club in Salt Lake City, saw Lambert, he was sure he was seeing a made-to-order WJBC member — clean-cut, handsome, courteous, and a terrific boxer. Marv invited Lambert to join with the best Depression Era offer he could think of — dues were free.

As he thought about Jenson's offer, Lambert, a high school

sophomore who was already 6-foot-1 and 175 pounds, captured the 1942 AAU heavyweight trophy without much trouble. He won all three of his bouts, all by easy decision. The fact that it was only the second tournament he'd ever boxed in didn't matter. He'd won the first one, too—at the previous year's Intermountain AAU Tournament, also at the Elks Club, when he fought as a middleweight (160 pounds) and not only won the division but the trophy as the meet's Most Outstanding Boxer as well.

"Maybe you'd like to box more than once a year," Marv said to Lambert.

★   ★   ★

Getting into boxing was no more planned than anything else Jay Lambert did while growing up in the wide open spaces at the Point of the Mountain, five miles north of Lehi, Utah, and 30 miles south of Salt Lake City. He was the fourth of four boys born to Joseph and Vera Lambert, and no matter what he did, his brothers had already done it first.

Joe and Vera ran a combination filling station/luncheon counter called "Point of the Mountain." Later, when State Street was widened and the route of the highway changed, they renamed it "Joe's Place." Equidistant between Salt Lake City and Provo, the Lamberts' business prospered, as did their four sons, who, when they weren't working the lunch counter or stocking the inventory, were shooting pheasants, hunting deer, fishing at the Jordan Narrows, or swimming in the Murdock Canal.

Or boxing.

Joe and Tony, the two oldest brothers, had started boxing at the American Legion hall in Price, Utah, where the Lamberts lived before moving to Lehi. When the older Lambert boys moved north, their boxing gloves moved with them. It was only natural that Clyde, the second youngest brother, and Jay, the youngest—almost eight years younger than Joe—would become sparring partners, sometimes unwittingly.

Athleticism ran in the family. Joseph Lambert, Sr., wrestled in college, winning an Intermountain AAU title in the 125-pound division at the 1915 championships in Salt Lake City. A proponent of fitness, he regularly got his four sons up before breakfast and took them on a run through the hills at the Point. "No matter what you boys are going to be involved in, you'll need good legs and good lungs," he told them as they ran.

All the Lamberts participated in football, basketball, and track at Lehi High School. Joe and Tony went on to play football at the Branch Agricultural College in Cedar City, the forerunner of Southern Utah University.

It was a male-dominated, sports-oriented, close-knit family that thrived at the Point of the Mountain during the '30s and '40s, a time that coincided with the Golden Age of American sports. During the Golden Age, boxing had a different hold on the public, and vice versa, than it would later in the century when the road to the ring would settle almost exclusively in urban areas, ghettos mostly, far from the rural roots and the West Jordan Boxing Clubs of the '30s, '40s and '50s.

The Lambert family was thus properly affected by the visit to the luncheon counter one afternoon of a trim, fit man in his early forties who liked the buttermilk so much he ordered a second glass. Before the customer left, Vera Lambert asked him to pose for a photograph with her four boys. They hung the black-and-white photo behind the counter where it would stay for years—Joe, Tony, Clyde, and Jay, all of them surrounding Jack Dempsey.

★　★　★

Jay was the last of the Lambert boys, and the biggest. At

Marv Jenson's West Jordan Boxing Club he started out at heavyweight.

Even if he was a high school sophomore, daily he would drive from Lehi to West Jordan, about a 10-mile trip, in the 1928 Model A Ford he bought from a customer who abandoned it at the service station because the starter motor was shot. Jay fixed the starter motor and drove the Model A back and forth to school, and to West Jordan, where he could box guys his own size, although they were often older.

The training and the increased competition in West Jordan had the expected results. Jay Lambert, who Marv Jenson said was blessed with the best reflexes of any boxer he ever saw, turned into a heavyweight to be reckoned with. As a junior at the Intermountain AAU Championships, he won his third straight title, this one even more handily than the past victories. No doubt he would have won his fourth title the next year, too, in 1944, and Lehi High might also have won that year's state basketball championship, except for one major hitch: World War II.

In the middle of Jay's senior year at Lehi, as he was leading the basketball team in scoring and getting ready for the AAUs, the draft board realized that he already had enough credits to graduate. He was off to the war in January, following in the steps of his three brothers who were already serving their country. He was happy to join them.

Twenty-one months later the bombs fell on Nagasaki and Hiroshima, and he came home. He hadn't boxed at all in the service. He returned as a 19-year-old looking more for a college education than a resumption of his boxing career. During his military training, first in California and then in Colorado, he had time to think about what he wanted to study and what he wanted to do with his life. He considered aeronautical engineering because he was in the Army Air Force. He also considered medicine, a subject that had always intrigued him.

Upon returning home, he asked his mother what she thought he should do.

"I think you'd make a fine doctor," she said.

It was all the encouragement he needed. He enrolled at the University of Utah for the winter quarter of 1946 and loaded up on pre-med courses. He also re-enrolled at the West Jordan Boxing Club.

★　　★　　★

Joe Lambert, Jay's older brother, came home from the war as fit as he'd ever been. Always a physical person, he had spent his youth in and around Lehi as someone who didn't duck a punch — someone with a reputation. He was of the opinion no one could whip him, and if someone thought he could, well, let him try.

After six years in World War II as a fighter pilot, that opinion was not diminished. Joe flew P-38s and P-39s in the Pacific Theatre. In 100 missions, from Guadalcanal to the Solomons, he never allowed the enemy a victory. He had to ditch once, put his plane in the ocean, and wait for a rescue. Even then, he said, the Japanese never laid a glove on him.

In 1948 his postwar assignment included test flights at the Dugway Proving Grounds. It was good duty. Get up early, drop some bombs on the desert, then have the rest of the day free.

One afternoon he went back to his parents' home at the Point of the Mountain. His little brother Jay was training in the backyard, preparing for some upcoming fights. Jay asked Joe if he would spar with him for a few rounds. Joe said sure.

They fought in the makeshift backyard ring, near the pole-vault pit they'd built when they were younger. They were wearing big gloves, pillows practically. In his mind, Joe reached back to his old boxing days, to the Cedar City AAU tournament he'd won in college as a middleweight. He threw a jab or two, looked for a combination. Then . . .

Crrraaaack.

Out of nowhere.

A moment later, Joe came to. Jay helped him up. Joe rubbed his jaw. The last thing he'd seen was a jab, coming from no more than 12 inches.

"Go find yourself another sparring partner, little brother," he said as he got back to his feet.

★   ★   ★

Commuting between the Point of the Mountain and the University of Utah, Jay soon found that Marv Jenson's ever-expanding club facilities in West Jordan — by now the mink shed had been replaced by a state-of-the-art gym — were conveniently in the way. Boxing was a welcome diversion from schoolwork, and Marv was always either promoting his own fight card or knew where a boxer could get a bout. When the annual Intermountain Intercollegiate championships came along at Idaho State in Pocatello, Jay represented the University of Utah — even though the Utes didn't officially have a team. He won college heavyweight titles for two years straight.

He also fought in all of the local AAU and Golden Gloves competitions that came along. It was in an AAU bout in 1947, against a heavyweight from Price named Pete Liapis, that Lambert lost the first fight of his life — by a technical knockout. Practically seven years without a loss, and finally it came. Jenson told Lambert to shake it off, he'd get Liapis another time. A few months later they met again, this time in Price, and Lambert got him.

In 1948, Lambert won the Intermountain AAU title and qualified for the National AAU Tournament in Boston. There, in the semifinals, he met a fighter named Coley Wallace, a huge black man many were calling the next Joe Louis. In a close three-round bout, Wallace was declared the winner on a split decision. The next night, Wallace went on to win the national amateur heavyweight title — about the same time Lambert and Jenson were arriving back in Utah.

Jenson told his fighter the same thing managers have been telling their fighters since the beginning of time: "You were robbed," he said. Then he added, "Now, there's this other tournament I'd like us to enter."

He was speaking of the U.S. Olympic Trials.

His promotional skills shining through, Jenson had managed to get Salt Lake City scheduled as the site for the first round of the trials. The road to London, where the 1948 Olympic Games were scheduled to be held, would begin in Utah.

After a 12-year Olympic layoff because of the world war, interest in the Olympics, and their resumption, was high. Jenson reasoned that Salt Lake fight fans would be excited to get a look at aspiring Olympians, and he was right. The first-round qualifying bouts, held at the Fairgrounds Coliseum, played to full house after full house.

Anxious that Lambert, one of the stars of his West Jordan club, would make it out of the first-round qualifying and move on to the Regional Finals the next week in San Francisco, Jenson turned strategist and at first suggested that Lambert fight as a light heavyweight. His weight was down after the AAU Nationals, and, perhaps sensing the formidable shadow of Coley Wallace at the end of the road to London, Jenson suggested that losing another five to ten pounds might be a good idea. By the time the Trials came to Salt Lake City, Lambert was down to 175 pounds.

But on a whim at the weigh-in, after looking around at the boxers who had come in from all over the Intermountain West, Jenson said to Lambert, "Fight heavyweight. Nobody looks that tough to me."

For two fights, Jenson was a prophet. Against Jay Horrocks in the opening bout and against Pete Liapis in the second round, the referee stopped both fights and sent Lambert breezing into the finals.

His opponent for the championship, and the right to move on to San Francisco, didn't look that formidable either. Rex Layne, a soldier recently returned from the war and a year younger than Lambert, had no reputation and a kind of pasty, pudgy look about him. A good-natured farm boy from Lewiston, Utah, Layne hardly came off as menacing when reporters asked him before the bout about his days as a paratrooper during the war.

"How many times did you jump out of an airplane?" they asked Layne.

"None," he said.

"You were in the service three years and you didn't jump once?"

"Nope," said Layne, "But I was pushed out 13 times."

A packed Fairgrounds Coliseum watched as the two men from Utah met in the ring, and Lambert opened the fight with a left hook more than the equal of the left hooks that had rendered Horrocks and Liapis unable to continue.

Layne barely acknowledged the blow.

In Lambert's corner, Jenson—who would later manage Rex Layne within one win of the heavyweight championship of the world (if only Rocky Marciano hadn't been in the way); who would watch him fight four former world champs and beat two of them (Ezzard Charles and Jersey Joe Walcott); and who would help him finish his amateur career with an AAU national championship the very next year—looked on with a mixture of horror and awe. There was more than just one great amateur heavyweight standing in the middle of the ring.

The three-round final turned from a breeze into a brawl. In the end, Lambert prevailed with his experience and his reflexes, winning on points. Later, he would say Rex Layne was the toughest man he fought all year, win, lose, or draw. And before it was through, he would fight many tough men.

★   ★   ★

To get to San Francisco and the next round of the Olympic Trials, Jenson loaded the four West Jordan fighters who qualified in Salt Lake City into his car and headed out through Nevada. Riding with Jenson were Lambert, a light heavyweight named Floyd Richardson, a 126-pounder named Van LePore, and, in the back seat, a promising young 16-year-old lightweight named Gene Fullmer.

Fullmer's age would cost him in San Francisco, where he lost in the second round to Johnny Gonsalves, a national AAU champion and hometown favorite from Oakland, who wouldn't realize, until a few years later, that he had survived a buzz saw of a fighter destined to beat Sugar Ray Robinson and twice reign as the middleweight champion of the world.

Lambert wasn't expected to survive San Francisco — and qualify for the Trials finals in Boston — either. Not even after he won his first bout rather handily, with a sharp left hook and an early knockout, over a fighter from Hawaii named John Contrades; because there, in the finals, stood the menacing figure of Clarence Henry, the national Golden Gloves champion who was supposed to be the next Joe Louis — if Coley Wallace didn't become the next Joe Louis first.

More than that, Henry was a Californian. He was fighting in his home state. He was surrounded by his home fans. He weighed over 220 pounds. And he was a southpaw.

A lot to overcome in three three-minute rounds. But the heavyweight from Utah was on a roll.

"When it's going well, they hit you and it doesn't hurt," Lambert said after winning the decision on points.

In the Olympic Trials finals at the Boston Garden, the new home of the Celtics and the Bruins, more than 12,000 fans

Left: Young Jay Lambert
growing up in Lehi

Below: Lambert and Marv Jenson
formed a winning combination

Above: En route to the 1948
Olympics, Lambert had to fight past
the country's best heavyweights

Left: Lambert used his hands to knock
people out but later used them
to get people back on their feet

packed the arena to see which boxers the United States would send to London. To get this far hadn't been easy. Finalists from no fewer than 11 separate regionals were entered. The Army and Navy alone had held elimination bouts among 67,500 troops. If amateur boxing had a heyday in America, this was the height of it.

In the heavyweight division, everyone expected that Coley Wallace and Jay Lambert were on a collision course for the final—including Lambert. But after successfully wading through the quarterfinals and semifinals without incident, Lambert sat at ringside and watched Wallace in his semifinal bout against another huge black fighter from Washington, D.C.

When Norvel L. Lee, the Washington, D.C., fighter, won, Lambert didn't know whether to be happy or mortified. He turned to his brother, Joe, who was stationed at a base in Maryland and had ridden the train to Boston for the bouts, and confessed, "Here I'm getting all nervous about having to fight one guy—then another guy who's tougher gets in the ring and knocks him out."

Against Lee, the only smart move was to knock him down first, which is what Lambert—after being cut on the chin in the opening round—did in the second round of their three-round final. After taking a six-count, Lee got back on his feet and fought back with a vengeance. But after a fierce and close fight the rest of the way, the points earned from the knockdown proved decisive for Lambert.

Back home in West Jordan, Marv Jenson—who hadn't made the trip to Boston because his wife was ill—wondered if even Lambert realized what he'd done in the past month. He'd beaten Rex Layne, the most promising new heavyweight in the country; he'd beaten Clarence Henry, the reigning national Golden Gloves heavyweight champion; and he'd beaten Norvel Lee, the man who'd hung the first loss on national AAU champion Coley Wallace.

If Lambert didn't appreciate what he'd done, a lot of other people did. Jack Mendonca, the head coach of the U.S. Olympic Team, told the Boston press, "Everybody's looking for a successor to Joe Louis. Let them look no further. Here is their boy." In New York, former champ Jack Dempsey, who had started his career in Utah as well, said in newspaper accounts that he had an interest in managing the young Utahn's career when he turned pro.

But all that would have to wait. Of immediate concern, Jay Lambert had a boat to catch and an Olympics to attend. And in London, the king of England was waiting.

★   ★   ★

In all of Olympic history, there may be no more poignant moment than when King George VI addressed the 84,000 people assembled in the Olympic Stadium in Wembley, England, in August of 1948, and said, "I proclaim open the Olympic Games of London celebrating the fourteenth Olympiad of the modern era."

Seven thousand pigeons took that as their cue to fly out of the stadium, as 21 guns fired in salute and 4,099 athletes from 59 countries cheered from the infield grass. Jay Lambert felt a chill run down his back. For an amateur boxer from Utah who was just trying to get through his pre-med courses, he had wound up in a strange and wonderful place.

The voyage overseas on the USS *United States* had taken a week. The boxers did their road work lapping the upper deck. Enviously, Lambert watched the sprinters work out, particularly Mel Patton, the great 100- and 200-meter man. Lambert had always wanted to be a sprinter, just as Patton had always wanted to own a great left hook.

Mendonca, a short, heavy ex-boxer from Honolulu nicknamed Curly, kept the team in good spirits. He proclaimed his boxers "the best the United States has ever sent to the

Olympic Games." He predicted that Lambert would win the gold medal, saying that Lambert's reflexes were second to none.

Once in London, Lambert, awaiting the start of the boxing tournament, toured the city with Utah's other '48 Olympians, distance runner Clarence Robison from Provo and cyclist Wendell Rollins from Salt Lake City. In his room in a barracks at a converted Royal Air Force base, he considered the twists and turns that had turned an air field into an Athlete's Village.

On Monday, August 8, he went back to work. His opening Olympic bout was against V.A. Dos Santos, a Brazilian. Lambert won handily on points. The next day, the London tabloids reported that the big Yank looked impressive.

In his second bout, Lambert faced F. Bothy, a Belgian. Again he won, and again without a lot of resistance—but with one exception. Frustrated at not being able to get to the American's chin, Bothy delivered a punishing blow to Lambert's body, a blow that damaged one of Lambert's ribs. In seven years of boxing, it was his first significant injury.

Later, as a physician, Lambert would know that the cartilage had been torn on the costal margin of his ninth rib. All he knew now was that it hurt. Prior to his quarterfinal bout against Johnny Arthur, a South African weighing in at 225 pounds, they shot novocaine into Lambert's ribs.

Three brawling rounds later, Lambert's Olympics were over. With Mendonca screaming about prejudiced judging against the Americans, Arthur won a split decision. (As it would turn out, the 1948 Games would not be at all kind to Yank boxers in London. None would win gold, just two would win silver, and all would lose at least one close split decision that had their coach fuming all the way home.)

Lambert, more philosophical than his coach, shrugged at the defeat and said, "He never hurt me . . . but I probably never hurt him either."

Arthur, who would go on to make a name for himself in South African and European professional rings, lost in the semifinals to the eventual gold medal winner, Rafael Iglesias of Argentina. The South African won the bronze medal in an easy final against Henri Muller of Switzerland.

So damaged were Lambert's ribs that in a post-Games tour of Ireland that included two exhibitions with Ireland's national boxing team, Norvel Lee, who was on the trip as the heavyweight alternate, fought in Lambert's place.

But the rib was feeling much better by August 31, 1948, when Lambert returned to Lehi and got his hometown's version of a ticker-tape parade. There was a reception at City Hall, a tribute read by Mayor L. Carlos Goates, the presentation of a three-foot high trophy, a banquet for 150 catered by Ralph's Cafe, and a dance that night.

In the midst of the celebration and the congratulations, people wanted to know two things: How were the ribs? And when was he going to turn pro and put the fear of God into Joe Louis?

★   ★   ★

In the harsh lights of the Hollywood Legion arena in Los Angeles in the fall of 1949, Lambert recognized the man whose left hand was pummeling his head. He had seen Clarence Henry before, in happier times, when they were amateurs, when Lambert was doing the pummeling. But Lambert's win in their Olympic Trials bout meant nothing now.

He had turned professional in the wake of the Olympic wave. And under the nurturing of Marv Jenson (who by now had a number of pro contenders, including Rex Layne and Gene Fullmer), he had come along nicely. He had won six of his first seven professional fights and tied the other one, and he had fought Joe Louis in an exhibition in Salt Lake City. He was making nice enough checks, too. Against Remo Polideri

in a bout in Salt Lake, where they packed the Fairgrounds
Coliseum, he got $1,500. Now, in this fight against Henry—a
bout regarded as pivotal for both in the climb toward the
heavyweight title of the world—he was making $700. But that
was the problem. Lambert was in it for the money now, not
the competition, and he knew it.

In the middle of the third round, Henry, with his new
manager, Jack Dempsey, watching in the corner, knew it too.
A flurry of combinations left the disillusioned Utah fighter
woozy on his feet. The referee said he knew enough when he
saw it, and this was enough.

Lambert went on to fight four more professional fights. He
won two and lost two. He was 8–3–1 as a professional and still
very much a contender in the spring of 1950. But he'd got what
he'd come for—a stake of nearly $5,000 for medical school.
He told Jenson, his friend and manager, that his fighting days
were over. Jenson was not surprised. He hadn't expected this
long of a run.

★   ★   ★

Jay Lambert got his degree from the University of Utah
medical school in four years. The $5,000 dwindled fast enough,
even in the 1950s, when $5,000 was still $5,000. But his parents
were there, as always. When the bills mounted, Jay cashed
some of the war bonds he had bought with his boxing winnings.
His parents redeemed them at what they would have been
worth at maturity.

He got married, started a family, and settled down. He
went to New York City for one year of residency, then spent
the rest of his residency as a general surgeon at LDS Hospital
in Salt Lake City.

A lot of people invest a great deal of time in a pursuit and
then are disappointed when they get there. Dr. Jay Lambert
wasn't one of them. As much as he enjoyed his first passion,

boxing, he enjoyed his second passion, surgery, even more. His practice flourished, and he felt a constant measure of satisfaction in helping people.

He especially felt it at the amateur fights, where he could not only stitch a nasty cut under a flyweight's eye but also tell him to keep his left up and snap his right when he countered.

He made the transformation all right — no one could argue that — the transition from ring to operating room. And it was in the emergency room they say he especially shined. His reflexes were the quickest anyone had ever seen.

PAULA JEAN POPE

BY DOUG ROBINSON

The directions are simple: Drive north out of Los Angeles for a couple of hours, make a right turn on the other side of Ventura, wind through a canyon past green pastures lined with perfect white rail fence and oak and eucalyptus trees, and you'll find the town of Ojai, tucked away like a secret in the Topa Topa Mountains. *Ojai* (pronounced OH-hi), means "The Nest" in the langage of the Chumash Indians. It is home to 7,000 people, although the outlying areas of the valley are home to many more. The town is a slice of Southern California heaven, where litter never blights the roads, where snow never falls (except conveniently in the mountains), where the sun always shines, where the air is clean, where tourists peek in the tiny shop windows that line the main street, where parking lots are converted into art exhibits on weekends, where every day feels like Saturday.

Make another right turn once you're in town and you'll find the Ojai Valley Racquet Club partially hidden in a thick stand of oak. It is six acres of tennis courts, swimming pools, a full-size basketball court, and a restaurant. Inside the combination office/pro shop is a small, red-haired woman hustling from one errand to the next. Paula Jean Pope — once known as Paula Jean Myers, or PJ, or just Paula Jean, or Diving Queen — co-owns and oversees the daily business of the OVRC. It's a big job. More than 2,000 people belong to the club, among them some Hollywood types who have settled in Ojai to escape urban sprawl. Mary Steenburgen, Malcolm McDowell, Eileen Brennan, Peter Strauss — they all work out at the club.

What some of them don't realize is that the little woman who runs the place was once a major celebrity herself. From 1950 to 1960, she was one of the best divers in the world, winning four Olympic medals and 17 national championships. She was big, and so was her sport. Even all these years later she still receives three or four letters a month from fans in Europe wanting an autograph.

Paula Jean could be a Hollywood story herself. Open with a scene of a young girl walking nervously past winos on the darkened streets of Los Angeles to catch a late bus home after another long day of school and training. Move in for a tight shot of her studying on the bus ride home, the overhead light shining on her books. Now cut away to a scene of her walking into the family house — a place almost devoid of furniture — to be greeted by her widow mother, tired herself from a day of trying to make ends meet. Run a slow-motion shot of the fearless young woman hurtling off a 33-foot-high platform with her pioneering 1 1/2 forward somersault with a double twist. Jump ahead a few years to a scene of her as an adult, cleaning teeth by day and diving by night. Zoom in for another close shot of Paula Jean — 5-foot-3, 126 pounds, short red hair, pert, pretty, cheerful. And now fade away for a moment as she stands at the edge of the platform in the 1956 Olympic Games. All she has to do is hit her last two dives and the gold medal is hers.

Paula Jean Myers married Karl Pope, a USC basketball player, in 1958. They had five children; after one of them died in infancy, they adopted another child, Sydnee. The living-room walls of the family house are covered with plaques and framed newspaper clips that chronicle the family's athletic feats — Dad in his USC days; Mom the Olympian; Darcy the protégée who won a diving scholarship to BYU; Thane and Stacy, who won college tennis scholarships; and Derrick, a nationally ranked high school tennis player.

Karl and Paula Jean opened the club 16 years ago. After it was on solid ground, Karl was ready to move on to other ventures, so he turned the operation of the place over to his wife a few years ago. After working 29 years as a dental hygienist, she was ready for a change. Like everything else she has done in her life, she has attacked her job at the club with a certain energy. She works 10-hour days there, to say nothing of the rest of her schedule. There's no time to sit. She is chairperson of the county Heart Association fund-raising committee; she coaches divers from three high schools; and she shuttles Thayne to and from tennis matches around the country and the state. It is the same pace Paula Jean has maintained since she was a young girl.

"I don't know what I'd do with myself if I wasn't busy," she says. "I'd be so bored. I don't know how people sit at home."

Paula Jean is 57 years old now, and, yes, she still dives on rare occasions. Every Fourth of July they hold a swimming and diving show at the club, and she wows them with a full twisting 1 1/2 or a double somersault. After all those years of training, do you think a body could forget how to do those things?

★   ★   ★

Paula Jean Myers was diving in the Pacific Ocean one morning when she was, in essence, discovered. Every summer the Myerses drove from their home in Covina, California, to Newport Beach, where they stayed with friends and vacationed. Paula Jean hung out on the beach, or, more accurately, on a diving platform that floated in the bay. She swam to the platform daily and dived over and over again, all day long. One day Paula Jean was turning somersaults and turning heads. She was only 11 years old, and she executed the dives with such grace and ease that friends suggested she join the Los Angeles Athletic Club. She took their advice, and just like that the course of her life was set.

To train at the club, Myers had to ride the bus from Covina to Los Angeles and back, 1 1/2 hours each way. The routine was so practiced that even now she can recite it in her sleep. She was released from class early, at 1:30, caught the 2:20 bus to Los Angeles, arrived at 3:45, trained for four hours at the club, and caught the 8:15 bus home. She had to walk six blocks from the club to the bus station in downtown L.A. for the return trip, a walk that took her past drunks, prostitutes, and other people of the street. By the time she reached the homestretch for the final two blocks on Main Street, she was usually running. She did her homework on the bus, ate dinner at 10:00, and then went straight to bed, ready to repeat the routine the next day, five days a week, for six years. On weekends, she trained three sessions a day—the high platform in the morning, the springboard in the afternoon, the high platform again in the evening. Her coaches can still remember having to kick her out of the pool at closing time. "Let's go!" they would yell at her. "Time to go!"

The LAAC was just the place for an aspiring athlete in those days. It was a haven for numerous Olympic athletes in track and field, swimming, diving, weightlifting, and fencing. Myers trained side by side with Pat McCormick, Sammy Lee, Robert Clotworthy, and Bob Webster—all of them past or future Olympic champions—as well as Lyle Draves, who coached his wife Vickie to two Olympic gold medals. They all came to the LAAC. For anyone with talent, the club provided training facilities, coaching, and travel expenses to competitions at no cost. It was the only way Paula Jean could afford club membership.

The Myerses had no money for such extravagances. Paula Jean's father, Paul, died of a brain tumor when she was six months old, and a brother died of a kidney ailment six months later. That left Blanche and her three surviving children — Richard, Robert, and Paula Jean — to fend for themselves. They had been well-to-do when Paul was alive, living in a large home in the middle of 20 acres of orange groves, but the money dried up soon after he died. Blanche tried odd jobs — catering, child care, working as a sales clerk, selling and tending oranges. The entire family worked in the orange grove when temperatures dropped below freezing at night. Blanche and the children lit smudge pots to keep the fruit from freezing. Then they tended them until morning, adding fuel when needed and guarding for fire.

Money was so tight that Paula Jean couldn't afford to buy hay for her horses, so she gave them grass that she pulled by hand from a neighboring field. Gradually, Blanche sold the furniture, one item at a time, until finally all that remained in the huge 20 x 40-foot living room was a Ping-Pong table and a juke box. Eventually, they lost the house, too, but not until Paula Jean, the youngest of the family, was gone to college. In the meantime, she kept her troubles to herself. Many of her closest friends never learned of her hardships until years later.

"I always thought she was a wealthy girl," says Sammy Lee. "She never talked about it."

When Myers first began training at the club, her coaches noticed that she arrived for workouts looking pale and wan. "What did you have for lunch?" they asked.

"Nothing," she replied.

After further prodding they discovered that she had been using her lunch money for busfare to save her family the added financial burden. From then on, her mother sent her to school with a thermos filled with hot soup or meat stew.

Despite the demanding schedule, Myers prospered. She pulled A's in the classroom, eventually won an academic scholarship to USC, worked odd jobs during holidays, improved steadily in her sport, and, in the face of coming fame and success, somehow kept her feet planted firmly on the ground when they weren't flying through the air. She was such a straight arrow that when she joined The Church of Jesus Christ of Latter-day Saints in 1973, she remembers, "I didn't have to make any life-style changes. That's the way I lived my life anyway."

She continued to train relentlessly. By the time she was 17, one writer calculated that she had jumped off towers and springboards 150,000 times and traveled 300 miles through the air and another 550 miles underwater.

"She came up the hard way," says Draves, who coached Myers for eight years. "She was a fighter. She wanted to learn, and she had courage. She was always a very determined girl."

Myers took up platform diving at the age of 14, which was an act of courage all by itself. The platform is 10 meters high — or about 33 feet (or three stories, if you prefer) — and to a diver standing up there looking down at another 15 or 16 feet of clear water, it looks more like 50 feet. Reaching a speed of 50 miles an hour, the diver has about 1.6 seconds of airtime to get his or her body into position to strike the water. Divers say that if you don't hit the water cleanly, it's like smacking your head into a mud bank. They enter the water with their thumbs locked to break the water and hit with such force that sometimes they emerge with bruised hands.

"I was scared," recalls Paula Jean. "But I decided I was

going to go places faster in the platform than in the springboard because people were afraid of it and because it's not as technical. It's as technical as the springboard in the air, but not in the approach. The approach and the takeoff are so critical in springboard. It takes longer to master."

Just one year after taking up the platform, Myers placed third in the event at the U.S. national championships. She was 15 years old, and for the first time in her life she began to consider the possibility of competing in the 1952 Olympic Games in Helsinki.

"She was very strong and aggressive, and she had a sharp mind," says Draves. "You could see the potential right away. She had that class, that willingness. She wasn't afraid to try things. She never had doubts. She had confidence."

Over the years Myers chipped six teeth, broke a hand, broke a foot, banged her head into the bottom of the pool, and scraped her legs on the board several times, all in diving mishaps, but she always came back for more. After missing her landing on one dive, she had to be pulled unconscious from the pool. But there were limits even to Paula Jean's courage. During one practice she was required to execute an arm stand cut-through reverse dive off the platform. She had to think about that one. Unlike the other dives in her repertoire, it was not a dive that she could practice off the three-meter springboard; there simply wasn't enough time to complete all the maneuvers before hitting the water. Myers sat on the platform, refusing to move. Lee, standing on the floor below, yelled up at her to dive, but she just sat there. Finally Lee hollered, "I'll send you a postcard from Helsinki!"

That did it. She jumped.

In the 1952 U.S. Olympic Trials, Myers placed third in the platform and fourth in the springboard, and she was just 17 years old. Even by today's standards, 17 is considered young. Diving is a technical sport, which favors experienced, older athletes. She was the youngest entrant in the Olympic diving events in 1952, but she was undaunted. On the day of the Olympic competition, the weather turned cold and windy. Between dives, the athletes huddled together, wrapped in towels, and soaked their feet in buckets of hot water. A screen was erected behind the platform tower to prevent the wind from affecting the divers' timing. It was all enough to make any diver lose her concentration, especially one as young and callow as Myers, but it didn't. She won the silver medal, finishing second behind McCormick, who earlier won the springboard event as well. McCormick, five years her senior, was at the peak of her career, but the kid was coming.

★   ★   ★

Diving was never a sacrifice for Paula Jean. The life-style — the hectic schedule, the bus rides, the late dinners, the hours of training — was fun. She had never even set out to reach the Olympic Games. For her, it was enough merely to train and compete and hang out at the club with the other athletes. Diving provided a second life, and it became an exciting one at that.

This was diving's golden age in many ways. The sport was in the spotlight in a way that it might never enjoy again. Pro sports had yet to take hold in L.A., and Myers and the other top female divers were celebrities. They saw their names and pictures regularly in the *Los Angeles Times* and *Sports Illustrated.* Myers was pictured on the cover of several of the nation's biggest magazines — *Look, Life, Parade.* Her name and picture turned up on the society pages of the newspaper. Magazines ran large, sequential pictures of her dives. Near the end of her career, she did television commercials and TV talk shows, and she was the celebrity guest on "To Tell the Truth." After she retired, she hired a neighbor girl to mount all the press clippings; they filled more than 80 2×3-foot pages.

Left: Young Paula Jean Myers

Below: Myers's fearless flying from the platform earned her three Olympic medals

Right: From 1952 through 1960, Myers climbed in and out of pools through three Olympiads

Below right: Myers wearing the U.S. Olympic uniform, Helsinki, 1952

In those days they held diving and swimming shows, and they packed in the crowds. When Myers agreed to participate in a diving exhibition in her hometown, the local newspaper ran headlines that covered one-third of the front page:

NATIONAL DIVING
QUEEN WILL GIVE
EXHIBITION HERE

Paula Jean and her high school friends went to the movies, and there she'd be, on the screen, an item in the newsreels, with the narrator describing her latest feats and her friends nudging her in the ribs. What young person wouldn't enjoy it all? Myers rubbed shoulders with the rich and famous. She attended Hollywood social functions and met Fred Astaire, Gene Kelly, Esther Williams, and Johnny Weissmuller. She attended a movie premier of *Alexander the Great* and sat with one of the film's stars, Frederick March. She attended society gatherings at Mary Pickford's estate. Twice she was included in the annual L.A. Times Woman of the Year selections—an honor that included, in the newspaper's estimation, the top California woman in each field. Myers was rated the top athlete, listed alongside the other winners, such as actress Rosalind Russell and future First Lady Pat Nixon. Myers was in the news. The 44th Infantry Division wrote her a letter requesting a copy of a picture of her in her swimming suit that had appeared in the newspaper.

This was all heady stuff for a teenager. So was her rise in diving. Many were calling her a favorite to win a gold medal at the 1956 Olympic Games in Melbourne. She was a natural athlete, but she wasn't without obstacles. Draves once told a reporter, "She has practically everything wrong with her. Can't get mad at the opposition. Giggles when I give her a fight talk. On top of that, she's so shy in front of a crowd that it hurts."

On one occasion, while diving for a movie-star crowd in

Beverly Hills, she needed only seven points on her final dive to win, but she froze at the end of the board. Finally, she rushed down the ladder and broke into tears.

Heights didn't scare her, but interviews and large crowds did. She once hid from reporters in a teammate's hotel room until Draves hauled her out. At a post-Olympic dinner, she was invited to introduce herself, but she stuttered and couldn't get her name out. She was merely young and inexperienced. Such problems were nothing that time wouldn't take care of.

McCormick was another matter. She was the reigning queen of diving. Myers lived with McCormick and her husband, Glenn, for two summers in Los Angeles to save commute time, and the two divers were friends. Everything was fine between them as long as Myers wasn't a threat. And suddenly she was.

A year after the Helsinki Olympics, the Draves took their professional diving show on the road, and Myers accompanied them to continue training under her coach. They stayed in Minneapolis, and between shows Draves worked with Myers. One day he asked her to try some daring new dives off the platform—a forward 1 1/2 somersault with two twists and an inward 2 1/2 somersault. She was shocked. No woman had ever performed such dives. Many of the men hadn't mastered them yet. Some thought that women simply weren't capable of such dives. Myers wasn't sure herself. There wasn't even an available intermediate platform from which to try the dives; she would have to go straight to 10 meters. Once again, Myers had to work things out in her mind. After two days of mulling over the matter, she decided she could do it. She climbed to the top of the platform and hit both dives cleanly, then continued to polish them for several weeks under Draves's direction. By the time she returned to Los Angeles she was ready to deliver them in competition.

Myers unveiled the new dives for the first time in the 1953 indoor national championships and upset McCormick to win the three-meter springboard title. The dives were a sensation. What did they feel like, her rivals wanted to know? Were they scary? Where and when had she learned them? Later in the year she used the new dives again at the U.S. outdoor national championships and upset McCormick once more to win the platform. But if the new dives and the winning brought more fame, they also brought new problems.

"It was different between Pat and me after that," says Paula Jean. "When I became a threat, it changed things. We were still friends, but after I beat her there was a feeling of tension. It was each girl for herself."

There was more tension to come. In 1954 Draves left the LAAC, and McCormick's husband, Glenn, was named to replace him as the club's coach. Myers saw this as a conflict of interest and left the LAAC herself.

"I didn't feel that having the husband of one of the divers as coach would work out too well for the other divers," Myers told reporters. "Also, I felt Lyle was the world's best coach. So I left too. . . . The other club members tried to talk me into staying. They told me I'd ruin the team. Some were so mad they wouldn't even talk to me."

Myers continued to train under Draves, but it wasn't easy. There were no indoor facilities in the area other than the LAAC, so they had to train outdoors, and even in L.A. the winters can be cold. During some training sessions she could wear a wetsuit, but when it came time for serious business she couldn't be bothered with it. At the 1954 national championships, Myers used the new dives again to upset McCormick en route to winning the platform. Myers was sick the following year and missed most of the competitions, but with her sole mastery of the advanced dives she looked like a favorite for the '56 Games.

There was just one more problem. The international governing body of swimming and diving—Federation of Inter-

national Athletics (FINA) — considered the new dives dangerous and outlawed them. The Amateur Athletic Union — the
U.S. governing body — accepted the dives for national competition, but FINA rejected them for international competition, such as the Olympics. Myers sent letters and films to try
to win approval of the dives, but FINA wouldn't accept them
until 1960, and by then everyone was doing the dives and
Myers's advantage was gone. She would have to face her rival,
McCormick, without her bread-and-butter dives in Melbourne.
If all this wasn't enough of a blow, Glenn McCormick was
named coach of the U.S. Olympic diving team.

★　　★　　★

Paula Jean arrived in Melbourne two weeks before the
Olympic Games and went to work. Every day, all day, she took
one dive after another. Climb the tower, dive, climb the tower,
dive, climb the tower . . . She took a quick break for lunch and
dinner and then was back on the board for more diving.

It was too much, but she didn't realize it. She should have
been tapering her training and resting for a big competition.
Other divers told her as much, but she wouldn't listen. She
was anxious to perform well, to produce her finest performance; she reasoned that the more she trained, the better she
would perform.

"I overtrained," she would say years later. "It was something I had never done before and never did again. I really
wanted the gold medal. I think also it was a case of wanting
to win it in spite of the fact that Glenn was the Olympic coach."

Perhaps if she had had a coach in Melbourne, she would
have calmed down. Draves, who wasn't an official U.S. team
coach, remained behind in California, and Myers was having
nothing to do with the McCormicks. She worked out alone at
different times than the rest of the U.S. team to avoid Glenn
and Pat.

If she was fatigued, it didn't show immediately. The competition opened with four dives and then resumed three days later with the final two dives. After the first day's competition, Myers was in first place, six points ahead of McCormick.

"I'm leading," she told Draves on the phone. "How should I handle it mentally?"

Unknown to Draves, Myers continued continued her rigorous training routine, diving nonstop during the next two days, even during the hours leading up to the finals. The regimen finally caught up with her that evening. She felt flat and fatigued for her final two dives. As usual, she refused to watch the other divers perform, fearing that the sight of a bad dive would rattle her own performance. She turned her back on her rivals as they dived, but she could hear the scores as they were announced. She knew McCormick was diving well. On her final dive, Myers's feet flopped over slightly on the landing, and she knew immediately, even as she swam to the surface, that she wouldn't be the Olympic champion. McCormick, who earlier won the springboard competition and would retire from the sport after these Olympics with four gold medals, won with 84.85 points; American Juno Stover Irwin won the silver, with 81.64 points; and Myers won the bronze, with 81.58 points.

When the winners were announced, Myers rushed over to congratulate her rival.

"I was so close to winning, to showing the world that I could do it," Paula Jean said later. "I smiled for the cameramen. What else could I do? It wasn't sportsmanlike to bust out crying. But afterward I went off by myself and cried till it hurt."

With McCormick gone, the diving world belonged to Myers during the next four years. In 1957, she became the second woman, along with McCormick, to win all five diving events in the national championships—the one-meter and three-meter springboard in the indoor meet and the one-meter, three-meter, and platform in the outdoor meet. She repeated the feat the following year. No one has done it since.

It was an amazing run, especially considering Myers's daily schedule, which was, as usual, frantic. She attended dental school from 8 to 5 each day and trained when she could at night, or on weekends and holidays. When school was out, she hit the training harder. Somehow she managed to round into shape just in time for the big summer competitions. In the 1959 Pan American Games she won gold medals in both the platform and springboard. Taking time off from her job as a dental hygienist, she won both dives again at the U.S. Olympic Trials, and *Sports Illustrated* rated her the favorite to win two golds at the Olympics. She flew to Rome with high expectations. McCormick was gone. She was in peak form. Who could stop her?

★   ★   ★

Paula Jean had never heard of East Germany's Ingrid Kramer before she arrived in Rome, but then who knew anything about the East Bloc athletes? They stayed away from international competitions, except for the Olympics, and even then they were aloof and unapproachable. The Eastern Bloc nations—namely the Soviet Union and East Germany—made their first appearance at the Olympics in 1952, and they were all business. They refused to stay in the Olympic village, and they trained in the middle of the night to avoid potential defections and contact with other nations. When Paula Jean tried to speak to a Soviet athlete, a third party showed up to intercept her. Talking and mingling with other athletes was forbidden.

As divers, the East Bloc athletes were pathetic in the early '50s. In the springboard competition, they actually stood at the end of the board, like children, and dived without making the standard approach. But they were anxious to learn. They observed almost every move the successful American athletes made, and they filmed them in practice and competition to learn their methods. Under such scrutiny, some of the Americans intentionally used erroneous techniques during training sessions to mislead the novices. One day a group of Russians followed Paula Jean everywhere she went, pointing at her and chattering among themselves and even patting her head.

"What are they trying to do?" she asked an interpreter. "Date me up?"

"It's not that bad," he said. "They want you to cut off one of your pigtails and give it to them for a souvenir."

By 1960 the Russians and East Germans were no longer novices. They had made tremendous improvement, and Kramer was living proof of it. She was blonde, blue-eyed, confident, and just 17, the same age as Paula Jean at Helsinki eight years earlier. Paula Jean first saw Kramer during pre-Olympic workouts in Rome, and she knew immediately that she was a threat. Kramer delivered one of the surprises of the Games by winning the gold medal in the springboard competition, 14 points ahead of Paula Jean, the silver medalist. It marked the first time an American woman had failed to win the event. It also made matters more difficult for Paula Jean in the platform. Where judges are concerned, a clear knockout is required to defeat an Olympic champ.

The platform competition was close. Kramer finished with 91.28 points, Paula Jean 88.94—first and second again. Ironically, Kramer clinched the competition with a final 1 1/2 forward somersault with a double twist—the very dive that Paula Jean had pioneered years before but had been banned from using in international competition. It was the highest scoring dive of the meet.

Life magazine captured the drama on its pages. One picture shows Kramer smiling, and in another Paula Jean is biting her nails. Then the final picture: Paula Jean bent over crying. "I never heard of Ingrid until two weeks ago," she says.

Looking back now, Paula Jean says, without bitterness, "I got beat in the springboard, but I felt I beat her on the platform. The East German and Russian judges gave her high scores."

Before she ever flew to Rome, Paula Jean had decided that she would retire after the 1960 Games, and so she did. She was at the peak of her career, but she had other things she wanted to do with her life. She was married now; it was time to start a family.

★   ★   ★

Paula Jean and Karl were driving through Germany in the summer of 1991 when they saw the sign for Dresden — Kramer's hometown. They had passed this way before, but travel had been restricted to the autobahn then. With the recent crumbling of the Berlin Wall, they were free now to drive wherever they chose. On a lark, they drove to Dresden to inquire after Kramer. They searched for public pools, and at the second one they found they were taken to Kramer's former coach, who put them in his car and drove them to Kramer's apartment.

Kramer opened the door, but there was no immediate recognition in her face. After all, she and Paula Jean hadn't seen each other in 39 years, and even then they had never conversed; the East German officials had seen to that. Paula Jean introduced herself, and Kramer's face broke into a big smile. Paula Jean and Karl stayed three days.

The women couldn't speak the other's language, but the men knew something of German and English, and they managed to piece together bits of conversation. The women looked over Kramer's scrapbook, which contained news clips from two Olympics (she won another gold medal in 1964), but, tellingly, there was little else. Kramer managed to tell Paula Jean that she had gained little from her career and her Olympic performances other than the medals and the fleeting publicity. She and her husband didn't live any better because of her athletic achievements. Now that free enterprise was legal, Kramer said she hoped to start an aerobics class.

Paula Jean couldn't help but notice the irony and the contrast of their experiences. Her career had been so vastly different a half-world away, even if she had won the silver medal and not the gold. "What a great life I've had," she says. "I got so much out of diving—the activities, the travel, the publicity. I wouldn't trade anything—except maybe for a gold medal."

From Dresden, Karl and Paula Jean eventually traveled to Helsinki, site of the '52 Games. They got out of the car and walked into the old stadium. Somehow it looked smaller than she remembered, no bigger than a public pool, but the memories were strong here. She got goose bumps as she walked around the old place, remembering the buckets of hot water and the cold wind whipping against her wet skin. This was where it had all started four decades earlier.

ROBERT DETWEILER

BY LEE BENSON

He didn't want to make an issue of it. His team, Navy, had just won the race, and the victory itself was plenty to cheer about. For Midshipman Robert M. Detweiler personally, it was one of the few races he'd been in that he hadn't had to climb out of the boat at the finish line, strip off his jersey, and hand it over to his counterpart on the opposing squad. It was a tradition in rowing—maybe a rather strange, rubbing-salt-in-the-wound kind of tradition, but, still, time-honored. You lost, you gave away your jersey.

The problem now was that Navy had beaten Yale—annihilated Yale was more like it—and the Yale rower who sat in the fifth seat, just as Detweiler sat in Navy's fifth seat, was nowhere to be found. He hadn't been in the finish area when the other Yale Eli's pulled off their jerseys and surrendered them to the varsity crew of the United States Naval Academy. All seven of Detweiler's teammates had Yale jerseys now, and all he had was a hot shower in the boat house locker room. He knew what the number 5 Yale rower looked like: biggest man on the squad, about 6-foot-5, muscle-bound, a senior. He had a menacing look about him, and, before the start of the race on the Housatonic River — Yale's home river — Detweiler made it a point, in the name of avoiding intimidation, not to look over.

Only now he wanted to see Yale's number 5 rower, because he had a jersey that belonged to him and . . .

The door to the shower room opened and there he was, Yale's number 5, the jersey in his hand. He bent down to the floor, sopped up as much water as the jersey would hold, stood up, and, without a word, pegged a fastball at Detweiler.

The jersey hit him square in the chest. To the victors go the spoils. And as far as Midshipman Detweiler knew, there was nothing to the tradition that said the jersey had to be dry.

★   ★   ★

Detweiler's first two years of collegiate rowing — make that first two years of rowing, period — had been mostly a clinic in humility. He had come to the Naval Academy expecting to be a football player. At Oberlin College in Ohio, where he went to school in 1949 to prepare for entrance into the Naval Academy, he was on the football, basketball, and wrestling teams.

But once in Annapolis he lost interest in football and was attracted, for what reason he wasn't sure, to water (perhaps because he was surrounded by it for the first time in his life). If he was to work at a sport at Navy — and there was no choice on that score, every cadet was required to participate in a sport — he determined that it would be crew. He was 6-foot-3 and 192 pounds, and he had a notion that rowing would be neither overly strenuous for him nor difficult. He was wrong on both counts.

His freshman year, he asked the crew coach, Commander Buck Walsh, if he could try out for the Plebe team, and his request was granted. He won a seat in the eight-man shell with the coxswain.

Soon enough he was to discover the intricacies of eight men weighing a total of more than 1,600 pounds, plus a 120–pound coxswain, trying not only to efficiently propel a shell 10 inches deep and 18 inches wide through the water but also to keep it from tipping over.

The Plebe team he was on in the spring of 1950 managed to master the art of not going for a swim every time they got into their shell. But, still, they didn't win a race. For some reason, Detweiler, a notoriously bad loser, didn't seem to mind as long as he consoled the losses with the realization that he was still learning the sport. By the time he graduated to the junior varsity in 1951, he was still on teams that won less than 50 percent of their races. As a sophomore, he and Navy had a new coach. Commander Walsh had contracted cancer and had to resign. Navy replaced him with Rusty Callow, a veteran crew coach who was approaching his 62nd birthday and had left the University of Pennsylvania after coaching there 23 years. Callow's inaugural season with the Middies met with fair success until the national championships of 1951, which were held simultaneously with a ferocious storm that hit the Ohio River at Marietta, Ohio.

On a day Callow referred to as "Little Pearl Harbor," the Naval Academy managed to swamp each of its boats at all three racing levels—Plebe, junior varsity, and varsity. "Navy Loses Three Ships at Marietta" was the next day's headline in the *Washington Post.*

That may have had something to do with Callow's decision the next season, 1952, to renovate Navy's program. In a sweeping top-to-bottom housecleaning, the coach relieved every returning member of the previous year's varsity of his duty, including the team captain. He announced that the new varsity would instead be six members from the 1951 Plebe team—a team that had lost only once all year, at Marietta—and two members from the '51 junior varsity, juniors Robert Detweiler and Frank Shakespeare. The only senior on the varsity would be 123-pound Dave Manring, the nonrowing coxswain.

Veteran Navy crew watchers looked at Callow, who wore floppy felt hats and lumpy overcoats, as if his ships weren't all he'd lost at Marietta. But after 30 years of coaching, Callow knew potential when he saw it, and in these eight, he saw it.

★   ★   ★

Potential was one thing. Reality was another. Racing the first race of the 1952 season on the road, as it were, in New Haven, Connecticut, against Yale, the defending conference champion, called for an easy-does-it approach. In his prerace strategy session, Rusty Callow assembled the members of his Navy team, none of whom had ever rowed in a varsity collegiate race before, and did his best to lower their expectations.

"I don't know how you'll do," he said, reiterating the fact that Yale was the defending league champion and most of the Eli team was returning. Further, this was Skimmer Day at Yale, the crew team's version of homecoming. And further yet, this race marked the beginning of the 100th season of rowing at Yale. Thousands of spectators, many of them former Yale crewmen, lined the banks of the Housatonic for the Centennial, their picnics spread on the lawn, their straw hats perched confidently on their heads. The atmosphere was festive. It isn't every day you coronate the start of a sport's second century.

"What I do know is this course," Callow told his Middies. "There's a big S turn that you'll go through first. Because of the position you're in on the river you'll think you're ahead. But don't be fooled. After you come out of it, don't look where the Yale boat is, just keep your heads down and row like mad."

With that he sent them off to sea.

Soon after the race was underway, there, as advertised, was the S turn. The Middies maneuvered through it and then, once clear, heard Manring, whose duties as cox were to sit in the rear and give the orders, yell from the back of the boat for power 10–10 strokes, as hard as they could give them. That done, Manring called for 20 strokes.

No one looked anywhere but straight ahead. As far as the Navy rowers knew, Yale was already at the finish line. But as they rounded the last curve and looked up to see the boathouse and crowds awaiting the finish, there was no sign of the Yale shell. Suddenly, beer cans and apple cores were coming their way from the shore, accompanied by abusive remarks. From the middle of the boat Detweiler risked a glance back down the river. There was the Yale boat, a good 100 yards behind, which, in a mile and three-quarter race, might as well have been 100 miles.

After showering and changing into their uniforms — and after securing the first opponents' jerseys of their varsity careers — the hardest part of the race remained for the Navy Eight. There was no bus waiting for them, as had been promised, and they had to walk across New Haven to the train station to catch the train to Annapolis. As they walked, they dodged a barrage of water balloons, sometimes unsuccessfully. They reflected on what had just happened. Unless Yale had had an off day — unless Yale had had a *very* off day — they might just be on to something.

★   ★   ★

Rowing suited Robert M. Detweiler. Disciplined by nature, he liked the discipline. Competitive by nature, he liked the competition. A teammate by nature, he liked the teamwork. Driven by nature, he *liked* it when Callow called for an extra five miles on the Severn River before dinner. The Severn, an estuary off the Chesapeake Bay in Annapolis, was where the Navy rowers trained. In that early spring of '52 they were on the Severn all the time — at least all the time when they weren't attending class, standing for inspection, standing for reveille, standing for dinner formation, and otherwise learning to be Officers and Gentlemen.

It was when he was out there on the river, ready to pass out, hearing the order for 10 more strokes, that Detweiler was in his element.

The thing he learned soon enough was that he had seven teammates just like him.

They came from eight diffeent parts of the country and were thrown together by sheer circumstance, but they soon sensed they were a matched set — born to row together.

Seated in the front, in the bow, was Frank Shakespeare, 6-foot-2, 165 pounds from Dover, Delaware. Behind him in the second position was Willie Fields, 6-foot-1 and 178 pounds from Forsyth, Georgia. At number 3 was Jim Dunbar, 6-feet and 178 pounds from Darlington, Indiana. At number 4 was Dick Murphy, 6-foot-3 and 188 pounds from Oaklyn, New Jersey.

Behind Detweiler in the sixth position was Henry Proctor from Independence, Oregon, the biggest in the boat at 6-foot-2 and 205 pounds. In the number 7 seat was Wayne Frye from Manchester, Ohio, 6-foot-2 and 193 pounds, and in the rear of the boat, in the stroke position, was Ed Stevens, 6-foot-2 and 168 pounds from Detroit, Michigan.

Behind Stevens was the coxswain's seat, occupied by Dave Manring, 5-foot-7 and 123 pounds from Cleveland Heights, Ohio.

Stevens was 19 and Manring 23. The rest were between 20 and 22 years old. With the exception of Stevens, none came from a big city and none from families of wealth. Their fathers were farmers or telephone linemen or salesmen. Detweiler's father was a coal mining engineer in Zeigler, Illinois, where Detweiler was born and raised.

In the postwar patriotic fervor of the time, a fervor that had the service academies bulging at their barracks, each of the eight had independently determined to secure congressional appointments to the United States Naval Academy. In later years, they would serve their country well. Five of them, ironically enough, would wind up in the Air Force, including Detweiler, who would win five distinguished flying crosses in Vietnam alone. But that was later and this was now, and for now they were Midshipmen. In Detweiler's case, literally.

In the balanced world of eight-man shell, with cox, rowing, the positions are as defined as the positions of guard, forward and center on a basketball team. The bowman, sitting in the front, and the number 2 rower in front of him are primarily responsible for keeping the boat on course. Together with the number 3 rower, they provide touch and finesse. The middle positions of 4, 5, 6 and 7, often called collectively the "engine room," are where the power comes from—seats reserved for rowers who have no compunction about getting their heads down and their heart rate up. The stroke, at number 8, is responsible for coordinating the entire effort and making sure the strokes are consistent from front to back. At the very back of the boat, the cox—by necessity the only man in the boat light enough to double as a jockey—sits with a megaphone and shouts orders to his crew as he oversees not only what his boat is doing but also what needs to be done in relationship to other boats in the race.

In the early spring of 1952, Shakespeare, Fields, Dunbar, Murphy, Detweiler, Proctor, Frye, and Stevens, with Manring in the rear, discovered that they complemented each other well. Within the confines of their Navy craft, they worked with a single mind.

Callow, their coach, at first wasn't above tinkering with their chemistry. At one practice, he moved Proctor to the junior varsity and replaced him at number 6 with Leonard Anton, a 220-pound upperclassman who could bench press 400 pounds. But in a practice race between the varsity and junior varsity, the junior varsity won. Anton was off, Proctor was back on. Another time, Detweiler was replaced, with the same result. After a time, Callow stopped fussing with his lineup.

Callow was the final ingredient in the mix, and the most colorful. He provided a significant contrast to the short-haired, well-mannered, and highly polished Navy men surrounding him. A civilian almost at retirement age in 1952, he wore baggy clothes and floppy hats, quoted Shakespeare, told jokes, and, when he was on the river, had a habit of losing track of time. For him, getting the men to mess formation every evening at 1900 hours took some getting used to.

Callow had himself rowed varsity at the University of Washington in the early 1920s, captaining the eight-man crew. He was also Washington's student-body president and was somewhat driven himself. As a college student he set a world record when he and a classmate cut down a pine tree four feet in diameter in a little less than seven minutes.

He coached crew at Washington from 1921 through 1926, winning national championships in 1923, 1924, and 1926. The University of Pennsylvania then lured him to the East, where crew wasn't just a sport but also a religion, and he stayed at Penn from 1927 through 1949, enjoying considerable success, although the winning of his fourth national championship eluded him. When Navy called in 1950 to replace Buck Walsh, he accepted the new challenge. He brought with him the layback stroke he'd developed at Washington and refined at Penn, taught it to the Middies, and settled back to see what might happen. When the Plebe class of '51 seemed to take to his coaching particularly well, he was inclined to promote most of that class, along with two junior varsity rowers, to the varsity in '51. When he dismissed all the incumbents from the varsity, he knew full well his sanity was being questioned.

But after opening the season with the win at Yale on Skimmer Day, his credibility soared, and by the midseason Adams

Cup, when Navy stomped the best boats in the East on the Charles River in Boston, all questions concerning his competence were answered.

Harvard, the host school for the Adams Cup, fell that day on the Charles. So did Penn. The Navy Eight won going away. They hadn't lost a race all season, and they had competed on water all over the East. In a few weeks in the national championships, they would be able to see what the West had to offer as well.

★   ★   ★

The national collegiate rowing championships of 1952 were held on Lake Onondaga in Syracuse, New York. But for Navy, the specter of the Ohio River in Marietta the year before was still fresh in memory—especially when the waves on Lake Onondaga kicked up the morning of the nationals and a two-hour delay was ordered. The last thing Navy needed was another storm and another disaster at sea.

But by midafternoon, when the varsity race was set to be run, the wind died down and the water assumed a glasslike surface. Humidity, a residue from the storm front that morning, hung in the air as heat waves rose visibly from the surface of the lake.

Fourteen qualifying boats from around the country lined up for the start. The national championship race would be contested over a three-mile course, a distance considerably longer than the usual mile and three-quarter or two-mile courses run during the year.

Starting in the middle of the shells, the Navy boat, undefeated throughout the season, might as well have had a bull's-eye on its side. Thirteen crews had their eyes focused on the Navy Eight as the gun sounded and the race began.

Not that Navy minded. Being the favorite sat well with Detweiler and his teammates. If anything, it helped them. In

Left: Robert Detweiler, age two

Below: The Great Eight honored by Parade Review at the Naval Academy in 1953 (Detweiler is fourth from left)

Far below: Detweiler (middle) and company never lost a race

BOW

TWO

THREE

OUR

A GREAT EIGHT
ROWS FOR NAVY

Olympic heroes still ripple along

The eight grimacing oarsmen on this page, having rowed some 2,000 miles together, are the most indomitable crew afloat. Their names appear in the 1952 Olympic records—bow, Frank Shakespeare; 2, Bill Fields; 3, Jim Dunbar; 4, Dick Murphy; 5, Bob Detweiler; 6, Henry Proctor; 7, Wayne Frye; stroke, Ed Stevens—as conquerors of the Russians at Helsinki. Now they are back at the Naval Academy dominating collegiate competition just as they did last year. Navy's rise as top boat came amazingly fast after hiring Coach Rusty Callow in 1950. His orders were "Row! Row! Row!" and the back-breaking hours bore fruit so quickly that six veterans in this boat still have another year to row for Navy.

CONTINUED ON NEXT PAGE

FIVE

IX

SEVEN

STROKE

the days leading up to the finals, Navy's rowers were conspic-
uous by their togetherness. They did nothing apart. They ate
breakfast together. If one went to a movie, they all went to a
movie. They sat around their barracks together. The other
rowers looked on with a certain amount of disdain—disdain
with respect perhaps, but disdain just the same.

Conscious of that disdain, when the race started Navy felt
the need to make a statement. From the back, Manring ordered
a strong start, and after 30 strokes, Navy had a lead of almost
a length and a half.

The Navy boat covered the first mile in five minutes—
rowing's equivalent to a four-minute mile. Detweiler, hearing
the time, shouted "Let's go for the record." He was referring
to the national three-mile record of 15:37. The championship
virtually secured, Detweiler didn't want to stop there.

They covered the second mile in just over five minutes.
"All right, let's go for broke," said Manring (who, by now, was
closer to 100 pounds than the 127 he had weighed at the start
of the season. His teammates would take him to breakfast, but
they wouldn't let him eat).

It was easy for him to say. In the boat, so heavy was the
workload and so heavy was the air that the sweat dripping into
the bottom of the boat was sloshing from front to back with
every stroke, affecting the shell's performance. Manring had
to soak up the sweat with a sponge and squeeze it out over
the side.

Just as the Navy Eight were testing the limits of their
drive—for the final mile they were up to 32 strokes a minute,
well ahead of their usual pace of 28 to 30 strokes and an
exhausting pace for the end of a three-mile course—they
crossed the finish line. Their time: 15:08—a three-mile record
that still stands, 40 years later (although, to be fair, the three-
mile distance has since been eliminated from competition).
The shell from Princeton finished a distant second, but, still,

at 15:20, ahead of the old three-mile record of 15:37. The Navy Eight grabbed Manring and threw him in Lake Onondaga. He was the only one not yet soaking wet.

For their next act, they would move on to a competition the following weekend at Lake Quinsigamond in Worcester, Massachusetts, where, on July 2–5, it would be determined which eight-man crew would represent the United States at the 1952 Olympic Summer Games in Helsinki, Finland.

★   ★   ★

For the first time all year — for the first time *ever* — Manring sounded worried. Detweiler, looking up from his number 5 slot, soon saw why. To the right of the Navy boat, practically dead even, was the boat from California — and the finish line was dead ahead.

It was the semifinal heat of the U.S. Olympic Trials, and Navy was paying for a case of overconfidence. After beating Princeton and Harvard easily in the previous day's opening heat — and Princeton, after all, was the national collegiate runner-up — the team had held a meeting and decided that the all-out effort to which they had become accustomed wouldn't be necessary the next day against Cal, a team that had finished a distant fifth the week before at the nationals in Syracuse.

"Let's just beat them, not destroy them," said Detweiler, the team captain and designated purveyor of the team's overall killer instinct. If Detweiler said it was okay to let up, it was okay to let up. He hadn't let up all year, not even in practice.

But it wasn't okay to let up, because Cal, electing to row the race close to the Lake Quinsigamond shoreline, to avoid any wind, had strategized itself into a position to win this race. Coached by Kay Ebright, who had taken Cal crews to three previous Olympic Games and won gold medals with all three (1928, 1932, and, most recently, 1948), the California shell was displaying a terrific game plan. The 2,000-meter sprint course—in conformance with the Olympic distance—was made to order for a team that was smart enough to take the path of least resistance. Here at Lake Quinsigamond, that path was next to the shore.

At the finish, Cal was up to 40 strokes per minute. Manring called for the same from Navy. The shells crossed the line in tandem, the outcome unclear. Only after much deliberation did the officials decide on a winner. It was the team from Navy, saved by a large rubber ball on the tip of their boat, attached there in the early spring so the boat wouldn't bang into the dock on the Severn River.

After the race, Detweiler called another meeting.

"Change of plans," he told his teammates. "I don't care who we embarrass. From now on until we're finished, we row all out."

He soon discovered he had seven teammates who felt the same way. In the final race the next day, Navy won by nearly 10 seconds—a millennium of time in a 2,000-meter sprint—over the next closest boats, from Princeton, which had come back through the loser's bracket and made it into the finals, and Washington. All the while, Manring, usually quite polite in his exhortations, yelled and screamed at his eight teammates sitting in front of him.

For his efforts, Manring was chucked into Lake Quinsigamond as soon as the boat docked. But this time he was joined by all of the crew. They were going all out in their celebration as well. The national champions were now Olympians and would soon be off to Helsinki, wherever that was. Going to the Olympics had not been paramount on anyone's mind just four months before. Making the varsity had been enough.

★   ★   ★

In the waters of the Meilahti Gulf just outside of Helsinki, the Soviet shell appeared to be in distress. From the shore, the American team watched with amused curiosity. On the Olympic course, warming up, was the eight-man crew from the Soviet Union. The Helsinki Games marked the first appearance by Soviet sportsmen in an Olympics since 1912 — an appearance not without fanfare. The Soviets, with their finely tuned, state-trained athletes, were expected to make a fine showing all around.

But the Soviet rowers didn't look finely tuned, or trained. Unlike typical eight-man teams everywhere else in the world — which tended to be close to the same height, gradually increasing in size from the front of the boat to the back — the Soviets were a collection of assorted shapes and sizes. Also, their coach doubled as their cox, and he weighed 165 pounds — the heaviest coxswain anyone had ever seen. And they didn't feather their oars when they brought them back for the catch. They brought them back every which way.

So it was that the Americans didn't have any concern about the Soviets when they drew them in the opening heat of the Olympics, no concern at all . . . until midway through the race and they were cruising through the Meilahti Gulf as if someone had tied them together. Manring would order "Go," and both boats would respond. Only at the finish did the U.S. boat, with a superior sprint, manage to pull ahead — shaken but still unbeaten.

In the second heats the next day, against Swedish and British crews that looked much superior to the Soviets and raced much slower, the U.S. team moved on without problem. That earned them a day off while boats moved through the loser's bracket to set up the finals the following day — between shells representing the United States, Australia, Germany, Great Britain, and the Soviet Union.

Respecting the Soviets was by now not a problem. As it would turn out, that was a good thing. Again, the two boats, one from the U.S. and the other from the U.S.S.R., rowed through the first part of the race as if connected by some underwater cable. But when the finish line came in full focus, with Manring calling for a 40-count, the boat from America surged ahead—winning by a length and a half.

On the dock, after the National Anthem was played and the American flag saluted, Finnish Olympic officials gave each Navy rower a spray of carnations and a box. Inside each box was a gold medal.

After the Soviets received their silver medals and the Australians, who placed third, received their bronze medals, the Navy rowers waited for the Soviets to hand over their jerseys. But when no move was made in that direction, and sensing the losers-give-up-their-jerseys tradition hadn't made it to Russia, the Americans quickly broke with tradition. They took off their jerseys and handed them to their Soviet counterparts.

As the Soviet Union's number 5 rower accepted his U.S.A. jersey, he looked at Detweiler and said through an interpreter, "It's a privilege to lose to you—you're good." After that, he and his Soviet teammates picked up the American team's shell and oars and carried them to the boathouse.

★   ★   ★

Back on the Severn, the Navy Eight went on to win every one of its races in 1953, at which point *Life* magazine, in its edition of March 18, 1953, wrote an article and published pictures about the team. It was entitled, "A Great Eight Rows for Navy."

The name stuck. They were the Great Eight and would be forevermore.

At the end of the 1953 season, the Naval Academy saluted the team with the only parade the Academy has ever given in honor of Midshipmen while still enrolled in school. The Great Eight stood at attention as the parade passed, and their classmates shouted three cheers five separate times.

Frank Shakespeare and Bob Detweiler, who was elected team captain again as a senior, won their commissions in the spring of 1953 and relinquished their spots on the team to two replacements for the 1954 season, when Navy would go undefeated for a third straight year — 33 straight wins in all. Coach Rusty Callow, who retired soon afterward, said it was the greatest team of rowers ever, and there should be a law against graduation.

Detweiler, after flight training, received an assignment to NATO in Paris and, while on furlough there in 1957, competed in the French National Rowing Championships and won the two-man shell with coxswain title, teaming with another Navy sailor and a Frenchman as cox. He later became a squadron pilot and a nuclear physicist and, by the time he retired, a full colonel. In 1965 he was named the Air Force's Scientist of the Year for research in solid state physics. In Vietnam he flew C-123s and was hit several times but never went down.

He joined The Church of Jesus Christ of Latter-day Saints in 1976, baptized by a former missionary to Finland, Keith Nyborg, who, while on his mission, was an interpreter for the American rowers during the 1952 Olympic Games. Nyborg was under strict orders not to proselyte, and he didn't, but a friendship with Detweiler, the captain of the team, developed and they kept in touch. When Detweiler was taught the missionary lessons in Washington, D.C., 24 years later, he telephoned Nyborg at his farm in Ashton, Idaho, and asked him to come East and baptize him.

The Great Eight had a 25-year reunion at the Naval Academy in 1977 and have gotten together every five years since. Each time, the Academy gives them a shell and turns them loose on the Severn and they row out again to the race course. In May of 1992, on the occasion of the 40th anniversary of their gold medal season, they rowed for the first time with the coxswain's seat empty. Dave Manring died the fall before, the first to pass away, and left a request that his ashes be scattered across the waves of the Severn—a request dutifully carried out by his teammates.

★   ★   ★

In 1989 the Collegiate Rowing Association of the United States commissioned the casting of a new trophy to be awarded every year at the occasion of the national championship to the team displaying the most teamwork and courage. Engraved on the side is a tribute to the 1952 Navy team that won the gold medal in the Helsinki Olympics—the team that provided the inspiration, and the name, for the trophy, which is officially called the Great Eight.

L. JAY SILVESTER

BY DOUG ROBINSON

The Olympic medal rests in the living room of the family home
in Orem, Utah. It's on the top shelf of the china cabinet, lying
inconspicuously in a huddle of figurines. You'd never know it
was there if you weren't looking for it. The children — grown
now — still take it out to look it over once in a while when they
visit. The medal's owner takes it with him occasionally when
he speaks to youth groups. A granddaughter took the medal
to school, along with the grandfather, for Show and Tell the
other day. But mostly the medal is forgotten.

That medal. Just think of the sweat and the heartbreak
and the sheer persistence it took finally to win one Olympic
medal, which now keeps all those Hummels company. L. Jay
Silvester, one of the greatest discus throwers in history, spent
the best years of his life pursuing that medal. Nearly two decades in all. Fresh off the farm, he set seven world records and
won six national championships, but what he wanted most of
all was the Olympic gold medal. He went to four Olympic
Games. He knocked himself unconscious in Tokyo, spent a
sleepless week listening to the best of Motown in Mexico City,

battled a severe slump in Munich, and made a curtain call in Montreal.

What is it that could drive a man to spend the prime of his life trying to throw a four-pound steel-and-wood disc from an eight-foot circle farther than anyone else? Certainly not money. There was something more.

Jay discovered the discus in his father's cow pasture quite by accident one day, little knowing what it would come to mean in his life. He was still a teenager when he invented a new way to throw the thing—a technique that would revolutionize the sport. Silvester loved to watch the discus fly, loved to master the implement with precision and skill, to "watch it pass through the atmosphere with energy I impart to it," he once said.

Silvester—intense, serious, introspective—sits in his office on the BYU campus and muses for a moment. On the wall is a picture of him making a world-record throw. The discus he used to set his first world record rests in a cabinet near his desk. When he finally speaks again, he measures his words carefully. "I see all of man the same," he begins. "Each has to find something to spend his energy against, to struggle against, to excel in. Some things just catch our fancy, they become us, we become them, we become attached to an endeavor. There is an internal force that drives you to do that thing, and it becomes an addiction."

These days Silvester struggles against golf, badminton, and racquetball, but the old addiction lingers faintly. He is 54 years old. The stomach is as flat as an ironing board. The stocky shoulders, the barrel chest, and the full face are gone. Shortly after he quit international competition, he dropped 35 pounds simply because he was uncomfortable at 250 pounds. *Who needs the weight if you're not going to throw heavy objects anymore?* But of course he does throw sometimes, just for the fun of it. Sometimes, after coaching BYU's throwers, he'll hang around the ring until everyone is gone, and it's like old times. It's sheer joy just to charge around the ring again, to blast off, to launch the discus. It's all so familiar, the motion and the power, even at 54. All the old feelings return in that ring. It could be any year. It could be 1972 all over again, and he's back in the ring at the Munich Olympics. His mind reels, remembering. He's there. On his next to last throw, he sends the discus deep into the grass field of Olympic Stadium and moves into first place. All he has to do is survive one more round and the gold medal is his. Oh, if only the big Czech, Ludvik Danek, and his attending shrink don't put it together on the last throw. He remembers again. Danek steps up, starts across the ring, whirls, screams, and launches the discus, and . . . No, we must wait, wait as Silvester did. We must start at the beginning.

★   ★   ★

In the summertime, the lights outside the Silvester house shined long after darkness had fallen. Ed nailed the lights onto the side of the house for the boys and built them a throwing ring in the garden. Shirrel and L. Jay stayed out late almost every night in the warm weather, throwing the discus and the shot put over and over again. They might have stayed out there all night if their folks hadn't finally called them to bed.

The Silvesters lived on a farm near Tremonton in the foot-hills of northern Utah. Ed was a farmer, the supervisor for county roads and a sometime bronc rider in the local rodeo; Della raised four children and worked in Cowley's department store. Each morning Shirrel and L. Jay awakened before dawn to begin their chores. They fed the livestock and milked the cows by hand, hustled off to school, then repeated their chores that evening after school and practice. This was their world. They rarely ventured elsewhere. They tried to leave once. They moved to Salt Lake City one summer, planning to attend the

University of Utah on football scholarships that fall, but they got so homesick that two weeks later they were back on the farm, and from there they commuted daily to Utah State. On his first road trip with the USU track team, L. Jay was homesick by the time they reached the town of Kemmerer, just over the state line in Wyoming. It was the farthest he had been away from home.

Shirrel was a year older than L. Jay, but they attended the same grade throughout school. They were the stereotypical big, robust farm boys, bound by blood and their odd names. L. Jay is the name. The L doesn't stand for anything — it's just L. Ed and Della were set to name him L.J., but a grandmother talked them into adding the "ay."

The boys were playing in their father's cow pasture one afternoon when Shirrel's buddy, Larry Chadaz, showed up with a discus for reasons no one can remember now. Nobody knew how to throw it, but they held a competition anyway. The most important rule was to watch where they stepped. Launching the discus out of the wrong side of their hands, L. Jay threw it 30 feet, Shirrel 35. L. Jay was hooked, at 13 years old.

The Silvesters starred in football and track at Bear River High. In football, they led the Bears to the state championship and earned all-state honors and scholarships. But the football career didn't last long. After a year at Utah State, L. Jay gave up the sport and devoted himself full-time to track and field, his first love. The long hours of football practice were tedious, and the sport too mean; he didn't mind hitting people — he just didn't like getting hit back. Coach John Ralston, who was building a national-class football team at USU, never got over the loss.

"What a tackle he would have made," Ralston once said. "It's a shame to waste all of that man on a little old iron ball and a wooden disc."

Silvester — bowlegged, slope-shouldered, long-armed — had

size, strength, athleticism, and, most important, speed—speed enough to run on the sprint relay team in high school, at 200 pounds. He also had an analytical mind that enabled him to learn and apply the minute details of technique in the highly technical art of discus throwing, as well as a fiercely independent nature that wasn't afraid to find a better way of doing things. He watched two movies side by side on the screen—one showing him throwing, the other showing a world-class thrower—and compared the various points of technique to decide which was best. Sometimes he preferred his own methods.

While still in high school, Silvester drove 15 miles to Logan regularly to train with Ralph Maughan, the track and field coach at Utah State and one of the event's most renowned teachers. He took what Maughan taught him back to the farm, put on his spiked shoes, went out to the cow pasture, and worked on technique tirelessly. He trained regularly with Maughan, but then one day he didn't show up for their usual session. For two weeks he didn't show up. While practicing in the pasture one day, L. Jay had noticed that Shirrel was throwing 170 feet—20 feet farther than he was throwing—and the state meet was coming up soon. Frustrated and desperate, L. Jay began experimenting with different ways to throw the discus, trying to beat his brother. Finally, he found one. He discovered that by using a wide stance and then a wide sweeping right leg action as he came around the circle, he created more speed and force. The accepted practice was to keep the right leg tucked in tight, but L. Jay was sure he was onto something. After three hours of throwing, he was too exhausted to throw any farther that day, but the new motion felt better. The next day he threw 170 feet in the pasture. He continued to perfect the new style on the farm for several days, and when he finally returned to Logan to resume training with Maughan, the coach watched one throw and noticed the change immediately.

"What are you doing?" he asked Silvester. "How come you're throwing that way?"

"It feels better. And I can throw it a lot farther."

"Well," said Maughan, "that's good enough for me."

The technique was one that every discus thrower in the world would adopt eventually. "Everyone was using a tight turn in those days," recalls Maughan. "He's the one who started it. All of them have patterned their technique after L. Jay."

Silvester won the state championship and set a state record of 170 feet, 4 1/2 inches with the new technique, then moved on to Utah State. He finished second in the shot put and third in the discus at the 1958 NCAA Track and Field Championships as a junior, but under the rules of the time he was ineligible to compete in the NCAA meet the following year because he had competed as a freshman.

Silvester continued to train during the next two years while serving in the Army. In 1960 he finished fourth in the U.S. Olympic Trials—one place away from making the Olympic team. He found consolation a few weeks later when he threw 190 feet in a pre-Olympic competition—just 6 1/2 feet short of Rink Babka's world record. For the first time Silvester realized he could break that record.

A year later he won the national AAU championships in New York and approached the world record with a throw of 195-8, but he had two fouls that went farther. In 1961 Silvester became a force. He went to Europe and won the shot and discus at the World Athletic Games in Helsinki, then won the discus again at the U.S.-Russia and U.S.-Germany duals. But he fouled several more world record throws. He also had world record fouls in London, Warsaw, and Berlin, and now the record was beginning to work on his mind. He was wondering if there were forces at work against him when he came to Frankfurt, Germany, on August 11. The discus competition was already underway when he finished—and won—the shot put, and meet officials told him that he would have to compete without warming up. Fearing injury, he declined. He was sitting on the infield watching the competition when one of the U.S. coaches convinced the officials to let Silvester warm up. Using a discus he borrowed from the Russians, Silvester launched a long throw that brought cheers from the crowd.

"I knew I had the record the instant the disc left my hand," he told reporters. The throw was 198-7 1/2, two feet beyond the world record. Nine days later he did it again, this time with a heave of 199-2 3/8 in Brussels, Belgium. Silvester returned home to Tremonton to a hero's welcome. Signs greeted him from the shop windows. He was honored at the county fair and the rodeo and in a parade. The press, meanwhile, was hailing Silvester as America's great Olympic hope.

"It's been my ambition to compete in the Olympics, but I can't say if I will now because it's still too far away," said Silvester. How could he have known that at 24 his career was still only in its infancy?

★   ★   ★

Silvester had just finished warming up outside Olympic Stadium in Tokyo, and he felt good. He had snap in his arm, and he felt explosive, powerful. He was ready for the 1964 Olympic Games. He left the practice field and entered the tunnel underneath the stadium to report for the qualifying rounds. Walking through the tunnel, he had to duck to avoid bumping his head on the heating duct that hung low from the ceiling. The Japanese could walk under the duct easily, but not a 6-foot-3 American. Eventually he came to a set of stairs. The stairs went up, but the duct didn't. Silvester slammed his head into the angle iron used to support the duct—and kept walking. He refused to acknowledge the distraction, even with blood running down the side of his face. Arriving at the athletes' holding room, he asked the team trainer to bandage his head. The trainer looked at the cut, then said, "Come with me." Silvester followed him down a hallway.

"Where are we going? I've got to get onto the field."

"You need stitches."

Silvester sat in a chair and stewed while doctors worked on his head. *This can't be happening,* he thought. *I'm getting stitches, and I'm getting ready for the Olympic Games.* Moments later he passed out. When Silvester woke up, he was lying on a table with smelling salts pushed to his nose and a coach telling him, "We've got to go now." Shaking like a leaf, he walked onto the field.

The competition had been held up for Silvester. He took a couple of quick warmup throws, both of which sailed out of bounds, wide to the right. So did his first official throw, but he threw far enough on his second attempt to qualify for the finals, which would be held later that night. Silvester returned to his room and rested. He had several hours to think about the finals.

Silvester had entered the competition as one of the favorites, but he was facing a formidable obstacle in Al Oerter, the two-time defending Olympic champion and a legend in the making. Oerter had broken Silvester's world record two years earlier, but Silvester had beaten Oerter by six feet while winning the U.S. Olympic Trials. Then there was the Czech, Danek, the current world record holder and winner of 45 straight competitions.

When Silvester returned to the stadium that evening, he was anxious about the six stitches in his head. How would he perform? He couldn't wait to find out. During warmups he threw hard—too hard. His throws were flying past 200 feet. On his last throw he threw over 63 meters, or 208 feet—which would be an Olympic record if it counted—and suddenly he felt drained. When the finals began, Silvester was flat. After four throws he found himself in third place, but up stepped Oerter, and fate seemed to be with him. Discus throwers love nothing more than to throw into the wind, which holds the discus aloft longer. The wind had been still all evening, but the moment Oerter stepped into the ring, the flag above the stadium suddenly stiffened, and the wind began blowing into his face. Silvester stared up into the sky. "I wondered if there was a glow from heaven for Oerter," he said afterward. Oerter threw 200-1, moving from fifth place to first, and then the flag went limp. Silvester finished fourth, one place away from a medal. He packed his bags and returned to his home in Smithfield, Utah. It was time to return to the insurance business.

★ ★ ★

Pursuing an amateur athletic career was never easy. Silvester thought his first Olympics would be his last, but the allure of the sport — the life-style, the training, the competition, the achievement, the success, everything about it — held him captive well into middle age. Still, he had a wife and three children to support. Silvester quit the Army and taught high school for a year while earning a master's degree in physical education. Then he sold life insurance in Logan for five years. Eventually he joined the physical education faculty at BYU, where he took a doctorate in exercise physiology and worked weekends as an Army reserve officer and world-class discus thrower.

There was never much money in discus throwing, and what there was of it Silvester wasn't taking. Under the rules of the time, so-called amateur athletes weren't allowed to be paid for their sport, but of course they were. But not Silvester. If anything, the sport cost him money, because to compete on weekends or on the summer European circuit meant leaving his job, without pay. Sometimes he didn't compete simply because he felt compelled to remain home with his family and to work. Sometimes he trained for 12 months just to compete

in a handful of meets in the United States, then stayed home
while the best in the world competed on the more important
European circuit.

Always he would wrestle with the notion of amateurism,
looking on as other athletes accepted money under the table
and wondering who was right and who was wrong. Sometimes
it was called appearance money or expense money, and sometimes it wasn't disguised as anything other than cold, hard
cash. Many athletes had no qualms about taking the money in
whatever form it came. They reasoned that there wasn't much
difference between a crystal vase, which could be accepted
legally, and the $500 the crystal vase was worth. They reasoned
that they were being exploited by promoters who filled 50,000-
seat stadiums for track and field meets but were required *not*
to pay the performers. Most did anyway.

In 1961, after Silvester broke the world record, a European
meet official asked him to compete in a meet in Stockholm.
Silvester declined. He had to return to his job in Logan, he
explained. "How much do you earn in a week?" the official
asked. Silvester told him: $160. "I'll pay you that if you throw
in the meet." Silvester agreed. After the competition the man
paid him, but Silvester felt guilty—so guilty that he tried to
persuade meet officials to keep the crystal vase they had given
him for winning. In the coming days his guilt grew to such
dimensions that he vowed never again to accept money.

"I knew some of the athletes were being paid," recalls
Silvester. "But in the Mormon culture we're taught to be hon-
est. All my life I had been told it was wrong for an amateur
athlete to take money for competing. I knew I couldn't live
with myself if I broke the amateur rules."

For the next nine years he refused all offers of money,
beyond expenses, but the question of amateurism continued
to nag him. Late in his career, Silvester began to accept some
modest payment for his performances, as he and his contem-

poraries helped pioneer the days when athletes could be paid. Inevitably, the hypocrisy of amateurism gave way to reform. By the early 1980s, athletes were allowed to accept money, but by then it was much too late to help Silvester.

"I could have been rich if I had been 'taking' those first nine years of competition," says Silvester. "It would have made my travels and standard of living a lot better in those days. Getting paid for my performances took a lot of pressure off myself and my family late in my career. Had I been free to train instead of work for a living, I doubt if anyone could have beaten me. But as it was, I didn't have the money for my family that we needed at times, and I had a feeling I was selfish in spending so much time in training and competition, in being away from my family. I came to the conclusion that someone had lied to me, had instilled in me a false set of values. . . . The system was set up by those in control to enhance their control. They deprived the athletes of their rightful share of their earnings."

Silvester's wife, Geneil, a small, trim, blue-eyed woman with beauty that defies her 54 years, sits in the living room of their small home in Orem and remembers. "We never had extra money," she says. "It was never easy. I wanted him to get on with raising a family and pursuing his career. I would look at these guys earning lots of money at times, and he couldn't work because he was going to meets."

Silvester was always driven. He was so focused, so devoted that during his many trips to Europe he rarely ventured out to see the sights. All he did was train and compete. Back home, he lifted weights in his basement, building his strength until he could bench press 465 pounds. He trained in the morning and sold insurance in the afternoon. Discus rings were often difficult to find or to get to, so he threw from sidewalks into vacant high school fields. In the winter he threw a rubber discus in an empty parking lot or indoors against a wall.

Above far left: At Bear River High, L. Jay Silvester
was a football hero

Above left: As a Utah State Aggie, Silvester threw the discus at All-American distances

Left: Silvester revolutionized the sport with a technique he
developed in his father's cow pasture

Above: Silvester's intensity carried him through four Olympiads
(photo courtesy *Deseret News*)

Family life and the discus were inevitably intertwined. Family picnics were sometimes trips to the track, where Dad threw and threw until finally the kids — Janet, Darren, and Lisa Dawn — and Geneil begged to go home: *"C'mon, let's go!"* And always the refrain: *"Just one more. Just one more."* Family vacations evolved around track meets. The Silvesters attended the Mt. SAC Relays in California annually, and from there they drove to Disneyland. While the kids swam at the hotel, L. Jay drove to the nearest field to throw. One day Silvester baptized Darren, and then the two of them were off to the track — L. Jay to throw, Darren to shag. In the summer Silvester left the family for weeks at a time to compete in Europe, feeling guilty for leaving Geneil alone to tend the children.

That's the way it would always be: Silvester pulled by the opposite forces of familial duty and sport, amateurism and money.

"Sometimes I wonder if it was worthwhile," says Silvester. "Any activity like that is selfish. All the time I was competing I was aware of more important things, such as family and church. I threw in a way that I hoped did not detract from my awareness of and attention to those other things."

★   ★   ★

Every night Silvester lay awake in his bed at Mexico City, stricken with the terror of insomnia. The 1968 Olympic Games was just days away, and he hadn't been able to sleep more than a few moments in the athletes' village all week. Twelve athletes were staying in one high-rise apartment, four to a room, and every sound reverberated through the concrete walls. In one room was a group of black athletes, one of them long jumper Bob Beamon, who would set a landmark world record in a few days. But right now Beamon and his friends were relaxed — too relaxed for Silvester. They played loud music until three or four o'clock every morning, and their friends were coming and going all night long. Silvester—31, married and accustomed to quiet nights—rested fitfully in the next room. He pleaded with American coaches to move him, but they refused. This was a time of racial tension in the United States. "We can't move you, or we'll be accused of segregation," the coaches told him.

Silvester had come to the Olympics as a sure bet to win a gold medal. He was in peak form, unstoppable. He had won 22 straight competitions; he had smashed the world record three times; he had won the Olympic Trials by a rout. He was so good that rivals were studying film and photos of his technique. *What was he doing?* Silvester added to the intrigue. He talked openly of a secret technique, which he owed to his old college coach, Maughan, but he wasn't saying what it was.

Only a year earlier Silvester had been abysmal. In the fall of 1967, after sitting out of competition for more than a year with a shoulder injury, he threw a meager 178 feet in a pre-Olympic warmup meet in Mexico City. It was his worst performance in eight years. In the off-season he spent hours studying film, trying to find the flaw in his technique, and experimented regularly at the Utah State track. But nothing worked. One afternoon, Maughan, who was putting his runners through a track workout, studied Silvester while he threw. After watching for a time, he finally approached the ring.

"Jay, you're not getting your weight over your left leg," he told him. It was jargon, of course, meaningful only to insiders. In essence, Maughan was telling Silvester that his mechanics were wrong. Frustrated and upset with his throwing, Silvester politely dismissed the advice, independent as always. And still the form wouldn't come. The next day Silvester returned to the track and struggled again. Then he recalled Maughan's advice. He tried it, and, like magic, it made a dramatic difference. "At 30 years old, to discover a significant technical key was very unlikely," he recalls. "But my entire body tingled when I let go of the discus. That has never happened before or since. Every cell in my body was cheering, '*That's how you do it.*' I worked hard on that movement. I was surprised that one little thing I had completely overlooked in technique could make such a difference. I had been stiff, but now I was like a whip uncoiling. Fluid and quick. It set up 1968."

This was Silvester's secret, and it made him unbeatable. At the Fresno Relays he set a world record of 218-4. At the Olympic Trials in Lake Tahoe, Nevada, all six of his throws bettered any by the runner-up, and he beat Oerter, the three-time defending Olympic champion, by three feet. Four weeks before the Olympics, in an all-comers meet in Nevada, Silvester produced the greatest series of throws in history, throwing 215-0, a world-record 223-4, 219-3, 207-1, a close foul of 230-5, and another world record of 224-5.

So he came to Mexico City as the favorite. He arrived six days early—and regretted it. With the music and the sleepless nights, Silvester could feel the strength draining from his body. If he complained to his roommates, he risked creating ill feelings and more distractions. Shortly before the start of the qualifying rounds, Silvester—normally intense and restless—lay down in the grass and fell asleep. His teammates had to wake him for the competition. His one and only throw sailed 207-9 1/2. It was an Olympic record, and it beat the other 11 qualifiers by nearly 10 feet. It also was several inches farther than Oerter had thrown in his life.

The final was set for the next day, and the competition would begin again from scratch. Silvester returned to his room exhausted, and again he endured another sleepless night. At three A.M. his roommates shut off their stereo, but he never did sleep. In the morning he looked out the window and noted the cloudy, overcast skies. When it came time to throw, Silvester was trembling as he walked onto the field. To his surprise, he felt ready. He removed his sweats, grabbed a discus from the rack, and was walking toward the ring when the rain began. It was a deluge. The discus ring filled with nearly an inch of water. The athletes continued to warm up in the downpour, but their throws were wild, crashing into the sides of the cage. The officials called the athletes together and asked for a vote. They voted for postponement.

The competitors returned to a holding room under the stadium to wait for the rain to stop. At an altitude of 7,000 feet, the concrete room was as cold as a cave. Silvester and the other throwers removed their sweatsuits and wrung the water out of them. They wrapped themselves in blankets, lay on training tables, and waited. Then a sleepless week began to overtake Silvester.

"I will never forget the physical collapse," he recalls. "It was shocking to lie down. I melted into the table. I was physically and psychologically exhausted. I could feel it. I said to myself, *Wait a minute, this is the Olympics.* I was scared. I could feel the strength draining out of me."

An hour later the athletes returned to the field. Silvester knew he was in trouble. He had no snap in his arm. Still, when the third round ended, he was in third place with a throw of 202-8. Oerter, who had lost to Silvester in six of their previous seven meetings, was in fourth place when he took his fourth throw. He threw 212-6—five feet farther than he had ever thrown. Silvester's final three throws were all fouls. He finished in fifth place.

Silvester met Geneil outside the stadium, where they embraced and cried. Before leaving Mexico City, they called their children at home to tell them the news, one at a time. They all cried for Dad.

A year later Silvester beat Oerter in three consecutive meets, and Oerter retired. But it was small consolation. More than 20 years later, Silvester would call the 1968 Olympics "the most painful experience ever in my life."

★　　★　　★

Even as a boy Silvester noticed that he didn't cope well with the pressure of competition. In Church basketball games, the basket seemed a little higher, the ball not quite so round. He couldn't shoot, couldn't pass, couldn't dribble the way he did in practice. He was so nervous that he couldn't perform. He became overly excited. Nowadays they call it choking, but Silvester wouldn't recognize it for what it was until years later.

He learned to deal with the pressure to a degree. After all, he did win the Olympic trials and all those national championships. But no pressure was as great as that at the Olympic Games. Nothing else was like it. And nothing could be done to prepare for it. There were no world championships for track and field in those days, only the Olympics, and so Silvester had no opportunity to grow accustomed to Olympic-like pressure except by attending the Olympics every four years. Another man—such as Oerter, the greatest of clutch performers—might have dealt better with the all-night hours of his Olympic roommates, might have better handled the rain delays and the six stitches in the head, but Silvester was already a high-strung, nervous sort. He always was. When he entered a ring, no one could move, no one could walk by, no one could stand behind him. Everything had to be just so. And so there was the pressure of the Olympic Games, where things happened that were beyond his control, and he couldn't or didn't cope with them.

"The Olympic Games were not my cup of tea," he says, reflecting. "I didn't understand it at the time, but I didn't know how to deal with the pressure. I had a tendency to get overexcited. As something becomes more important to you, the anxiety rises. You must learn to control it, to deal with it."

After the '68 Olympics, Silvester continued to compete for the love of the sport, but the Olympics were always on the horizon. "I've never given up the dream of winning a gold medal," he said.

★   ★   ★

Silvester arrived at Munich in 1972 a week before the Olympic Games in the worst slump of his life, and this time it was his own fault. He had coached himself all those years, and now what he really needed was Maughan, but the coach was in Utah, thousands of miles away. Silvester was desperate. He couldn't even break 200 feet. It was amazing, really, that he had even managed to make it to the Olympics.

Silvester had been in the form of his life only one year earlier. In 1971, he threw 230-11 to become the first man in history to break 230 feet. It was a world record, sort of. The meet director had failed to mail a letter of sanction to the International Amateur Athletic Federation, track's international governing body. As a result, the IAAF refused to sanction the meet or recognize Silvester's mark as an official world record (although most experts, including *Track & Field News,* recognized the mark anyway). A month later, Silvester set another world record of 229-10, but there was another complication. The meet had been registered only as a national event, not as an international event, and a Swede had competed in the discus. Once again the IAAF refused to recognize the meet and the record. All this silliness and paperwork aside, there was no doubt that Silvester was king of the ring. He lost just one competition all year and was ranked number 1 in the world for 1971.

Silvester was so far ahead of the rest of the world that he was without challenges. *Where can I go from here?* he wondered, once the season ended. How can I improve? He decided to try a new technique. Some throwers were using 1 1/2 turns instead of the traditional 1 1/4. Silvester was intrigued. He worked on the new technique during the winter and took it into competition with him in 1972, but he was erratic, and the throws were inferior to his marks of a year earlier. One month before the Olympic Trials he returned to his former style — and couldn't find it exactly. He won the national championships with a throw of 213 feet, and he won the Olympic Trials for the third consecutive time with a mark of 211 feet, but even those throws didn't feel right. They were labored and forced, not flowing and smooth. When his performances declined in the coming weeks, he grew panicky. He went to Europe and was beaten badly. Out of desperation, he threw the discus three or four hours daily trying to discover the technical flaws. One day in Oslo he stayed out in the rain for three hours throwing repeatedly. He knew he was overtraining, but he was going to solve the problem or die trying. That was his style, and it had always worked before. But this time he couldn't find the problem, and he was exhausted from trying.

With the Olympics one week away, he decided to gamble: he wouldn't touch a discus the rest of the week. He needed to recover from the fatigue of all that training. For a week he rested and avoided the discus, but the day before the qualifying rounds he could stand the suspense no longer. He went to a practice field alone and threw 213 feet. He was encouraged. The next day he qualified easily for the finals.

Silvester returned to the Olympic village to wait for the next day's finals and to wonder if he would choke again under the pressure. Now more than ever there was pressure. At the age of 35, with two nonmedal performances behind him, this might be his last chance for the gold medal. And finally Oerter was gone.

Silvester prepared his wife for the worst: "Don't get your hopes up," he told her. A devout, lifelong Mormon, Silvester prayed that night, "I've put in the effort. Help me to perform to the best of my ability."

Silvester stepped onto the Olympic field, and to his surprise he felt strong. He felt none of the fatigue and weakness or any of the other by-products of anxiety that he had felt at the previous two Olympics. Even if he was battling a slump, at least he felt good.

The experts figured that with Oerter in retirement, the competition for the gold medal was between Danek and Silvester. They were both 35 and both had been overshadowed by Oerter. Danek, a towering Czech, had won silver and bronze medals in '64 and '68, respectively. Danek and Silvester had competed against each other 24 times, with Danek winning 12 and Silvester winning 12. It was an even match.

Silvester stepped into the ring for his third throw and began a practiced routine. He spat on the discus, spat on his hands, studied the landing area for a moment, gauged the wind, and then whirled through the ring. He unleashed a throw of 208-4 to move into first place. Discus throwers rarely if ever talk to each other during competition, but Sweden's Ricky Bruch, a longtime rival, approached the intense Silvester smiling. "Jay, I like that," he said. Silvester was curiously moved by Bruch's simple gesture.

For the next two rounds, Silvester maintained his hold on first place, but he felt vulnerable. Danek stepped into the ring for his final throw. He was having a bad day. He was in fifth place with a mark of 206 feet. But as Danek entered the ring, Silvester remembered something the Czech had said to him at a meet earlier in the season. Danek had been followed everywhere on the European circuit that summer by a goateed psychologist. "We are trying to make every throw a good throw, especially the last one. *Especially* the last one," Danek had explained to Silvester.

Danek blasted across the ring, whirled through a tight and violent turn, and hurled the discus 211-3. He was in first place. Silvester had one more throw, but it fell short. After the competition ended, Danek threw his arms around Silvester, then

Bruch threw his arms around both of them, and there they stood in a collective silent embrace on the field. Danek won the gold, Silvester the silver, Bruch the bronze.

After the meet, Silvester called his wife, who was waiting for the news in Orem.

"Honey, what do you think of a silver medal?"

"I think that's fantastic!" she said.

With that, Silvester returned to Orem, content. He had done his best. It was time to return to family and work.

★   ★   ★

Silvester returned to the Olympics again four years later, old enough to be the father of many of his teammates. He didn't compete in 1973 or 1974, but he competed on the European circuit again in 1975, calling it his "last fling." Seeing that there was no clear favorite to claim the third spot on the U.S. Olympic Team in 1976, he entered the Olympic Trials and finished third. A month shy of his 39th birthday, he competed in his fourth Olympic Games and finished in eighth place. Countryman Mac Wilkins, who used Silvester's sweeping leg action and was coached in the technique by Silvester himself years earlier, won the gold medal.

By then Silvester's place in the sport was secure. In at least one book devoted to discus throwing, his technique is listed as one of five milestones in the sport. It changed the sport. So did his performances. When Silvester first began throwing the discus, 200 feet was considered a barrier comparable to the four-minute mile. For the next two decades he was always there at the front, pushing the record forward. His last world record was some 32 feet farther than his first world record, 10 years apart.

In 1980, after a three-year layoff, Silvester competed in the Olympic Trials again, finishing eighth with a throw of 195-11. He was 42. After that, he gave up national-class competition for good. By then he was finally ready to find other things to spend his energy against.

PETER VIDMAR

BY LEE BENSON

As calmly as possible under the circumstances, Peter Vidmar watched as Tim Daggett finished off the best horizontal bar routine of his life with a full twisting double layout and hit the mat like a panther. The crowd in Pauley Pavilion erupted, but that was nothing compared to what they did when the judges flashed Daggett's 10 on the electronic scoreboard. It didn't get any better than that.

The United States men's gymnastics team was on a roll in 1984, a roll unprecedented in Olympic gymnastics history. As far as men's gymnastics was concerned, for almost a century the United States had been the doormat for the world. In team competition the history was a succession of coming up short, mostly way short. But now, in Los Angeles for the Games of the 23rd Olympiad, all that had changed, and the men's team from the United States was not performing down to tradition.

Vidmar, America's top gymnast, the team's anchor man, waited for Daggett's ovation to die down and approached the bar. So this was it, this was what 12 years of training—minus one week once for a break—came down to. This was why your coach insisted that every time you did a routine you did it as if a judge was watching and it mattered—because there would come a time when the trick was to do it as if you were still in practice and it didn't matter—do it just as you'd done it a thousand times before. Knock down a who-cares, get-this-over-with-and-we're-outta-here routine, and no matter what the Chinese, the perennial bullies of gymnastics, did, they couldn't catch up. Give this one final high bar routine your best shot, and the United States could not be stopped from winning its first men's gymnastics gold medal in history.

★   ★   ★

Doris Vidmar had the newspaper article in her hand as she and her 11-year-old son, Peter, wearing a blue jacket that said DODGERS across the front, walked into the Culver City Junior High School gym. They were looking for a Mr. Makoto Sakamoto. He was the coach mentioned in the article in the *Santa Monica Evening Outlook* that read:

FUTURE GYMNASTS GET AID IN CULVER
This weekend, the Culver City Dept. of Parks & Recreation will hold the first experimental gymnastics program designed to develop future Olympic champions. Selection will be made from boys 10–13. No experience necessary. Founder of the program is international gymnastics champion Makoto Sakamoto. Only five boys will be chosen to train under Coach Sakamoto. Tryouts and selections at 11 A.M. at Culver City Jr. High Girls Gym.

★   ★   ★

John Vidmar, Doris's husband and Peter's father, had seen the article two nights before, after John had come home from his job in downtown Los Angeles, where he was an engineer with the Byron Jackson Pump Company, and settled onto the couch to read the evening paper. John had been a gymnast himself, at L.A.'s Dorsey High, and his brother, Dick, had been a conference champion at USC. John had since had a battle with polio, a battle he had won but not without a limp to show for it. He knew how much he enjoyed the days when he had done backflips and somersaults and run everywhere he went. He also knew that his youngest son, Pete, had similar inclinations, an opinion verified by various pieces of broken furniture lying around the house. So he clipped out the ad and gave it to his wife.

Mr. Sakamoto was not hard to identify. Actually, as it turned out, there were *two* Mr. Sakamotos—Isamu, or Sam, who had been running the gymnastics program for the Culver City Recreation Department for several years now, and Makoto, or Mako, Sam's younger brother who had just returned from the 1972 Olympic Games and was retiring from competition. It was Mako who was looking for a few good protégés, five of them at the most, to turn into champions. (Until now, the Culver City program existed for girls only. As the Vidmars walked into the gym, Peter, all 4-foot-9 and 69 pounds of him, was the only boy in sight).

Mako, who'd torn a biceps muscle and still managed to finish the Olympics all-around competition in Montreal, was having a hard time leaving gymnastics cold turkey. He had a full-time job, working for an import firm, but he'd been an active gymnast since 1957, when he was 11, and it was in his blood, and he needed to do *something*. With Sam as his coach, he'd been a United States national champion (he was born in Tokyo but soon moved with his family to Los Angeles) seven different times. He'd won his first national championship when he was 16 and had competed in three Olympic Games, the first as an 18-year-old in Tokyo in 1964 and the last just weeks ago in Munich, where he captained the U.S. team. At his peak, he'd been among the top dozen gymnasts in the world. What he wanted now, closer to 30 than 20 and over the competitive hump, was to train someone else, someone who could go even further than he had.

In all, 20 boys, and their mothers, signed up for the five spots Mako Sakamoto had opened to tryouts. He put all 20 through a variety of tests, many of them seeming to have no connection at all with gymnastics. He tested intelligence, memory, obedience, and other intangibles. He also tested strength, flexibility, and coordination. The boys with the top five scores qualified. The blond kid in the Dodgers jacket turned out to be the class valedictorian.

Peter Vidmar didn't have terrific leg strength. That could be, and would be, a problem. But his upper body strength was exceptional and, even if he was 11 and blond and looked like he should be outside somewhere chasing frogs, in Peter Vidmar Coach Mako saw himself.

Not that Peter was a gymnast, or anywhere near a gymnast yet. The Sakamoto brothers' philosophy began with the notion that no one was a natural. "You can be born fast, but you're not born doing a handstand," Mako told his five future champions. Sprinters were born, but gymnasts were made in the gym. When he joined the Culver City Club, Peter's proudest gymnastics maneuver was a back handspring he'd learned at Westchester High School during open gym nights. One of the first things he said to Sam Sakamoto after he'd been accepted into the club was, "Watch this," after which he did his backflip. Isamu just stood there and grinned.

★   ★   ★

They were in one of the roughest sections of downtown Los Angeles, in Queen Anne Park. It was where Mako had grown up. He had brought the five members of his Culver City Gymnastics Club here, to his roots, and, more specifically, to the track that surrounded the park, for one of his mini camps.

Mako was fond of his mini camps. Periodically, he would take his Culver City gymnasts away from their homes, put them up in his apartment, and have them spend the next two or three days concentrating on something specific — like strength. And at Queen Anne, that was the theme. The gymnasts looked at each other and rolled their eyes. Peter Vidmar wondered what a white blond kid, like himself, was doing in this part of town anyway.

Mako — he never asked his gymnasts to do anything he didn't do right alongside them — explained that for today's strength workout they would do squat jumps around the track. Put your hands behind your head, get into a catcher's crouch, and jump. With every squat jump, you could move about three feet.

After the first 20 feet around the 440-yard cinder track, even the coach sensed he might have gone too far this time. But a goal was a goal, and they kept squat jumping, going in a circle that felt like a straight line. It took over an hour to finish — and a week after that for their quadriceps muscles to recover. The next day at the gym, they all had to use the handrails to walk downstairs. Even Mako.

"You know, that was really stupid, what we did," he said. "But it builds character, doesn't it?"

Such was the Culver City Gymnastics Club — as unstructured as it was structured; as unassuming as it was assuming. The club's headquarters alone, in the girls' gymnasium of the Culver City Junior High School, was enough to fool the world that world-class gymnastics was the Sakamoto brothers' object. The gym was on loan only at night. All the gymnastics equipment had to be moved out of closets every evening before workouts and moved back after workouts were finished. The coaches had no offices. And getting rich wasn't even remotely in the picture: dues were $20 a month.

Discipline was the only clue that this was a serious business;

and not just the kind of discipline that cost you two laps around the gym if you walked in five minutes late. Discipline to gymnastics, period. Every workout, without fail, started with an hour of stretching, balancing exercises, handstands, and a little ballet. And every routine, without fail, started with a salute to the judges, who they pretended were there. Most of the time there was also a Snicker's bar waiting on the mat if you landed upright, and there was always plenty to joke about. The atmosphere wasn't oppressive, just devout. To thrive in the club was simple enough: all you had to do was love gymnastics as much as the brothers who ran the place.

Peter loved every minute of it. He looked forward to practice. When Mako — "Mr. Mako," to Peter; from day one he called him that and never stopped — asked if they could increase his workouts from every other day to four days a week, he said fine; from four days to five, fine again; from five to six, no problem.

But there was a problem when Mako, sensing Peter's potential, suggested adding Sundays to the schedule. Peter had just turned 12 and had been ordained a deacon in the Aaronic Priesthood. Much as he loved gymnastics, he couldn't in good conscience put the sport ahead of his priesthood and of Sunday.

He told Mako that he couldn't train on Sunday and hoped he would understand. Mako didn't. He responded the way you'd expect a coach to respond: he dismissed Peter from the team. If Mako was willing to give 100 percent to a developing gymnast, a gymnast he believed had world class potential, and that gymnast wasn't willing to give 100 percent back, then they had a problem.

Mako, suspecting the decision not to practice on Sunday had been made by Peter's parents, visited them soon afterward. John and Doris Vidmar explained that Peter's decision was completely his own, and that it wasn't based on a lack of loyalty

Left: Peter Vidmar, age six, with his puppy Taffey

Below: As a motivational speaker, Vidmar and his pommel horse are never far apart

Above right: On the pommel horse in 1984, Vidmar was perfect

Below right: Vidmar and Tim Daggett were good friends and teammates at UCLA and the Olympics

Below far right: At Los Angeles in 1984, to the victor went the spoils

to the Culver City Gymnastics Club. To the contrary—his quandary was wondering how he could be loyal to both God and gymnastics if they each wanted him on Sunday.

If anything could sway Mako Sakamoto, it was commitment—any kind of commitment. He saw this as commitment. He asked Peter to rejoin the club. And Peter rejoined the club.

With the exception of the Fourth Commandment, virtually nothing could keep Peter from working out. Before he went on the six-day schedule at the Culver City Club, he used to return to Venice High on his "off" nights for its open gym nights. He kept the undisciplined workouts a secret from Mako, just as later, when he was a teenager, he would keep his surfing days a secret. During the summer, Peter and another member of the club, Sam Tipp, would take their surfboards and board a city bus bound for Manhattan Beach, where they'd surf all day. At nights, back at the girls' gym working out, Peter's strategy was to work harder than ever, a strategy driven by a fear his coach would guess he'd spent the day surfing and order him to stop.

Energy, he had. Strong legs, that was another matter. In all other respects, he was a prototypical gymnast: five-foot-five inches tall, 115 pounds, broad shoulders, narrow hips, naturally strong shoulders and arms. But the legs were skinny and always had been. And since it was another of the philosophies of Sam and Mako Sakamoto that you attacked your weaknesses head-on (and that the only truly superior gymnasts were those who turned their weaknesses into their strengths), they drew attention to this particular weakness by calling Peter "Chicken Legs."

To make up for what he lacked in bulk, at least visually, Peter responded by coming to practice wearing two or three layers of socks. However, in an effort to openly acknowledge his nickname (if not the ruse), at a novelty store he bought a pair of gag socks that looked like chicken legs. He wore those socks on the outside. The first time he finally managed a backward somersault that went higher than four feet—finally getting close to the border for the requirements of world class floor exercise—he was wearing them.

★   ★   ★

In his 17th year he took a leave of absence from his high school classes at Brentwood School to compete in the National Gymnastics Championships in Westwood at UCLA. Competition wasn't something Vidmar was used to. No one who belonged to the Culver City Gymnastics Club was a competition junky. Mako didn't believe in a lot of intersquad meets during the formative years. Every practice was a simulated competition in its own right. Beyond that, you mostly used your imagination.

So it was that even after six years of intensive training with Coach Sakamoto, Peter Vidmar wasn't sure just where he stood in relation to the rest of the nation—just as nobody else was sure how they stood with him. Going into the 1978 Nationals was only the 11th time he'd competed against anyone, period.

But as the competition wore on, he became more and more pleased with where he stood. In each of the events—horizontal bar, rings, floor exercise, parallel bars, vault, and his specialty, pommel horse—he held his own, most often against gymnasts older than himself. When the competition was over, his all-around score was 13th best in the meet. Because the top 14 finishers made the national team, he qualified to travel the world the following year as an official member of the U.S. Gymnastics Team.

Before they held the ceremonies to announce the team, Mako pulled Vidmar aside and said two things: (1) Congratulations, and (2) Don't join the national team.

It was Mako's belief that the worst thing Vidmar could do at this stage of his development was take off on a year-long schedule of international competitions. It would retard the kind of progress he could make if he stayed in the gym and competed for Snicker's bars. And worse than that, at the highest levels of competition, against the Soviets or the Japanese or the Chinese, he would be massacred, and what good would that do for an aspiring Olympic champion?

It was the first time anyone associated with the U.S. Gymnastics Federation could remember someone turning back his national team uniform. Mako did say it would be all right if Peter joined the U.S. junior team and competed in their meets. But when Peter sent in his papers for their training camps and competitions, the junior team officials sent them back, saying he hadn't gone through the proper channels and couldn't be considered.

As Peter would find out a year later, giving up a year on the national team wasn't the hardest part. The hardest part was when he returned for another national championships competition, this time in Dayton, Ohio. Convinced he'd sacrificed his soul, worked twice as hard as the team members, and had plenty of gratification coming, he was stunned when they added up his scores . . . and he still placed only 13th.

He returned to Culver City displeased and disgusted — with himself. He did not take what he perceived as a defeat lightly. He cranked up his workouts to eight hours a day, training with both Mako, who was by now coaching at UCLA, and with Sam Sakamoto.

The UCLA Bruins had done their homework. Knowing that one of the country's brightest young gymnasts lived four miles away, in Culver City, and knowing that he and his coach were living a real-life Karate Kid existence, they went after the coach first. They offered Mako the assistant's job when Vidmar was entering his senior year of high school. It wasn't the money — only $500 a season — that enticed Mako, but the chance to work with college gymnasts and, hopefully, continue to work with Peter if he decided to matriculate to UCLA the following year. The next year Vidmar did just that, turning down offers from virtually every gymnastics power in the country as well as a full-ride scholarship offer from BYU.

In his post-Nationals funk, Vidmar would work out with Mako and then jump in his car and drive to Culver City, where Sam was waiting with another four hours. Week after week he kept up the grind, determined that if he couldn't out-perform the world he could at least outwork it.

Three months later he improved from 13th to sixth on the U.S. Team, qualifying for the sixth and final spot to compete in the 1979 World Championships. By the occasion of the next U.S. National Championships, in Columbus, Ohio, in 1980, at the age of 19, he won the USA all-around title. Heading into the Moscow Olympics, Peter Vidmar was either America's top gymnast or close to it.

That America wouldn't be going to the Moscow Olympics wasn't necessarily awful news to either Vidmar or his coach. There were still steps to climb and lessons to learn.

★   ★   ★

The crowd filling the gymnasium in Budapest, Hungary, did not know where to hide their eyes. Even if the young gymnast who had just lost his grip on the high bar was an American who looked as if he might win the world championship, it was still hard to know how to act when one minute, there he was, flying through a routine that was borderline incredible, and the next, he was on the floor, looking at his hands like a shortstop who couldn't believe the ball had gotten through the infield.

The horizontal bar was Peter Vidmar's final routine in the World Championships of 1983. He was in second place in the individual horizontal bar standings. Just hold on and a silver medal was the worst news he could get. In the stands, John and Doris Vidmar sat in anticipation, John wearing the pink cowboy shirt he always wore when Peter competed, believing it was lucky.

The shirt had enjoyed quite a run the past three seasons, through two NCAA collegiate all-around championships for Peter and the UCLA Bruins, and through yet another USGF national championship and two titles in the national trials for the world championships. That Peter Vidmar had turned himself into the best gymnast in American history was becoming unarguable. He had become the anchor of the U.S. team.

The high bar routine started out smoothly enough. Vidmar knew it well; he'd done it often enough. His ever-present coach looked on from just across the mat, expecting the best. But in the middle of his routine, when Vidmar released the bar for a flip and then reached back to grab the bar again, all he got was a handful of . . . thin . . . useless . . . empty . . . Budapest air.

It was the first time in 11 years Mako Sakamoto saw Peter Vidmar lose his composure; the first and only time he ever saw a hint of life-isn't-fair sentiment in his eyes. He was near tears as he looked up from the heap he was in on the floor.

"Mr. Mako," he said, "I released the bar, and I went for it, and *it was not there.*"

He dropped to seventh place in the final standings, just another casualty in the unforgiving world of the gym. At least the team competition had gone better. The team from the United States placed fourth, one out of the medals, behind the gold medal team from the People's Republic of China, a team that rode the superior individual talents of its top gymnast, Li Ning, to victory over the favored Soviet national team.

Considering the history of men's gymnastics in the United States, fourth place was reason enough for dancing in the halls back at the United States Gymnastics Federation offices in Colorado Springs. But for the six members of the U.S. team,

it was only reason to return to America and work harder—
hard enough to climb the international ladder to the next
rung—the medal rung. The Olympics of 1984 would be the
next time the best men in the world would gather in the same
gym—and that gym would be familiar enough. It would be
Pauley Pavilion, on the campus of UCLA.

★   ★   ★

Watching Daggett's perfection on the horizontal bars gave
Peter Vidmar a curious case of déjà vu as he rubbed the chalk
on his hands and prepared to begin the routine that would
decide the 1984 Olympic team championship. Daggett was his
best friend. They had worked out daily the past four years as
UCLA teammates, along with Mitch Gaylord, yet another
Bruin on the national team. The rest of the U.S. team consisted
of Scott Johnson and James Hartung from the University of
Nebraska and Bart Conner from the University of Oklahoma.
The blending of the best gymnasts from the three schools that
had gone tooth and nail at each other for the past four years
was at first feared to have disaster written all over it, but instead
it created probably the most cohesive men's team ever.

Vidmar and Daggett habitually ended their workouts at
UCLA by turning off the radio, moving to the horizontal bar—
traditionally the final event in competition—and simulating
the finals of the Olympic Games. Daily they'd do this. First
Daggett would approach the high bar, and Vidmar, doing his
best Jim McKay, would say, "Next up from the USA is Timothy
Daggett," after which Daggett would salute the coach standing
there, usually Mako, as if he were the head judge, and launch
into his routine. That done, Daggett would be Jim McKay,
Vidmar would assume the ready position, and the procedure
would be repeated. If they nailed their routines, practice was
stamped a success; if they didn't, they kicked themselves all
the way home for losing the Olympic Games.

Now they were doing it again. Only now it really was the Olympic Games. And Daggett was taking a deep breath in great appreciation for the 10 he'd just scored, and this time Vidmar was not saluting Mako (who was now an assistant coach with the U.S. team) but the real head judge of the Olympic Games. And when the announcer said, "Next up from the USA is Peter Vidmar," he really meant "Next up from the USA is Peter Vidmar."

Vidmar went airborne and grabbed the bar, his teammates standing like a net off to the side. Since Scott Johnson, the first American on the high bar, had experienced difficulty and scored a less-than-acceptable-under-the-circumstances 9.5, the United States team, in the best-five-of-six scoring system, already had its throw-out score.

Hartung followed Johnson with a 9.8, and he was followed by Conner with a 9.9. Then came Gaylord with a 9.95 and Daggett with his perfect 10. On the next mat over, competing in floor exercise for their last, and best, event, the Chinese, the defending world champions, were purposefully racking up high score after high score. But they needed someone from the U.S. to falter.

Winning this medal wasn't going to be easy; another Budapest for Vidmar and the Americans would be bowing to their conquerors from the East. But this wasn't Budapest, this was Pauley Pavilion in the heart of UCLA, less than four miles from Culver City — four miles that required 12 years of sacrifice and dedication to cross. You don't just toss that out. You can't just toss that out. Some things you've earned and you know it, and Vidmar knew he'd earned this.

He flew around, under, through, and over the high bar as if they'd been born together. The Pauley Pavilion crowd — where Vidmar joked he had "more relatives per capita" than anyone else in the Olympics, where his sister was an usher; his wife, Donna, was a film crew technician; and his parents,

Doris and John, sat in the middle of it all, John wearing the pink cowboy shirt—looked on in a collective trance as the All-American boy-next-door performed his routine.

He sailed through his final double reverse flip, arched high in the air, and touched down on the mat, unwavering. The crowd erupted again, as it had for Daggett, sensing it didn't need to wait for the judging. Soon enough there was proof of that when Vidmar's score, a 9.95, flashed on the screen. Unless the Chinese could somehow come up with a score of 11—on a scale of 10—for their final floor exercise routine, America's gymnasts would soon rule the world.

After acknowledging the crowd, and after standing at attention as the American flag was raised and the national anthem was played, and after having gold medals draped around their necks, Conner, Gaylord, Hartung, Johnson, Daggett, and Vidmar were pushed into a limousine and rushed by police escort—16 motorcycles and four squad cars—to the ABC television studios in Hollywood. Jim McKay wanted them for that night's Olympic nationwide wrap-up.

★   ★   ★

In the meantime, Mako did what a coach does—he fretted. There was still the issue of the Olympic all-around individual competition to determine the world's number 1 gymnast, as well as the issue of the individual apparatus championships. There were still routines to complete.

Riding the wave from the team championship—the crown jewel in international competition—Vidmar came into the next night's all-around suddenly on par with the outstanding Chinese gymnast, Li Ning. Event by event they slugged it out. Vidmar drew first blood with a perfect 10 on the high bar. He followed that with a 9.8 on the floor. After two events, he and Li were tied.

In the third rotation, Vidmar scored a 9.9 on the pommel

horse and Li a 9.9 on rings. They were still tied. Focusing on each other, neither immediately noticed the emergence of Japan's Koji Gushiken. After three events, Gushiken, the leading member of the Japanese team that had won the bronze medal the previous night, had moved within .025 of the two leaders.

In the fourth rotation, all three gymnasts scored a 9.9, and nothing changed. Then, in the fifth rotation, Li slipped on the parallel bars and scored a 9.8. Vidmar scored a 9.9 on the rings, and Gushiken, suddenly moving up strong from behind, scored a nearly perfect 9.95 on the horizontal bar to take the lead.

Twenty-five thousandths of a point separated Gushiken and Vidmar as they came to the sixth and final rotation – the parallel bars for Vidmar, the floor exercise for Gushiken.

Approaching his final routine, Vidmar remembered back to early that morning, when he had come to Pauley Pavilion to warm up for the all-around finals that night. He had expected to be alone. But Gushiken was there too. Twenty-seven years old and considered by many to be past his prime after the 1980 Olympic boycott (Japan didn't go to Moscow either), he had come to Los Angeles the old man of the competition. In his 16-year career, he had recovered from serious, career-threatening ankle and Achilles tendon injuries. He was a survivor. And now, in the morning solitude of the Olympics arena, the gymnast from Japan was reading a book of philosophy. He looked up and saw Vidmar, and they acknowledged one another, then moved to their separate areas of the arena.

Now they were side by side. After Gushiken scored a 9.9 on the floor, it came to this: A 9.95 or a 10 on the parallel bars would win the gold medal for Vidmar.

He was on that course, the gold medal there in the cross-hairs, until his dismount, when again a slight hop on the landing cost him the .05 he needed. The 9.9 the judges gave him meant he had missed the gold medal by that 25-thousandths of a point. He and Gushiken had staged the closest all-around championship in Olympics history.

The next night capped the competition with the crowning of individual champions in each of the six gymnastics disciplines. Vidmar finished seventh in floor exercise — privately, he knew it was his biggest accomplishment, to come from a chicken-legs beginning to seventh best in the world — and then he moved on to the pommel horse.

The horse had always been his favorite, and best, event. Here his natural ability shone through, and his legs, for the most part, just came along for the ride. At times, riding the pommel horse, he felt completely free, as if he were skiing perfect powder or surfing the perfect wave.

He found that feeling now. He had to like his timing. An Olympic medal was on the line. He thought about that as he sailed from side to side on the horse. He thought about that at the finish, when he dismounted as if he were landing on an egg.

The judges gave him a 10. The Olympic Games gave him a gold medal.

Was there any question where this medal was going? Peter Vidmar walked across the mats of Pauley Pavilion as he dusted off memories of the chalky mats of the Culver City Junior High School 12 years ago, of the article in the Santa Monica *Evening Outlook,* of the person who had made all this possible. He gave the medal to Makoto Sakamoto.

★   ★   ★

Epilogue: Coaching the most decorated U.S. gymnast in Olympic history did not turn Mako Sakamoto into an unwanted commodity. Among the several offers that came his way following the Los Angeles Games of 1984 was one from the New South Wales Gymnastics Association in Sydney, Australia. They asked Sakamoto to be the director of their program —

with an eye toward developing future Olympic gymnasts for Australia. He accepted and stayed in Australia until 1987, when the head gymnastics coaching job at Brigham Young University opened. Peter Vidmar first heard about the opening and told BYU officials they could do no better than dash off a telegram to Sydney and hope Mr. Mako would say yes. They did, and Sakamoto has been spiraling BYU's men's program upward ever since.

Peter Vidmar retired from active gymnastics competition after the 1984 Games and has since turned into one of the country's most sought-after motivational speakers. Especially well received is his pommel horse routine, which features a gymnastics demonstration and a philosophical discussion on the similarities between gymnastics and life. There's still a lot of the coach in the protégé.

DOUG PADILLA

BY DOUG ROBINSON

As the 14 runners toed the line for the start of the 1984 Olympic 5,000-meter run final, Lynette Padilla strained to see her husband Doug among the line of lithe men gathering courage for the 3.1-mile race. What Lynette saw through her binoculars from the stands of the Los Angeles Coliseum only confirmed her suspicions. Doug was fraught with nerves, his pale, colorless face a blank mask of fear. As the TV cameras panned the finalists, he was caught in a deep trance. Lynette recognized this as his anxious look, but she had come to expect it. The night before the race, as they lay in bed, she could feel the mattress trembling. "What's that?" she asked, but she knew the answer even before she heard it. It was no California earthquake, just Doug wiggling his toes in his sleep — an odd habit he has when he is high on anxiety.

Doug had been in big races before. A year earlier he had finished fifth in the World Track and Field Championships in Helsinki. But it was one thing to be prepared for a big race; it was another to be struggling with anemia, as Doug had learned he had at the doctor's office two weeks earlier. He was convinced there would never again be anything in his life that would make him so nervous, so fearful, as the Olympic Games. He had been unable to eat anything since breakfast, and now it was evening, with the sun low and warm and breaking over the Coliseum.

At the sound of the gun, Padilla, the lone American in the race, broke for the front, tucking in behind the leader, Portugal's Ezequiel Canario. He had hoped for a slow pace, which would better enable him to maintain contact with the leaders and then use his strong kick to carry him to the finish, but he soon realized he would have no such luck. The first lap was 62 seconds, and Padilla, wanting no part of it, faded quickly to the back of the pack. The pace refused to slacken. Portugal's Antonio Leitao took charge after two laps and pushed a pace that, if maintained, would shatter the Olympic record. After a mile, which the leaders covered in 4:12, Padilla began to feel the strain of the effort. *Help me to hang on,* he prayed silently, as he often does at such moments. *Help me not to hurt so much. Help me not to give up . . .*

★   ★   ★

Who could have foreseen that Doug Padilla would be here, an Olympic athlete? He had grown up some 400 miles north of L.A. in San Leandro, a tiny, sickly child. His rise to world-class runner was almost too much to be believed; it was a cliché, the stuff of movies. Unable to make his college cross country team, unable to win an athletic scholarship, he had left running for two years to serve a mission for the LDS Church. Upon his return he was never the same runner again.

Certainly, nothing in his early history suggested Olympic prospects. When Doug was one and a half years old, his parents, Joe and Gerry, noticed a distinct wheezing sound as he struggled to breathe. They took him to the doctor, who diagnosed the problem as asthma. Throughout much of his schooling, Doug would become so ill each spring that he would stay home for sometimes two weeks at a time, and at the least he had to remain indoors during recess and P.E. classes.

Doug began receiving weekly allergy injections that would continue until his mission. Later, when Doug was in junior high school and decided to try competitive running, his worried parents returned to the doctor.

"Should we let him run?" they asked.

"Yes," the doctor replied. "It will probably be good for him. But he'll probably never be any good at it."

It is, after all, one thing to be a football player with asthma; it is another to be a distance runner, pulling in great gulps of air for miles on end.

"We had to keep an eye on him," says Joe now. "We gave him vitamins. He was always so small, and he had the asthma. We had to take him in to the doctor a lot."

Asthma wasn't the only strike against him. When Doug was still a boy, Joe and Gerry dragged him back to the doctor about another matter: his feet. The doctor looked at the right toe angling sharply toward the left foot and decided to place both feet in casts. A week later the Padillas were back. Doug had broken both casts into pieces and bloodied his toes.

"That's not going to work," said the doctor, so he came up with a new plan. "Put his shoes on the wrong feet. That should straighten them."

For the next year and a half, Doug wore his shoes on the wrong feet, much to the dismay of well-meaning passersby, who constantly pestered the Padillas: "Excuse me, did you know your little boy is wearing his shoes on the wrong feet?" Eventually the feet straightened, and Doug, as he grew older, took the usual interest in sports, even if sports didn't reciprocate.

"In P.E., when they picked teams, there were always three

or four guys left at the end nobody wanted," recalls Padilla. "I was one of those guys."

That was at least partly because Padilla was always the smallest of his classmates, even smaller than the girls. By his freshman year in high school, he was 4-foot-11, 82 pounds— the gift of genetics and a 5-foot-2 father. "I was hardly an imposing figure on the athletic field," says Padilla.

That didn't stop him from trying out for the basketball team in ninth grade. The coaches eyed this tiny specimen and quickly found a place for him—on the bench. The school had four basketball teams, with selections based on size and ability. Doug made the lowest of the four divisions simply because they didn't cut anybody, but even at that he sat the bench. After each game they played a fifth quarter to let the scrubs play, and there were times when Doug didn't play even then.

"I never had any sports heroes," recalls Padilla. "To have heroes, you have to be able to picture yourself doing the things they're doing. I could never do that. I was always the little guy."

Doug, the second of the Padillas' four children, turned his interests elsewhere. He was a good student, participated in church activities, became an Eagle scout, dabbled in cooking (he sometimes cooked dinner for the family), and doted on his family. He left loving notes for his parents to find under their pillows when they turned down their bed at night, and he brought them breakfast in bed, complete with a menu and a bill ("one hug").

For all of his physical shortcomings, there was something Doug never lacked: energy. He had so much of the stuff that his parents were convinced he was hyperactive. Almost nightly for a time, Joe and Gerry awakened in the middle of the night to the sound of footsteps thumping around in the darkness of the house. "It's Doug again," Joe would say. Doug was running laps through the house. Joe would climb out of bed and wait for Doug in the hallway. He wouldn't even bother to chase him; he'd just wait for him to pass by, sweep him up in his arms, and take him back to bed. The Padillas returned to the doctor to inquire about this hyperactivity. The doctor prescribed medication that was supposed to calm Doug, but it only made him worse. As a last resort, the Padillas finally tied Doug to the crib with a scarf to keep him from escaping at night.

Doug was so active, so filled with energy, that he never had time for television and never had the patience for walking. On Sunday, dressed in a shirt and tie, he ran to church. Years later, he would run between classes at Brigham Young University, and to this day he runs from the gas pump to the cashier to pay for his gas.

Joe and Gerry went to the track to walk and jog, and Doug, still a young boy, tagged along. He ran circles around them like a puppy, or lapped them, or ran backward ahead of them, shouting encouragement: "C'mon, Dad. C'mon, Mom!"

And so what better sport than running? Or so it seemed. The girls beat Doug regularly during races in junior high school, but he was undaunted. He went out for the high school track team and won a small race near the end of his freshman year. "It was significant to me," recalls Padilla. "I had never been the best at anything in my life." Still, he ran mostly for the junior varsity team — not the varsity — through his junior season. By his senior season, victories were becoming more frequent, to the endless surprise of all.

"You're not varsity, are you?" his opponents would ask the boyish-looking, 5-foot-6 Padilla as they lined up for the start of a race.

Joe, standing beside the track during races, eavesdropped as onlookers gawked at his tiny son. "Look at that little kid!" they'd say. And then, once the race began: "Look, the little kid is winning!"

Padilla was unbeaten in cross country and finished 13th in the state two-mile race. Privately he took great pleasure when he was named Marina High School's Athlete of the Year, ahead of all those big, stunned basketball and football players.

Padilla attended Chabot Junior College the following year and improved his mile time 10 seconds to 4:10.7, which was good enough to win the Northern California Championships. He transferred to BYU the following year and tried out for the cross country team, uninvited and without a scholarship.

★   ★   ★

The word spread fast. One day, during a small, low-key meet in BYU's Smith Fieldhouse in January of 1981, an unknown runner named Doug Padilla ran a 4:02 mile. The word was that he had run it solo—no one had been able to stay close enough to Padilla to offer a challenge that probably would have made him run faster. What's more, he had run it at an altitude where the thinner air was supposed to make four-minute miles nearly impossible. No one had ever run a four-minute mile in Utah, and yet Padilla had approached that mark on the tight, slow turns of an indoor track, virtually alone. That night, Bob Wood, a Salt Lake City–based coach and running afficionado, received calls from friends, telling him of Padilla's race.

"I had seen Doug run cross country, but I had no idea he had that kind of smoke," recalls Wood. "I felt like I had wandered onto a playground and found a 7-foot-4 kid no one had ever heard of."

First thing Monday morning, Wood, convinced Padilla was on the brink of something big, called organizers of the L.A. Times Invitational and tried to enter Padilla in their meet. They refused; they had never heard of Padilla. So Wood called Al Franken, meet director for the annual Sunkist Invitational, one of the world's top international indoor track and field meets.

"I've got this guy here who's running at BYU who's run 4:02 indoors at altitude by himself," Wood told Franken. "I think he'd be dynamite if you'd get him in the two-mile."

If nothing else, Franken realized Padilla was a bargain. He wouldn't have to pay him an appearance fee because he was a collegian, and the airfare was cheap.

"OK, we'll get him airfare and see what happens," said Franken.

For Padilla, the Sunkist race would be the ultimate test. He would compete against the great Suleiman Nyambui, who had won the silver medal for his native Tanzania at the previous year's Olympic Games. Padilla and Nyambui were no strangers. Both had competed in the Western Athletic Conference — Padilla for BYU, Nyambui for the University of Texas–El Paso — but they weren't exactly rivals. Padilla had never beaten Nyambui, hadn't even threatened to beat him. For that matter, no American had ever beaten Nyambui at two miles.

Padilla didn't expect to challenge him in the Sunkist meet either, but when Nyambui moved to the front of the pack after three laps, Padilla went with him. That's the way they ran throughout most of the 22-lap race, with Padilla running so close on Nyambui's heels that no one — though they tried — could get between them. With three laps to go, Nyambui grew uneasy. He surged, hoping to shake Padilla, but the upstart went with him. The biggest surprise was yet to come. With two laps to go, Padilla shot past Nyambui at the top of the turn, brushing his arm as he went by. Padilla had two steps on Nyambui before he was able to respond, and by then he was in full flight and uncatchable. Padilla won with a time of 8:27.

"Can you talk to the L.A. Times people," Padilla joked with Franken afterward. "They wouldn't let me in their meet."

Above: Doug as a seventh-grader

Below: Doug Padilla

Doug Padilla beating marathon world record holder Alberto Salazar in the Millrose Games in Madison Square Garden

That wouldn't be necessary. The next day Wood received a call from chagrined L.A. Times officials, saying that they would like to have Padilla in their meet after all.

"I beat Nyambui," Padilla wrote in his journal that night. "I still can't quite believe it. It seems unreal."

It was all happening so fast. Only a few years earlier, Padilla had come to BYU and failed to make the cross country team. Three months later he left for a mission in El Salvador, uncertain of what the future held for his modest running career. For two years he all but abandoned his running to knock on doors and proselyte. His mission president allowed him to run but only with a companion, and it was a rare missionary companion who wanted to awaken at 5:30 in the morning to run two miles.

Padilla returned from El Salvador to BYU in March of 1978 with few expectations. His coach, Sherald James, remembered Padilla before his mission as "a scrawny little guy," but his practiced eye took in the long legs, the seemingly oversized set of lungs in that small frame, and the long, light-footed gait that reminded him of a deer, and he knew the kid had talent. "When he ran he just touched the high points of the track," says James. Padilla had uncanny speed for a distance runner. He could turn a 47-second 400. The problem was that he had no measurable strength—the ability to sustain a hard effort. If the workout called for just one sprint, Padilla would win, but more than one—forget it. He finished dead last during interval workouts on the track.

But something happened upon Padilla's return to BYU. He fell in with a group of teammates who were determined enough to train every day, without exception. Before his mission, Padilla had trained alone and often talked himself out of workouts, seemingly for every ache and pain. His training had been erratic, at best. But now, caught up with being part of a group, Padilla ran daily for the first time, and he ran hard, with the leaders. With startling quickness, his strength began to improve. That fall he not only made BYU's cross country team, but he also became the Cougars' number 1 runner. By the time the spring track season arrived, he had established himself as BYU's best distance runner.

There are two types of runners in the world: kickers and strength runners. The kickers have great finishing speed; they must stay close to the leaders to outkick them to the finish line at the end of the race. The strength runners have little speed; they must wear out their faster rivals in the middle laps to escape their kick. Padilla was clearly a kicker, but he rarely kept himself within striking distance of the leaders. That kind of running requires the greatest of willpower, and Padilla could not make himself endure the pain of the middle laps long enough to maintain contact. He repeatedly let the leaders escape him in the middle laps, only to have his stinging kick left at the end but no one to catch. Over and over, his coaches urged him to maintain contact, only to watch him fade.

"It's been the crux of his whole career," says James now. "We as coaches [at BYU] were exasperated almost to tears."

James, a warm, philosophical man, likes to say that running—or sports—is discovering one's self. Padilla, he says, was still searching for his identity. He was still the tiny, underrated, non-athlete of his youth, the kid who was beaten by girls and couldn't play basketball in the fifth quarter.

"Self-discovery is the best teacher," says James. "In trying to discover who he is, Doug Padilla found out that he was a lot tougher than he really knew."

For Padilla, self-discovery came during a dual meet at the University of Oregon in 1979. He lost the first race, a 1,500-meter run, but afterward he was convinced he would have won if he had maintained contact with the leaders on the third lap, which of course is what his coaches had been telling him all along. Angry at himself, he vowed it wouldn't happen in his next race of the day, which would pit him against University of Oregon superstars Alberto Salazar and Bill McChesney in the 5,000-meter run. Salazar and McChesney did their best to break the neophyte Padilla. They took turns sprinting every other backstretch, while Padilla's teammates exchanged bets on the sidelines over which lap he would drop off the pace. Padilla was feeling the pain—he had already set a personal record for two miles with a time of 8:55 and there was still more than a mile to go—but this time there would be no dropping off the pace. With a lap to go he actually took the lead, bringing the crowd to its feet. Salazar and McChesney caught him on the homestretch, leaving Padilla a close third with a time of 13:43—a full minute faster than his personal record.

"That race reaffirmed that I had to maintain contact," said Padilla. "That was my big challenge."

The following year, when the same race unfolded again in Oregon, Padilla was strong enough to take the lead and keep it in the homestretch, clocking 13:36. By 1981, he was one of America's rising young distance runners, but he and his countrymen had one great challenge. The older, African distance runners were dominating the collegiate races; the Americans were simply no match for them. One day, Padilla told James, "Coach, those Africans can be beaten. I'm going to do it."

And so he did, at the Sunkist meet. Had it been a fluke? After losing to Padilla, Nyambui urged his new challenger to race him in New York the following week, but he declined, and Nyambui set a world record. Two weeks later, Padilla won the L.A. Times Invitational two-mile in the Forum, clocking 8:26.0—the fastest time in the world so far that year. The following week, he tried the mile in the San Francisco Examiner meet and finished a close third to American record holder Steve Scott and Olympic champion John Walker with a time of 3:56.6—a personal record by some eight seconds.

One week later, at the Western Athletic Conference indoor championships, Padilla and Nyambui met again in the two-mile run, and Padilla, taking the lead with one lap to go, outkicked his rival to the finish again.

Two weeks later they met once more, this time in the NCAA Indoor Championships in Detroit's Joe Louis Arena. "For the first time we have an American who is going to challenge Suleiman, and his name is Doug Padilla," the TV announcer said before the race, fully aware that Nyambui, in three years of competition, had never lost an NCAA championship race.

As they stood at the starting line, Nyambui, who was normally all smiles before a race, shook Padilla's hand solemnly and mumbled something unintelligible. As expected, Nyambui took charge early in the race, and Padilla, his shadow, settled in behind him. For days Padilla had tried to determine his strategy. In their two previous meetings, he had beaten Nyambui by waiting to kick somewhere during the last two laps, but this time he had the distinct feeling that he should make his move with five laps to go. He resisted it at first. He knew that passing Nyambui that early would prolong and heighten the pain, and he was uncertain that he could go the distance. But he couldn't ignore an almost spiritual feeling that he must do it anyway. Lap after lap, Padilla stalked Nyambui, and with five laps to go, and with considerable trepidation, he moved into the lead, taking everyone by surprise.

"Look at this, Padilla is taking over early!" exclaimed TV announcer Larry Rawson. "This is a change in tactics. This is really interesting. I'm very surprised at that move."

"You should have seen the change in expression in Nyambui's face when Padilla went by him," said Rawson's sidekick, Ralph Boston. "He was really surprised, as if to say, What's going on?"

"I can't believe he tried it," said Rawson again. "I just can't believe it."

Round and round they ran, matching each other stride for stride. On each homestretch, Nyambui pulled up to Padilla's shoulder, trying to regain the lead, and each time Padilla held him at bay, forcing him to fall back slightly and run wide on the turns. They were running so closely that at times Padilla used his forearm to prevent Nyambui from drifting into his lane. With two and a half laps to go, Padilla was hurting, and for a moment he was tempted to ease up and surrender the lead. Nyambui began to edge in front of him, but Padilla caught himself, fought off the pain, and edged in front again just as they reached the turn. "Look at the stride and the speed and the confidence of a man who trains only 50 to 60 miles a week!" gushed Rawson. Padilla and Nyambui had picked up the pace so dramatically — they covered the final half-mile in 1:58 — that they were lapping the other runners.

With a lap to go and the suspense building, the crowd came to its feet. At the top of the homestretch the two runners made one last surge, but Padilla held on and won by a scant six-hundredths of a second.

Doug Padilla was the national collegiate champion, and it was just the beginning. A year later he set the first of his national records, at two miles, 3,000 meters, and 5,000 meters, and he won the first of seven indoor and five outdoor national championships. In 1984, Padilla won the 5,000 in the U.S. Olympic Trials. Combined with Paul Cummings's victory in the 10,000 and Henry Marsh's victory in the 3,000-meter steeplechase, Padilla's win gave BYU alumni a clean sweep of the distance events at the Trials. The stage was set for the Los Angeles Olympic Games.

★   ★   ★

Lap after lap they swung around the Coliseum track, and

Padilla was fading. The Olympic final was getting away from him. "That's a fast pace," Joe Padilla said to no one in particular. The Padillas were sitting in the stands, where they had set up a card section spelling their son's name.

Padilla let the leaders go, and for several laps he ran next to last, in 13th place. With five laps to go, he was still only 12th.

It was just as James had feared, having observed Padilla in the days before the race. "You could see it eating away and eating away at him," recalls James. "All that stress. He couldn't eat, he couldn't sleep, he had cramps. And there was nothing you could do about it."

The first six runners broke the Olympic record, led by winner Said Aouita, who finished with a time of 13:05.59. Padilla, with his usual kick, rallied late in the race to place seventh in 13:23.56. "I was disappointed," he recalls. "I knew I could have done better."

Once again he had failed to maintain contact with the leaders. For an afternoon, all the old self-doubt had returned with a worldwide audience looking on. Padilla was still learning, still making his way through James's journey of self-discovery. Surely, there would be better days ahead.

★   ★   ★

There were better days. In 1985, a year after the Olympic Games, Padilla produced the best season of his career. He won nine of 10 major races—including the World Cup—recorded a personal record of 13:15.44, ranked second in the world at 5,000 meters, and won Track and Field's overall World Grand Prix championship, which was worth $35,000. Padilla used the money to make a down payment on a large Tudor-style home on an acre-size plot in Orem, Utah.

Shortly after Doug, Lynette, and their three children moved into the home, his problems with allergies returned, and his running career began to decline. He has never made the world rankings again and has rarely broken 13:30 for 5,000 meters, although he has still managed to rank consistently among the top three Americans. He won the Goodwill Games and another national championship in 1986, but he faltered in Europe, and Nike, which had been paying him $40,000 to $48,000 annually for three years, cut his contract almost in half. After another poor season, he managed to win another national championship and the U.S. Olympic Trials in 1988, but he didn't make the finals at the Seoul Olympics, and at the end of the year Nike cut his contract completely.

The Padillas have struggled to make ends meet since then, sometimes living from race to race. In the summer of 1991, Padilla flew to Europe to rabbit (serve as a pacesetter) for a couple of world-record attempts to earn some quick money. "The week before that, I couldn't even afford to go to McDonald's," says Lynette. The Padillas have had to borrow money from their parents on a couple of occasions to survive.

Padilla is considered an enigma on the running scene. His rivals consider him exceptionally gifted, even by their high standards. With just the slightest amount of training, they say, he can achieve world-class fitness. They've long marveled that he can compete at such a level while running only 40 to 50 miles a week in training — compared to 60 to 70 for most 5,000-meter runners.

"He's like a thoroughbred," an Olympic distance runner once noted. "All you have to do is run him around a little bit in the corral and he's ready. He has awesome talent. There is no doubt he could be a world record holder."

All such talk irritates Padilla. It implies, he says, that he doesn't train hard. He and James claim that his health has prevented him from increasing his mileage. "If I do any more, I tend to break down," he says.

Padilla's health continues to be delicate. He is forever

suffering from allergies and picking up every cold and illness that comes along. Sometimes there are flashes of the old Padilla, but the good times are often followed by the bad. In 1989, he ran a personal-record 3:54.2 mile to win the Jack In the Box Invitational in Los Angeles, but otherwise he had a poor season. He won the 1990 overall national Indoor Grand Prix championship, which was worth $15,000, but after winning the national championship he floundered outdoors. He competed so poorly in his first race on the European circuit that he canceled the rest of his schedule and returned home. In 1991, he finished 18th in the national championships — a performance so poor that he was unable to gain entry into the European meets.

In the fall of '91, with the Olympics once again on the horizon, Padilla sent his family to live with his in-laws for a few weeks so he could rest, regain his health, and concentrate on training. He bumped his training mileage up to 60 and 70 miles a week, and presto! He finished second in two big road races — a 5K in Rhode Island and a 10K in Phoenix. Over the years he has avoided road racing to concentrate on the track, but not anymore. "Now I can't afford to," he says. Later that winter he won another indoor national title at 3,000 meters.

Padilla will be nearly 36 years old for the 1992 Olympics. Time is running out for continuing the old career and for beginning a new one. "We feel in our hearts that there is something more for him to accomplish in running," says Lynette. "It's worth the struggle. We don't feel it's time to quit yet. It's a gut instinct. We're just waiting to see how things unfold."

HENRY MARSH

BY LEE BENSON

Leaning against a wall in the runner's warm-up area outside the Los Angeles Memorial Coliseum, Henry Marsh sized up where he stood. The race he was about to compete in, the 1984 Olympic steeplechase final, was the biggest of his life . . . He had waited almost 10 years to run it . . . He was the heavy pre-race favorite . . . A prime-time national television audience and a worldwide audience of close to 1 billion, would be watching . . . Nike, his sponsor, had a $40,000 check waiting for him if he won the gold medal . . . And, to add to the drama, he had been bedridden less than three weeks ago, only a week ago he'd almost fainted while trying to jog, and he still wasn't feeling terrific.

By any standard, these were a lot of ingredients going into one race.

But before he began his warm-ups, Marsh wanted to make sure he was square on one thing: Winning didn't matter.

What did matter is that he would give this race, due to start in less than an hour, his best and let it go at that. Then, after running slightly more than seven laps in slightly more than eight minutes, he would have no alibis. He wouldn't pull off to the side with a fuzzy head or a cramped stomach. He wouldn't hold back just to be certain he'd last. Nothing less than red-lining this race would do. All-out. If he did that and lost, so what? If he could walk past a mirror the rest of his life and say absolutely that he gave it his all, that would be enough. It was all he would expect of anyone else. It was all he expected of himself.

Satisfied that his pregame speech — not so much Win One for the Gipper as Give Your All for the Gipper — was over, he jogged two steps and cleared a hurdle. He had forgotten to zip up the flaps on his warm-up pants, however, and as his left foot came up it caught in the flap and spiked his right leg, drawing blood. He went down in a heap as a medic rushed over.

Marsh got to his feet, unhurt. "Hey," he said, smiling. "This is the easy part."

INSIDE THE STADIUM, the crowd was getting into a bad mood. In the race preceding the steeplechase, the women's 3,000-meter final, there was a collision between Zola Budd, the South African running for Britain, and the crowd favorite, Mary Decker Slaney (America had two veteran sentimental gold-medal favorites in these Games of the 23rd Olympiad — Decker Slaney and Marsh). While Decker Slaney — in tears, her medal hope dashed — was attended to by her husband, officials reviewed tapes of the race and told the steeplechasers to wait.

Marsh turned away from the scene, using the time to assess the hand he'd been dealt. Thirty-six of the world's best steeplechase runners had come to Los Angeles. In two trial heats these 12 had survived.

The best part, Marsh knew, was who *wasn't* here. Patriz Ilg of West Germany, the top-ranked steeplechaser in the world and the defending world champion, had tonsilitis. Boguslaw Maminski of Poland, ranked number 3, was a no-show because of the Soviet Bloc boycott. Also, Britain's Graeme Fell, ranked number 6, failed to qualify in his country's trials, and Filbert Bayi of Tanzania, the silver medalist in Moscow in 1980, was injured.

Under normal circumstances (that is, not having to run in tandem with a virus), Marsh, number 2 in the world rankings and top-ranked two of the past three seasons, would have preferred Ilg and Maminski (who had never beaten Marsh) to be in the final, and all the rest. Now, he would take the edge.

He would be racing against a field of mostly unknowns. Only Joseph Mahmoud of France, ranked fifth, and Britain's Colin Reitz and Roger Hackney, ranked fourth and eighth, respectively, were established names. Brian Diemer, Marsh's U.S. teammate, also had credentials—newfound credentials. Marsh—the national champion seven straight years and the U.S. record holder, America's Sir Steeplechase—hadn't lost to Diemer through those seven championships. But in the last race before L.A., at a pre-Olympic warmup meet in Eugene, Oregon, Marsh was sick. Diemer beat him on the final lap, and the streak was ended.

It was the Kenyans who worried Marsh the most. Often inexperienced in international competition, they could be jittery and unpredictable runners—as Julius Koriuki had demonstrated in setting an insane-for-qualifying pace in the second heat (Marsh, to his chagrin, had been in it) three nights previous. Worse than that, Kenyans were usually fast. They had won two of the past four Olympic steeplechase races, and in 1978 it was a then-unknown Kenyan named Henry Rono who had set the world steeplechase record of 8:05.4 that still stood six years later. Given his current condition, Marsh hoped no one would be chasing that rabbit of a record tonight.

As Mary Decker Slaney was taken to the training room,

the steeplechase runners were called to line up. Marsh, light-headed, took his place among them. He had paid nine years' worth of dues; he could pay another eight minutes. And he had his game plan ready. This concept of running his best and living with the results wasn't a new notion, and it had gotten him places before . . .

★   ★   ★

The first thing Henry Marsh noticed when he returned to the Brigham Young University track team in January 1976 was that no one noticed. He walked onto the indoor track in the Smith Fieldhouse, where the team held its winter workouts, and none of his teammates looked up. No one asked where he'd been. No one said, "Henry's back," or "Nice tan."

He had quit the track team two weeks earlier. Tired of the grind, discouraged because the half-scholarship he'd held before his mission to Brazil had disappeared into no scholarship at all, and with an eye on his nontrack friends who spent the winter skiing and dating and staying up late, he walked away from practice one day and decided not to return. He skied, he dated, he stayed up late.

But he had a nagging thought: What if he had abandoned his running talent before he'd given it a fair trial, before he'd found out what his best was? The question wore on him. It wouldn't let him rest. To satisfy his own conscience, he had to see what he could do.

So he came back—to no one's surprise as it turned out—and, for motivation, the first thing he did was set a goal. His personal Mount Everest that spring would be to run fast enough in his event, the 3,000-meter steeplechase, to qualify for the NCAA national championships in June. The qualifying time for the NCAA meet was eight minutes and 55 seconds. He had to run better than that. Marsh's all-time best was a 9:25 he had run as a college freshman two years before. He had 30 seconds to trim in four months—the rough equivalent of transforming a Volkswagen into a Porsche. To that 8:55 end he trained throughout the indoor season, a rebel with a cause.

He had come to college as an aspiring distance runner and miler—in high school in both Texas and Hawaii he had been something of a sensation; at Honolulu's Punahou High he was the Athlete of the Year his senior year. Upon his arrival at BYU he had barely heard of the steeplechase, a race of 1.8 miles—a little more than seven laps around the track—that included hurdles, barriers, and a water jump and required a combination sprinter, plodder, hurdler, and masochist.

The coaches weren't sure where to put him, so they him in the steeplechase. His mile times, though near four minutes, weren't exceptional for a college runner, and at 5-foot-10 and closer to 160 pounds than 150, he didn't look lean, like a long-distance runner. He looked more like a linebacker. Assistant Coach Pat Shane, a former steeplechaser, thought Marsh had the toughness it took to be a steeplechaser, and he took it upon himself to teach him the nuances of this new event.

Then Marsh went to Brazil, and they took away his scholarship.

Back to school in the spring of 1976, Marsh set about losing the last of the 25 pounds he had gained on his mission—and set about turning himself into a more efficient steeplechaser. To that end, he did two things he hadn't done in 1973: He ran on his toes, and, with Shane's help, he learned how to hurdle off either leg (before, he could only lift off with his right leg, creating constant stutter-step problems). His thinking was that if he could make up time on the barriers, if he could become a technician, it could compensate for any lack of raw speed.

By April, at a meet against Arizona State in his first college race in three years, he had no idea where he stood. If this race bombed, he might call it a career. If it didn't, he might call it a miracle.

He ran 8:57—twenty-eight seconds faster than his best-ever—only two seconds above the NCAA qualifying standard.

To get to 8:55, Marsh believed he needed a fast and competitive race, preferably at an oxygen-rich sea-level location. He asked Clarence Robison, Brigham Young's head track coach, if BYU would consider sending him to the Penn Relays in Philadelphia. Robison said no, too expensive. He asked about the Drake Relays in Iowa. Robison again said no, too expensive. Finally he asked about the Mt. SAC Relays in California. The coach relented and sent Marsh to the meet, alone. A one-man team.

He ran 8:43, fourteen seconds faster than before. Twelve seconds under the NCAA qualifying standard. Just two seconds above the BYU school record. And at the Modesto Relays two weeks later, Marsh ran 8:40 and got the school record.

The people he was beating were amazed. The coaches were amazed. Marsh was more amazed than any of them. He was forced to set a new goal for the NCAA meet he qualified for at Franklin Field in Philadelphia in early June: Why not a top seven finish, a time of 8:36, and All-American certification? Why not find out where this meteor was going to land?

He ran 8:27. He very nearly won the meet and the national title, and he would have if not for the presence of a world-class Kenyan, James Munyala of UTEP, who managed to out-kick the unheralded BYU sophomore on the final lap. Not only was Marsh second, and not only was he an official All-American, but by running faster than 8:32, he qualified to compete in the U.S. Olympic Trials later that month in Eugene, Oregon. That hadn't even been a goal.

On the plane ride home, Robison pulled Marsh aside. "Have you thought about the Olympics, Henry?" he asked.

"Who, me, coach?" Henry answered. "The guy who's not on scholarship?"

Time flies when you're on a roll. Three weeks later, in

Eugene, Oregon, Marsh found himself at the Olympic Trials, facing the best steeplechasers in the country. He ran 8:27 again, the same time as Philadelphia, finished second to Doug Brown, and qualified for the U.S. Olympic team. Ten months since returning from Brazil and six months since he quit (and rejoined) the BYU track team, he was bound for Montreal and the 1976 Olympic Games. Of the 4,834 competitors going to the Games of the 21st Olympiad, no one, Henry Marsh was convinced, was more surprised than he was.

Once he got to Montreal, he may also have been the loosest athlete in the village. He came to the Olympics without expectations and with the best sound system in the American sector. His eight-track console stereo, as it turned out, would play a key role in Bruce Jenner's gold medal win in the decathlon. At night, Jenner, who roomed with Marsh, would listen to Jethro Tull on Marsh's eight-track as Marsh, his competition over, got Jenner's food from the cafeteria. Inspired and rested, Jenner then spent his days setting a world decathlon record.

In the steeplechase, Marsh was the only American to make it through the heats and qualify for the 12-man Olympic final. He ran 8:23.9, just seven-tenths of a second off the American record, and placed 10th.

"Tenth is good," Jenner, his new soulmate, told him. "That's where I finished in 1972."

★   ★   ★

THE STARTER'S PISTOL CRACKED through the Los Angeles twilight mist, and, as television commentator Marty Liquori said on ABC, Henry Marsh assumed "his customary position in the rear." On his best days, Marsh eschewed the lead, or even the front of the pack, in the early part of a race, content to drift well behind the front-runners. As his coach, Bill Bowerman, who coached 25 seasons at the University of Oregon,

said, "He doesn't run to win a lap. He runs to win the race."
Marsh was fond of efficiency. He liked to conserve his energy,
time the hurdles, and avoid the rush-hour mentality of the
pack. It was a strategy that had served him well, although it
did tend to give anyone watching him ulcers. Even when he
was running easy, he wasn't a pretty runner, and every race
started with Henry lagging behind and looking as if he were
doomed. This race, the Olympic final, was no exception.

He felt odd, then, when he rounded the water jump at the
far end of the first lap and sensed that he wasn't running last
anymore. Either someone new was behind him or one of the
Kenyans was already lapping him, and he wasn't *that* sick.

With the final barrier of the first lap now in front of him,
Marsh tried to concentrate on what was in *front* of him, but
he knew that sound to the rear, and that sound was footsteps.

The footsteps belonged to one Llewelyn Phelan of Berkeley, California. Phelan, wearing a tank top and yellow running
shorts, was carrying a fig leaf in one hand and a banner in the
other that said, "Our Earth at Peace, One Human Family."
He had leaped over the railing at the bottom of the stands
near the water jump and joined the race. If he could get close
to Henry Marsh, he could get air time.

The Coliseum's security force soon gave chase. Phelan gave
them a race down the home straightaway before he was caught
and sent off to be at peace with the human family at the L.A.
County Jail.

Meanwhile, Marsh, last again, settled into his stride. The
runner immediately in front of him, Tommy Ekblom of Finland, had glanced back at Phelan, but Marsh never did. It had
been his experience that if you pay attention to adversity, it
can drag you down . . .

★   ★   ★

It was 1983, the World Championship steeplechase finals

in Helsinki's Olympic Stadium, and Patriz Ilg was worried. He
was very worried. The finish was 50 yards ahead. That was the
good news. The bad news was that coming up, on his right
shoulder, out of his blind spot, was Henry Marsh—the very
last person the German wanted to see 50 yards from the finish
line. Anyone but Marsh. Marsh had momentum at the end of
races like a Ferrari pulling out to pass on the autobahn.

They had one barrier to go, and then the sprint. The two
leaders got to the hurdle almost simultaneously, well ahead of
the field. Marsh went up . . . and came down in a heap. Too
anxious to start his final kick, he had failed to jump high enough
and had jammed his right knee into the unforgiving, heavy
wooden barrier. Ilg, past the barrier and grateful, sprinted
ahead. Marsh got up, climbed over the barrier, and finished a
distant eighth.

The best steeplechaser America ever produced was defi-
nitely not its luckiest. Here was further proof. What had happened in Helsinki was nothing new, just another chapter to
add to the book.

In his first World Championships, in 1979 in Montreal after
winning two straight national championships and setting an
American record, Marsh came down with mononucleosis and
finished fourth.

In the 1981 World Cup in Rome he finished first only to
be disqualified by a jury that ruled he had run around the final
water jump (Marsh appealed, saying he was pushed around
the water jump—he lost).

And now, here in Helsinki, in the 1983 World Championships, ranked number 1 in the world in both 1981 (despite
the disqualification in Rome) and 1982 seasons, he self-
destructed just 50 yards from practically a sure victory.

Also, there was the U.S. Olympic boycott. In 1980 Marsh,
then 26, set yet another American record (8:15.68) in winning
the U.S. Olympic Trials and was a good bet for an Olympic

medal in Moscow — if only President Jimmy Carter had allowed him (and the rest of the U.S. team) to attend.

The resulting picture, no question, was of a runner running under crossed stars, a runner wondering just when and where it was that he broke the mirror.

After Helsinki, Marsh was feeling more than unlucky. He was feeling angry. He was in the best shape of his life and ought to have something more to show for it than cracked ribs and a swollen right knee — if not a world championship, then at least the fastest time of his life.

The next international meet on the European circuit was in four days in Berlin. X-rays of Marsh's knee showed it was only bruised, not damaged. As for the ribs, they would be painful for weeks, but the doctors told him there was no danger of further damage.

"Okay, if it's just *pain,*" said Marsh, and he caught the next plane for Berlin.

He couldn't breathe very well, which made running difficult at best. He managed three and a half miles in training on Monday and about four miles on Tuesday, the day before the meet. He told the officials he was 50–50 to run, and that was an hour before the race.

But there was something in him that wouldn't let him return to the hotel, take a Jacuzzi, order everything on the coffee-shop menu, and catch the Concorde to New York. Something that couldn't stand the thought of all that preparation being wasted. Something a lot like the urge that caused him to rebound from the mononucleosis at the 1979 World Championships and set a new American record the next spring at the Olympic Trials, when he was named the meet's Most Outstanding Male Athlete. Something like the urge that sent him on a two-year worldwide winning streak after the disqualification at the 1981 World Championships. And some-

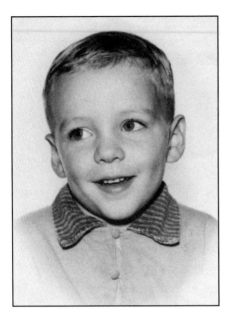

Left: Henry Marsh, age three

Below: Marsh's attention to hurdling technique vaulted him to the forefront of the world's steeplechasers

Above: For 12 straight years Marsh ranked among the top 10 steeplechasers in the world, capturing first place three times

Left: Henry Marsh smiles as he comes off the final barrier en route to victory at the 1984 U.S. Olympic Trials

thing closely related to whatever it was that wouldn't let him quit the BYU track team in 1976.

When the race started, so did Marsh. He settled into his customary position in the rear, looking even worse than usual, listing slightly to the right to ease the pain in his left ribs. Britain's Graeme Fell grabbed the lead and set a hard pace. Marsh struggled to hang on, trying to convince his ribs that this would be over soon. The good news was that his legs felt fine. If only they weren't connected to his brain!

Poland's Boguslaw Maminski, one of those who had passed the fallen Marsh at Helsinki (Maminski placed second to Ilg in the World Championship final), took the lead from Fell at the beginning of the last lap and kept driving. But somehow, through six and a half laps, Marsh hadn't lost touch with the leaders — and he wasn't going away now.

It was on the backstretch that Marsh caught Maminski. Stride for stride they took the water jump and turned for the final straightaway. There, directly in front of him, stood the final barrier. The European crowd of 56,500 fans, knowledge-able in the ways of track and field and fully aware of what had happened in Finland four days earlier, watched pensively. So did Marsh. He slowed down perceptively as he approached the barrier.

As a result, Maminski took the lead. But now Marsh, safely over the final hurdle, had his end-of-the-race sprint left, his trademark, and, as he hoped, he *was* in the best shape of his life. He passed Maminski a few strides before the finish, win-ning in 8:12.37 to 8:12.62. A measure of redemption was his, along with a new American record — almost three seconds faster than the previous best steeplechase ever run by an Amer-ican (also Henry Marsh). On the victory stand he saluted the crowd as it roared in approval. He raised only his right arm; he couldn't raise the left.

★   ★   ★

THE PEACE INTRUDER WAS GONE, and Marsh heard no more footsteps behind him on the Coliseum track. All his worries were ahead of him. The 1984 Olympic final had settled into a nervous start, with none of the runners eager to take the lead or push the pace—an indication of the relative lack of experience in this race. Peter Renner from New Zealand, a long shot, took the lead for the middle laps, dogged by the Kenyans with the same first name, Julius Kariuki and Julius Korir. Korir had come to America for the 1982–83 season on a track scholarship at Washington State University. At the recent 1984 NCAA Track and Field Championships he had won his specialty, the 5,000-meter run, and placed second in the collegiate steeplechase final with a lifetime best of 8:19.95. All of 24 years old, he had potential written all over him. But now he was looking nervous, checking ahead to the leader, behind at the pack, and to the side at his countryman, Kariuki, not knowing for sure if he was where he wanted to be.

Marsh wanted no part of the chess match at the front. He had no desire to make Olympic history in the manner of Decker Slaney just an hour before. Or, for that matter, in the manner of Jim Ryun, the American mile champion who was eliminated in the heats of the 1,500 meters in the 1972 Olympic Games after a collision and a fall on the far turn. Ryun had been Marsh's first real track hero. He had read his autobiography in high school and had been sufficiently impressed to determine that he would become America's next great miler. In the years since, he had often wondered why he had chosen to emulate a runner with such a star-crossed Olympic history.

He sensed the pace tonight was on the slow side and didn't know if that was good or bad. He guessed bad, since it could make for a frantic second half, and the last thing he needed at this point was a lengthy flat-out final sprint. He concentrated on the leaders, keeping them within reeling-in distance. The race, the real race, was to begin soon . . .

★   ★   ★

The homes on Santa Monica Boulevard were moving, and Henry Marsh wasn't. He sat on a curb and tried to clear his head and make sense of what was happening. The 17 days of the Los Angeles Olympic Games were already underway. He had marched in the opening ceremonies in the Coliseum just two days ago. His first steeplechase heat was scheduled in seven days, and now, on a training run through the residential section of Beverly Hills, he was having a hard time focusing, let alone running. Either the world was spinning or his head was. He sat down on the curb to find out.

The dizziness and nausea had begun six weeks earlier. One day he was winning the U.S. Olympic Trials, also held in the L.A. Coliseum. The next he was back home in Bountiful, Utah, to watch as his wife, Suzi, give birth to their second son, Henry Andrew. And the next day he was flat in bed. At first he had thought it was because of the rather hectic pace of winning a track meet on Saturday, staying up almost the whole night afterward, traveling to Utah on Sunday, and waiting for Henry Andrew to come into the world at seven o'clock Monday morning. But by the middle of the week he was feeling worse. Whatever it was, it was no respecter of Olympic qualifiers — and it wasn't going away.

The steeplechase final at the U.S. Trials had gone well. Marsh was running where he wanted to be, dead last, going into the final lap. Then he blew by all the runners, passing Brian Diemer and John Gregorek, both of whom would also qualify for the Olympics, on the final straightaway. His 8:15.91 time was the third fastest ever by an American — and by Marsh. "Everybody's goal in the steeplechase is to be Henry Marsh," said Gregorek. Including Henry Marsh.

It had been another triumph in a year of triumphs. Ever since hitting the hurdle in the 1983 World Championships in Helsinki, Marsh hadn't lost.

To begin the 1984 season he went into what he called his Olympic mode. He changed his diet, his work schedule, his travel schedule.

A practicing lawyer in Salt Lake City with the firm of Parsons, Behle & Latimer — after graduating from BYU Marsh had received a law degree at the University of Oregon — he cut back more than 50 percent from his practice. He took a part-time sportscasting job with KSL-TV, the CBS affiliate in Salt Lake City, but tried to limit his duties there as well. The main emphasis in his life in the spring and summer of 1984 were the Olympic Games. He arranged for weekly huddle sessions with his personal coach, Bill Bowerman, either by telephone or in person. Following Bowerman's instructions, he traveled periodically to Laguna Beach in Southern California to train at the Olympic altitude and atmosphere. Together they worked on refining his already refined techniques. He trained religiously, alternating his workouts between hard and easy. He stayed away from junk food, ate balanced meals, and got plenty of sleep.

Then he got sick.

Viruses had been something of a recurring nightmare for Marsh during much of his competitive career. There was always a fine line between being in top shape and going over the edge — in his case, a very fine line. He didn't train with the fanaticism of many other world-class athletes. His weekly mileage rarely exceeded 50 miles and never approached the 100 miles routinely turned in by distance runners.

But somehow, for all his preventative measures, he had crossed that line now. With his competitor's mentality, after almost a week of it, he decided the best way to beat it was with a good workout. At home in Bountiful, he climbed out of bed and got on the treadmill in the workout room in the basement. He ran 10 miles at a 6:10-per-mile pace. He got off

62 minutes later and did a nosedive back into bed. "Not feeling 100 percent," he wrote in his training log.

The next day, after a Nautilus workout and a three-and-a-half-mile run at the Deseret Gym in Salt Lake City, he wrote, "Sick."

On it lingered, whatever "it" was. Doctors said it was a virus, which one they weren't sure, and rest was the answer. That was easy for them to say. They didn't have an Olympics knocking at the front door, an Olympics that came around only every four years whether you were healthy or not.

At the age of 30, Marsh came to L.A. far from the rookie Olympian he'd been in 1976. This time he had expectations. This time he wanted to see if he had the game to win the gold medal. With Bowerman's blessing, he decided — and this was long before he got sick — not to stay in the athlete's village at UCLA. He didn't need the distractions. No Jethro Tull this time around. Through a mutual acquaintance, he arranged to stay in a quiet section of Beverly Hills at the home of Gerald Grinstein, the president of Western Airlines. The Grinsteins had a guest room, a pool, a fully stocked refrigerator, and a big-screen TV. They were happy to have an Olympic runner stay with them, and Marsh was happy for the solitude.

He marched with the U.S. team in the opening ceremonies on July 28. Ronald Reagan declared open the Games of the 23rd Olympiad, Rafer Johnson lit the torch, scalpers outside the stadium got $300 and more for tickets with a face value of $50, a human rocket flew through the air Hollywood-style, and the 92,000 people in the Memorial Coliseum greeted the first Olympic Summer Games on American soil since the 1932 Games of the 10th Olympiad, held also in this Coliseum. The Olympics had arrived. Henry Marsh, dizzy in the infield, didn't know whether to laugh or cry.

The reclusive life in Beverly Hills helped, and he began to feel better. By the first part of August, he could run again without constantly feeling like he was going to faint. By Friday, August 3, he went through a full workout at UCLA and wrote in his log, "Felt much better." The next day, after two short runs, he wrote, "Felt really good." He was forcing himself to train as much as possible, to simulate the three races he would run—he *hoped* there would be three—on August 6, 8, and 10—the preliminary race, the semifinal, and the Olympic final.

But on Sunday, August 5, after a two-mile run, he wrote, "Not feeling well." The Olympic preliminary was the next day.

He ran 8:29.23 in his heat, placing fourth. The first six advanced to the semifinal. On Tuesday, he jogged a mile and a half and prayed. On Wednesday, in the semifinal, he ran 8:20.57—an exhausting time under the circumstances, necessitated by the winning time of 8:19. He placed fourth and qualified for the final, which they would run in 48 hours. On Thursday, Marsh kept warm by running another mile and a half. He wrote the distance dutifully in his log book. But for the first time in a month, he wrote nothing about how he felt.

★   ★   ★

THE KENYANS WERE TRYING TO TAKE CONTROL of the race. Korir had gone to the front and Kariuki, at his shoulder, was close behind. Less than two laps remained, and the 1984 steeplechase final was turning frantic. Peter Renner, who had had to set a personal record in the semis just to get this far, faded down the straightaway approaching the bell lap and fell out of contention. Korir and Kariuki were joined by Colin Reitz of Britain, Joseph Mahmoud of France, and Henry Marsh and Brian Diemer of the United States. On the ABC telecast, Marty Liquori said, "This is an amazingly close race for the Olympics. It should be made to order for Henry Marsh."

Coming into the first turn of the final lap, Marsh moved around Diemer and Kariuki on the outside and ran up to Korir's right shoulder as ABC's Al Michaels shouted, "And here comes Marsh!" The burst of speed 300 yards from the finish was trademark Henry Marsh. From this juncture he had won race after race the past nine years.

Korir glanced at Marsh but did not break stride. The Kenyan had been in the lead or near it throughout the race and never looked physically troubled. He didn't look troubled now. He and Marsh ran stride for stride for several yards as Mahmoud and Diemer dogged them.

Korir splashed through the water jump first, followed by Marsh, Mahmoud, and Diemer. There were barely more than 100 yards now to the finish line. Three medals were waiting there, the gold, the silver, and the bronze. Unless they tripped or stopped, three of these four would win them.

The Kenyan, running free now, running loose, never looked back. He streaked to the finish line, creating behind him a frenzied scramble for the silver medal. Just before the final barrier, Marsh's hamstrings started to protest. Mahmoud inched past. Marsh was the slowest over the final barrier. Mahmoud sprinted on, the silver medal his.

On the outside now, Diemer hurdled the barrier behind Marsh but with momentum. Diemer would say later he had never experienced before, or since, the concentration he had for the final 120 yards of this race. He didn't know whom he was passing, he only knew why. The finish line straight ahead had an Olympic medal waiting for the next person there.

Diemer slid by Marsh 20 yards from the finish. He won the bronze medal by 19-hundredths of a second, clocking a personal best of 8:14.06 to Marsh's 8:14.25. Mahmoud was second in 8:13.31 while Korir won in 8:11.80, the fifth fastest steeplechase time ever run.

Once across the finish line, Marsh's body quit. It had had quite enough. While Korir took his victory lap and Diemer paid a curtain call to the Americans in the crowd of 92,000, Marsh collapsed on the Coliseum track, unconscious but still

breathing in lunging breaths that could be seen from the top
row of the stadium.

Half a dozen medics rushed to his side, wringing towels to
drip cold water onto his body. The rest of the runners, finished
by now, looked curiously at this runner that had flown past
them just minutes before, now lying motionless on the ground.

Finally an ambulance arrived and took Marsh from the
arena. He was rushed to a temporary infirmary just outside
the Coliseum entrance. Doctors checked his vital signs while
he was still unconscious. Nothing was wrong. His body, totally
spent, had taken matters unto itself and simply shut down. At
last, some rest. If the owner didn't know when to quit, his body
did.

Thirty minutes later, Marsh returned to full consciousness,
cleared his head, realized where he was, and climbed off the
hospital table. It was a far cry from a parastyle. He walked
silently to the parking lot and drove himself back to Beverly
Hills.

By the next afternoon, he was again at the track, dressed
in casual clothes, a spectator now. He still didn't feel completely well, but now it didn't matter so much. A newspaper
writer approached cautiously, not sure if there was a mourning
time and if it should be violated by asking for a reflection on
the race.

But Marsh wasn't mourning anything. "Fourth place, the
worst possible position," he said, joking. "You don't get a
medal but you still have to go through doping control."

He said he ran as well as he could. He said he thought he
would win on the final backstretch, when he came to Korir's
shoulder. He said he just didn't have enough left at the end.

"I had my shot, my day in the sun," Henry Marsh said.
"How can I be unhappy? I gave it everything I had."

★   ★   ★

Epilogue: He would have retired if he had won the gold medal in Los Angeles — picked up his $40,000 from Nike, hopefully several endorsements, and done a Bruce Jenner — walked away on top.

But he didn't retire. After a lengthy period of rest and relaxation with his wife, Suzi, and their family that fall in Bountiful, he plotted his comeback in 1985. Just what he was coming back from he wasn't sure, but there were still unanswered questions about his running and how far it could take him.

By the time the U.S. National Championships arrived early in the summer of 1985, he was back in shape. He knew Brian Diemer would be there, and he knew there had been an unspoken passing of the steeplechase baton in L.A. the summer before. Healthy now, he was prepared to give Diemer a chance to become America's best in their event. But only a chance. He was also prepared to give himself a chance to reclaim his customary position at the front. In a lot of ways, it was the biggest race of his life.

He ran an 8:18.35 to Diemer's 8:20.06.

He got Joseph Mahmoud in Berlin the next month. Competing on the same track that had given him his American record in 1983, he outkicked the Olympic silver medalist down the homestretch.

The next week, in Koblenz, Germany, he took aim at the 8:12.37 American record he'd set in '83. His 8:09.17 clocking lopped 3.2 seconds off the record and made him the fifth steeplechaser in history to run under 8:10.

He never did race Korir again. But he won 11 of the 12 races he entered in 1985 and at the age of 31 was once again ranked number 1 in the world.

He ran in one more Olympics, in 1988 in Seoul, where, at the age of 34, he finished sixth in the overall fastest steeplechase race of all time — won in 8:05.51 by Julius Kariuki, the young Kenyan who had faded on the final lap in Los Angeles four years before. The youth of the world were finally passing him by.

In a way, his Olympic finishes — tenth, fourth, and sixth, along with a boycott no-show — belied an otherwise unparalleled domination of a race often regarded as track and field's most demanding single event. For 12 straight years, Marsh was ranked in the top 10 in the world. His accumulated ranking points for his career rated him the second most prolific and consistent steeplechase runner in history, finishing just one point behind Bronislaw Malinowski, the Pole who won the gold medal in the Moscow Olympics in 1980.

The virus continued to come and go. In fact, the bouts became more frequent. Additional research by physiologists suggested that Marsh's body was extremely susceptible to stress-related viruses, and that his continued competitiveness weakened his immune system, which was being continually shut down in favor of what they called the "survival response." It explained why he got sick more often than other athletes. It explained why the sicknesses lingered.

Oddly enough, if he had been born a decade later, when the study of physiology had a chance to catch up with the intricacies of his body, he could have better known how to ward off the viruses. No matter. After that last race in Seoul, before he left the Olympic Stadium, he knelt down and kissed the track. There were no hard feelings.

PAUL CUMMINGS

BY DOUG ROBINSON

The alarm clock rings, and Paul Cummings starts from his sleep. It is dark and still and 5:30 A.M. He stretches and rises from his bed. In a practiced routine, he stumbles to the closet, slips into a sweat suit and shoes, sneaks out of the bedroom past his sleeping wife (careful not to wake her), and tiptoes downstairs and into the kitchen for a quick bowl of cold cereal, while the family dalmatian, Sparky, wags his tail anxiously. After breakfast, Sparky pulls Cummings out the front door, and they disappear into the pre-dawn darkness. The air is cool—it is autumn now—and it stings Cummings's nose as he starts jogging up the road, past the darkened homes of neighbors. He runs slowly at first, allowing his body to awaken, but Sparky tugs on the leash to go faster. Gradually, Cummings's pace quickens as he warms to the task of an eight-mile run.

He is 38 years old. The lines have begun to appear in his handsome, moustachioed face. A few gray hairs have turned up lately in his thick, tousled mass of black hair. Like a middle-aged couch potato, he wages his own battles with weight gain—as recently as last spring he actually had a slight paunch—but he is slender and fit now, if not always healthy. There are allergies, always those. Twice a day, six days a week, Cummings trains, logging up to 100 miles or more, even though the good races are getting further and further apart. Something drives him on, but certainly it's not money. With his continued health problems, Cummings is no longer able to earn a living with his swift legs, so he drives 30 miles from his home in Lehi, Utah, to Salt Lake City, where he oversees the employee fitness program at LDS Hospital. To reach work on time, he must squeeze in these morning runs before dawn. He runs again at lunchtime. By the time he gets home, it is often dark again.

Cummings keeps running and running. It has always been so. Through allergies, through big paydays, through no paydays, through family troubles, he has always kept running, even when no one understood why. For years he labored beside fiery hot furnaces in a Provo steel mill, and still he kept training by running to and from the mills, in all kinds of weather, at all hours of the day or night. He suffered from layoffs and long stretches of unemployment while trying to feed a family, living off savings and a prayer and what money could be scraped up cleaning carpets. But he kept running. Finally, when the system changed and allowed a runner to earn money for his sweat, he devoted himself full-time to running. His running took him to wealth and, after two previous failures, to the Olympic Games, only to have his body betray him again. Three years later, he was battling financial troubles and allergies again, and this time something more: Time.

How good could this man be if fate ever dealt him a good hand? Probably no one will ever know, but Cummings keeps running just the same.

★   ★   ★

The 1974 NCAA Track and Field Championships was held in Austin, Texas, in the worst of conditions. It was early June, nearly 100 degrees and deadly humid. It was the kind of heat that could kill a distance or middle-distance runner. The mile was held at midday under a cloudless sky. Paul Cummings, a slight, scholarly looking student from BYU with round wire-rim glasses, knew it would not be a day for fast performances. He was considered one of the favorites, along with North Carolina's Tony Waldrop, who had been a national sensation indoors, and Texas–El Paso's Wilson Waigwa, a world-class import from Kenya. No one wanted to run hard in this heat, and the leaders covered the first half-lap in a pedestrian 35 seconds. Hearing the split time, Cummings, who had been running in the back of the pack, sprinted into the lead and picked up the pace, not wanting the race to be decided by a mad sprint at the finish, especially with Waldrop and Waigwa in tow. This was the mile, not the 100-yard dash. The field gave chase, but when Cummings turned a 57-second third lap, no one went with him. That pace was crazy in this heat, and there was still a lap to go. Surely Cummings would return to the field, they reasoned, but he didn't. Covering the final lap in 59 seconds, he finished first with a time of 4:01, then collapsed, overcome by heat exhaustion. Someone threw a wet towel and ice on him. BYU coaches picked him up, carried him to the end of the track, and placed him in the steeplechase water jump to cool his body temperature. Cummings was the national champion, even if he didn't feel like one.

Cummings, only a junior, had improved steadily and methodically every year since taking up the sport. As a freshman at BYU, he knocked eight seconds off his best mile time, running 4:02. As a sophomore, he ran 3:59, breaking the four-minute barrier for the first time. As a junior, he clocked 3:56.4 and ranked 11th in the world and second in the U.S. His future seemed assured. In the NCAA race, he had demonstrated courage, boldness, and strength to run from the front on a dangerously hot day against a talented field, not to mention a

toughness that took him to the limit of his strength. He had
the makings of becoming America's next great miler, but a
year later, his career looked all but finished.

In the spring of 1975, Cummings was on a training run
near his parents' home in California. He ran past a man mow-
ing his lawn, and two blocks later he felt something in his eye —
pollen or grass, he was never sure. His eye was tearing, and
by the end of the run it was swollen shut. He was taken to a
hospital and given a shot of adrenaline. The eye recovered,
but Cummings would never be the same again. It was the
beginning of a battle with allergies that would forever haunt
his running career.

"From then on I started having problems," he says. "I
never got in sync that year. I felt tired and weak. I had conges-
tion and extreme fatigue. It was like flipping a switch. It was
that dramatic."

"I can remember him coming to the track for a workout,
and he couldn't even run two quarters his asthma was so bad,"
recalls BYU assistant coach Willard Hirschi.

The 1975 NCAA Championships were held at BYU, and
Cummings, the defending champion in the sport's glamor
event, was burdened by the expectations of all those hometown
fans and media and the gnawing realization that he was in no
shape to please them, beset as he was with allergies. Cummings
bravely took the lead for the first three laps, but on the gun
lap Villanova's Eamonn Coghlan passed him, among many
others, and Cummings faded badly, to seventh place. It was
the beginning of a career that would be marked by extreme
highs and lows.

★   ★   ★

Day and night Cummings worked in the Geneva Steel
Mills, wielding a six-foot crowbar in the stifling heat that ra-
diated from the open hearth furnaces. His back was stiff, his

arms ached, and sweat ran off his blackened face as he pounded and pried at the brick walls of the furnaces. Exposed to the 2,000-degree heat used to melt steel, the walls eventually decay. Cummings and the rest of the crew tore down the decayed walls and rebuilt them. Sometimes the hearths were shut down, and Cummings and the rest of the crew climbed on top of them to repair damaged brick. They knocked a hole in the brick and then filled it in while staggering 200-degree heat rushed into their faces. At other times, Cummings worked under the bed of a hearth, knocking away brick that was encrusted with several inches of soot that soon filled the air. The dust was so thick that he couldn't see the guy next to him. Cummings, unlike many of his co-workers, wore a respirator, but it didn't help completely. He'd go on vacation, and a week later black stuff would still be coming out of his nose. By the end of the day, Cummings looked like a coal miner. His clothes were saturated with sweat, and his face and hands were covered with a thick black grime. If he rubbed hard enough, it would wash off.

After his shift, Cummings showered, put on a sweat suit, and, while his co-workers climbed into their cars, ran home.

Cummings had graduated from BYU several years earlier, in 1976, with a degree in physical education, but he quickly realized that the teaching profession wasn't for him, not with the low pay and long hours, which would leave little time for running or family.

In those days few track athletes continued their athletic careers after college graduation, especially those with a family. Under the archaic amateur rules of the time, they weren't allowed to be paid for their sport, and they received no help from their government, as did East German and Russian athletes. In essence, the amateur rules prevented Cummings from earning a living in his sport, and earning a living prevented him from pursuing his sport. With an eye on the 1976 Olympic

Games, Cummings continued to train anyway. After graduating from BYU, he held a series of odd jobs as a construction gofer, grocery store bagger, and BYU grounds crewman. During the racing season, he quit his job to compete indoors or on the European circuit, then returned to Provo and found another job. In spite of the amateur rules, Cummings and other top athletes were paid for their races. It wasn't much—a few thousand dollars—but combined with the money from his odd jobs during the off-season, it was enough to sustain Cummings and his growing family.

In 1978, Cummings, seeing an opportunity for better employment, camped out all night to get a job at Geneva. Even at that, an official in the BYU athletic department had to pull strings to get Cummings the job. The money was good and the job was in high demand. For three years, Cummings worked graveyard, swing, and daytime shifts on a weekly rotation. Layoffs came regularly, usually in late fall or winter. He worked five or six months, and then he and his co-workers were laid off two or three months.

Cummings continued to run and race. He ran seven miles to the mills, worked his eight-hour shift, showered, changed back into his running clothes, and ran the seven miles home, his energy sapped by the heat and the hard work. That was how he trained. If he was working a graveyard or swing shift at the time, it meant running to and from work in the middle of the night. Whenever he could, he worked double shifts so he could clear weekends for races. Once he got off work on a Friday evening, drove straight to Salt Lake City International Airport, flew to Philadelphia, arrived at his hotel in the wee hours, slept most of the next day, won the Penn Relays mile that evening with a time of 3:58, and then flew home the next morning, arriving in Provo just in time to report for the swing shift that afternoon.

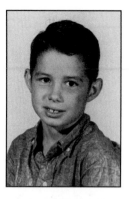

Left: Young Paul Cummings

Below: For years the only way Cummings could train was to run to and from his job in the Provo steel mills day and night, but eventually he put the mills behind him (photo courtesy *Deseret News*)

Above left: At the 1984 Olympic Trials, Paul Cummings took the lead on the final lap and never gave it back (photo courtesy *Deseret News*)

Above: Celebrating victory at the finish line at the 1984 Olympic Trials (photo courtesy *Deseret News*)

Left: Cummings wears the Olympic uniform at last

"I just loved to run," recalls Cummings. "I wanted to improve."

Among others, Sherald James, Cummings's coach at BYU, tried to rescue him from the mills. He rallied support from the community to finance Cummings's training. "All For Paul," they called it. Aided by a local radio station, the program raised only a few hundred dollars, which didn't go far. "Here was this great runner who should be given the opportunity to reach his potential," says James. "But it was almost impossible to run while working over an open hearth like that." Cummings himself tried to escape the work-and-run routine. In 1979, he talked with officials from the Nike shoe company about paying him to run for their club; they told him he was too old. He was 26.

Cummings's career was mostly floundering. He ranked among the nation's top 10 milers three of the previous four years before taking the job at Geneva, then dropped out of sight. What few good races he did produce were usually during the winter indoor season. He was safe from pollen and allergies indoors, and the layoffs often coincided with the indoor season, which allowed him to train more. Despite such circumstances, he set two national indoor records in the metric mile — 1,500 meters — during layoffs, both of them at the Muhammad Ali Invitational in Long Beach, California. In 1978, he finished first with an American record of 3:38.6. In 1979, both Cummings and Olympic champion John Walker broke the world record, but Walker beat Cummings to the tape by a mere .2 of a second, in 3:37.4, after passing him on the final homestretch.

But if Cummings was able to hold his own indoors, he was rarely heard from outdoors, where he was susceptible to allergies and burdened with his job as a steelworker. In 1980 he failed to finish the national cross country championships, and the following year he failed to make the finals at the U.S.

trackchampionships. An injury prevented him from even competing in the 1980 Olympic Trials.

"I nearly quit," says Cummmings. "I thought, this is it. I just didn't have time to train properly."

And spare time was becoming even more difficult to find. In 1980, he invested his life savings, $10,000, to be a partner in a running store called Paul Cummings's Second Sole. For 18 months he worked two jobs — and, of course, he ran. He ran to Geneva, worked a shift, ran to the store, worked several hours there, then ran home just in time to go to bed and start over the next day — a total of 17 miles. But even his endurance was wearing thin. He was working so hard that he was unable to sleep. His hands trembled as he lay in bed at night.

★   ★   ★

Cummings grew up the silent, withdrawn third child in a family of 13 children. His mother Lee was still having children when Paul left for college. His father, David, a former sprinter at Arizona State, struggled to support his family on a music teacher's salary. He taught school band and gave music lessons on the side, and in the summer he worked odd jobs as a route truck driver, salesman, forest ranger, and whatever else he could find. He sold the family home almost annually to make extra money, hustling the children from one house to the next. Money was always tight. Each child was given one pair of shoes, one pair of pants, and two shirts to last an entire school year. "We grew up differently than most people, but we didn't know it then," says Paul. "It was normal to us. But it was tough when I look back on it."

Lee did her part to save money. She pushed health foods onto her children before they were in vogue, largely to keep the family healthy and avoid medical bills. She lined up the kids for daily doses of cod liver oil and vitamin E and fed them whole grains, fruits, vegetables, and no sweets.

Paul was and always would be the quiet one. He was so bashful that one day his college roommate would be required to ask his eventual wife, Gaye Anhder, for a first date simply because Paul couldn't imagine talking to a girl he didn't know. When coaches brought Paul to the BYU campus on an official recruiting trip, they were baffled by his silence. No amount of questioning could draw him out, beyond yes and no.

As with so many athletes, Paul's talent was discovered in a physical education class, and perhaps just in time. As a ninth-grader, he had arrived at a crossroads. One path led to education and the Church; the other to trouble. "I was on my way to becoming a juvenile delinquent," he recalls. "I was hanging out with my older brother, Dave, who had dropped out of school. I was skipping school and trying cigarettes and alcohol. But then I got interested in running. Success changes a lot of things."

Despite having to stop and walk a couple of times, Paul won a mile run in P.E. class one day with a time of 5:25, which was a freshman school record. Seeing this, coaches invited him to join the track team. But after enduring the team's first workout—a set of repeat 220-yard sprints—Paul nearly quit right then. He won the first cross country race he entered, again walking and stopping en route to the finish. "It was the first time I won anything," he says. "I was hooked."

With the lure of running and success, Cummings resolved to take school seriously and to adhere to his Mormon upbringing, which meant refraining from alcohol and tobacco. "I didn't want to do anything that would hurt my body," he says. His friends made sure that he lived his own standards, even if they were non-Mormons. When someone offered Cummings a drink at a party, they intervened: "No, he doesn't drink; he's a Mormon."

The following year the Cummings family moved, as always, this time to Santa Maria, California. The family remained in the Santa Maria area the remainder of Paul's high school days, although they continued to change houses regularly. Paul attended Righetti High, where he met Dick Ballou, a large, kindly, humorous man who coached the school's track team. Ballou knew relatively little about runners and running, but he recognized Cummings's talent quickly and began to study training technique. He also became his friend and mentor. After learning that Cummings was too poor to buy a pair of spiked track shoes, Ballou approached Cummings one day and handed him $25. "Somebody gave me this money," said Ballou. "He's seen you run, and he wants you to use this money to buy some track shoes. He wants you to be the best you can be. He has faith in you."

Says Cummings now, "I still don't know who did that. But I think it inspired me to take running more seriously."

Despite a lengthy bout of pneumonia, Cummings ran a 4:19 mile as a junior. The following year he ran 4:10.7 and finished second in the California state meet. He was recruited heavily, which was fortunate since the only way he could afford to attend college was with a full-ride scholarship. He finally chose BYU over Arizona State and USC.

"He was so quiet we never knew what he was thinking," recalls James. Unlike so many of the star runners who developed at BYU, Cummings's ability was obvious from the beginning. "We all knew he was a tremendous talent," says James. "We knew he could be great."

★   ★   ★

Cummings might never have reached greatness if not for a dramatic turn of events. When the usual layoffs at Geneva came in 1981, there were indications that this time the workers wouldn't be rehired. If that weren't bad enough, Cummings's partners in the running store forced him out and refused to pay him the current value of his one-third share. Cummings was devastated.

"I've never seen Paul break down and cry like he did then," says Gaye. "They told him his name wasn't worth anything anymore, that it meant nothing to the store."

"In some ways it strengthened my resolve to run well again," says Cummings.

But now he had other motives. Cummings was unemployed and deeply in debt, and Gaye was pregnant with their third child. He started a carpet-cleaning business, but still he was forced to sell their two cars to pay debts. "We played beat the bank," says Gaye. "We just prayed the money would come through before they got the check. Everything went on the charge card to the hilt."

"It was all we could do to keep food in the house," says Cummings. "There were plenty of times I didn't know how we would make the next house payment."

The answer was there all along, although the Cummingses didn't see it at first. Running was merely a source of contention at home, not a way to pay bills. Even in the best of times, Gaye wondered why her husband ran. He was already gone so much to work, and then running . . .

"There was a time when I was going to leave Paul," says Gaye. "I never stopped loving him, but . . . he was always gone, either working or running. I thought he was just obsessed with running. I felt like I was competing for time."

Then the bad times hit, and Cummings was still running. "I ran to release tension," says Cummings. "It got my mind off my problems. But I also felt like I still had a future there. I didn't know where or what, but I knew I hadn't given it my best shot."

Cummings had never considered running as a way to make a living, and he never would have if fate hadn't cut off every possible alternative. Geneva was gone. The store was gone.

He tried unsuccessfully to find other work. He applied for a job as a route truck driver for Frito-Lay but was turned down, and so he accepted unemployment checks. "I had to look at myself," he says. "What can I do? The only thing I had done well my whole life was run. It's the one thing I really excelled at. I knew people were making money out there now."

The running boom was reaching its peak, and some runners were actually earning money in road races. Cummings decided to abandon the mile and convert himself into a distance runner, partly because he had been outkicked at the end of so many mile races and partly because that's where the money was. "I saw guys I knew I could beat who were making a reasonable living road racing," he says.

Cummings checked out books from the library on physiology and consulted with a BYU exercise physiologist to learn how best to train himself for the distance races. He increased his training and his mileage, and in December of 1981 he finished sixth in the Las Vegas Half-Marathon, not far behind the winner, and won $500. "It helped a lot at the time," he says. "It was the first time I had made money in that way." Cummings's time of 1:02:59 attracted attention. New Balance awarded him a contract worth $10,000 to endorse its running shoes.

Suddenly Cummings's running career took off. A few months later he finished fourth in the Nike Marathon in Eugene, Oregon, with a time of 2:12, which was worth $4,000. During the next two years he reached peak form and became one of the nation's busiest and most successful runners. He often raced once a week or more, year-round, anytime, anywhere, any distance. In one three-week period alone he ran the 7.1-mile Bay to Breakers race in San Francisco; a track 5,000 in Knoxville, Tennessee; the Salt Lake Classic 10,000; and a marathon in Stockholm, claiming a first, two seconds, and a third, respectively. In one weekend he ran three races, placing second in a road mile in Salt Lake City, winning a 5K race in Modesto, California, that night, and then finishing fifth in the Pepsi Invitational two-mile in Los Angeles the next day. In all, Cummings placed third or better in 21 races and sixth or better in 33 races in 1983, set a world record in the half-marathon, an American record at 15,000 meters, and earned money well into six figures.

With his new-found wealth, Cummings, the laid-off steel-worker, bought a customized van and a 5,500-square-foot home in Orem, complete with a Jacuzzi and basketball court. In 1984, Converse, the athletic shoe company, signed him to a six-figure endorsement contract. At the age of 30, Cummings had ar-rived—and the Olympics were coming to America.

★　　★　　★

For 24 laps Cummings had stalked the field, waiting for the right moment to jump the leaders, and at the start of the final lap he saw his chance. The 10,000-meter run at the 1984 U.S. Olympic Track and Field Trials had come down to a sprint, and there was little doubt now about who would win. Matched against Cummings and his miler's speed, the others never had a chance. In two swift strides Cummings burst past Garry Bjorklund and moved into the lead. He surged down the backstretch to the roaring approval of 21,000 fans in the L.A. Coliseum. As he hit the final straightaway, Cummings glanced over his right shoulder and then, satisfied with the huge gap he had put between himself and his pursuers, he smiled. By the time he hit the finish line, both arms were raised triumphantly above his head, his fists clenched tightly.

At last, after years of frustration, he had made the Olympic team, and even the normally mild and bashful Cummings couldn't resist savoring his moment on stage. He waved to the crowd and took a victory lap that lasted a full five minutes.

Along the way he hugged his grandmother and shook hands and waved to well-wishers.

Cummings, who earlier in the season had run the fastest time in the world for 10,000 meters, 27:43.7, looked like a solid bet to win an Olympic medal. What other distance runner had his combination of speed and strength? Only New Zealand's Rod Dixon could match his versatility. Cummings had run everything from a 3:54 mile to a 2:12 marathon.

But soon there would be problems. Cummings's allergies had bothered him on and off for years. Some years were bad, others good. At the 1976 Olympic Trials, his allergies were so bad that he didn't even qualify for the finals. In 1981 and 1982 he ran free of allergies. In 1983 they were back, and by then Cummings's living depended on his health. For years, well-meaning people, having read of Cummings's troubles, wrote letters to him or sent books offering advice on how to cure his allergies. He tried injections, herbs, drinks, vitamins, and diets, but nothing worked until 1983, when he tried one shot of cortisone. The results were dramatic. The drug significantly improved his condition and allowed him to train hard and race well, but there was a price to pay. Following the Olympic Trials, a U.S. team doctor warned him of cortisone's side effects: namely, damage to tendons. Cummings, who had noticed recent soreness in his Achilles tendons, quit taking the cortisone at the doctor's advice. He reasoned that he could get by without the injections since the Olympics was just six weeks away. But three weeks later he realized he was wrong. All the old symptoms returned. Two weeks before the Games, he began taking large doses of cortisone, hoping to make up for lost time, but it was too late. He retained water (another side effect of the drug) and gained 10 pounds. By the time the Olympics arrived, he knew he was in trouble. During the heats of the 10,000, he was only a mile into the race when he knew this wouldn't be his day. He finished ninth with a slowish time of 29:09.82 and failed to advance to the finals.

"If I had kept taking the cortisone, I would have been a medalist," says Cummings calmly. "I know it. I should never have stopped taking the shots."

★   ★   ★

The alarm clock rings and Cummings rises from his bed. It is 5:30 A.M., and the routine begins again. In a few minutes, Cummings and Sparky are running the darkened backroads of the Utah countryside. The man who was once so awkward and bashful around people never feels so good, so tranquil as during these simple moments of running. He likes the simplicity. He likes being lean and fit. He likes doing the one thing at which he's always excelled. And always he is drawn by potential and the endless search for the perfect race.

"If I ever got healthy enough, I still think I could run the best race I've ever run," he says.

Old dreams die hard. It's been four years since his last good race. He ran well through 1986, but a year later his health soured and the cortisone lost its magic, after his body developed a tolerance to the drug. His performances declined, the prize money stopped coming, he lost his shoe contract and most of his money in bad investments. Two years later, he ran out of savings and filed for bankruptcy. He had to sell the big house in 1989, move his wife and four children to Lehi, and take a regular job, at the hospital. In many ways, he is back to where he started years ago, only older.

"I feel real good about what I've done," says Cummings. "But I still think it's not over. Maybe that's not true, but I'll continue to run. I expect I'll be running about the time I kick over dead."

KARL TILLEMAN

BY LEE BENSON

The phone call came in the early summer of 1986, when Karl Tilleman was serving a mission in Arcadia, California. Jack Donahue, the coach of the Canadian National Basketball Team, was on the line, from Ottawa. It had been almost two years since they last talked, but Donahue didn't waste time catching up.

"They put in your shot," Donahue said to the best long-range shooting guard he had ever coached.

"They what?" said Tilleman.

"The three-point shot," said Donahue. "They approved the three-point shot for the Olympics. When are you getting home? I think we could still use you."

Due to conclude his mission in less than a month, Tilleman put down the phone and considered his good fortune. Anything over 20 feet, six inches, would now count three points, not two, in international competition — and he never liked to shoot any closer than that anyway. Couple the three-point line with a zone defense, and you had his version of a perfect world.

So he was going to have the chance to play in another

Olympics after all. The Summer Games in Seoul, Korea, were yet two years away—plenty of time to get ready. Canada still wanted him, even if he had never owned a pair of ice skates.

*   *   *

He moved to Canada when he was 12, and he was sure it was the end of life as he knew it. His father, Bill Tilleman, walked into the front room of their home in LaCrosse, Wisconsin, and, out of the blue, said, "We're moving to Calgary," and Karl immediately went into a prolonged depression.

The youngest in a family of seven, Karl wasn't by nature a brooder. But at the age of 12 he was already addicted to basketball, and he foresaw no basketball in Canada. Any hour of the day in LaCrosse you could find him at the basket at the end of the cul-de-sac, shooting alone, finding a game, whatever was there. He wasn't sure they even played the game north of the border. "The only thing they do is whack each other with hockey sticks," he said to his father, an accounting professor at the University of Wisconsin-LaCrosse who had accepted a similar position on the faculty at the University of Calgary.

Before Wisconsin, the Tillemans had lived in Washington Terrace, a suburb of Ogden, Utah. When Karl was four, and his older brothers Bill and John were nine and seven (the two oldest in the family were sisters Cherie and Sharon), Bill, Sr., who graduated with his Ph.D. from the University of Utah in Salt Lake City and took his first teaching job at Ogden's Weber State College, nailed a redwood backboard and rim above their garage on 279 West 4775 South. From the start, even at four, Karl shot at that basket incessantly. He shot two-handed at first, then one-handed, and no one was sure where the infatuation came from, only that it was there.

Bill Tilleman didn't cave into his youngest son's protests that they not move to the naked north where all the gym floors were allegedly covered with ice. But before moving to Calgary, a city in Alberta of 200,000 about to strike oil and turn into a city of 500,000, he did inquire about which schools paid the most attention to basketball, and the family moved to that part of the city. As a further concession, he struck a deal with the custodian at the University of Calgary gymnasium that Karl could play basketball there whenever he wanted.

True, basketball wasn't as developed in Canada as in the states, and they *did* whack each other with hockey sticks, but Canada didn't prove to be the Siberia of basketball Karl had feared it would be. He soon enough found games and courts and other players. The baskets were still ten feet high. He was feeding his habit, playing on the team at H.D. Cartwright Junior High by afternoon and in the U. of Calgary gym with the college players by night. Toward the end of his ninth grade season at H.D. Cartwright he scored 79 points—in one game.

That summer, in 1976, Karl was at home lying on the couch watching television when a basketball game from the Montreal Olympics came on between the Canadian National Team and the team from the United States. Intrigued, he sat up and moved to the edge of the couch. His hands were sweating. He found himself rooting for the good guys. Fifteen years old and three years removed from never wanting to leave the United States, basketball's birthplace, for the barren basketball waste-land of Canada, he immediately set the first real and serious basketball goal of his life—to play for his national team: the *Canadians.* There was just one problem: he wasn't Canadian.

★　　★　　★

He didn't find that out until five years later, at the con-clusion of his second season at the University of Calgary. One afternoon he got up the courage to phone the head coach of the Canadian team, Jack Donahue, at the offices of the Ca-nadian Amateur Basketball Association in Ottawa, to ask about tryouts for that year's team. Donahue—who, through inquiries, already knew Tilleman was an American — told him there was no loophole around Canadian citizenship. That rule was black and white. You had to be a Canadian to play on the Canadian National Team, or, for that matter, to try out.

The next day Tilleman went to the Canadian Consulate in Calgary and filed for dual U.S.-Canadian citizenship.

Ever since his arrival from Wisconsin, Canadian basketball had been good to him. At Sir Winston Churchill High School he was all-Canadian two straight years and helped the team win the city final his senior year. Churchill almost won the Provincial championship as well, losing in double overtime to a team from Lethbridge. From there, Tilleman signed to play with the University of Calgary Dinosaurs. He had several scholarship offers from U.S. schools, including one from Washington State University in Pullman, Washington, where he had attended summer camps. The one stateside school he was most interested in, Brigham Young University, wasn't interested in him, however. In 1979 BYU had a full contingent of guards, including Danny Ainge, who would go on to be an NBA All-Star.

Karl's high school coach, Skip Morgan, thought Tilleman should play for Dean Smith at the University of North Carolina — and went so far as to telephone Coach Smith.

But ultimately when it came time to make a college decision, Calgary was the most appealing, partly because the school was in Karl's hometown and his father taught there, and partly because two players on the team, Steve Atkin and Rommel Raffin (a transfer from Penn State), had been members of the Canadian National Team that Tilleman had watched on television in 1976. That team, the first coached by Jack Donahue, took fourth place in the Olympics, losing to the Soviet Union in the bronze medal game. It was the highest finish ever for a Canadian basketball team in the Olympics.

Tilleman's introduction to national-caliber basketball in

the summer of 1981 was encouraging. After securing his citizenship and traveling to Ottawa, he played well enough in tryouts to be put on the B team and that summer played in a handful of junior varsity-type scrimmages for the Canadian B squad. By the time he went back to the University of Calgary for the start of the 1981–82 season, he was confident about his chances for advancement to the A squad the following year.

After the 1981–82 season, he was more than encouraged. In his third season with the Calgary Dinosaurs, he led the team in scoring at 32.9 points per game and scored a grand total of 657 regular season points to set an all-time Canada Interuniversity Athletic Union record. Tilleman won the Mike Moser Award as the best college basketball player in Canada. Statistically, there had never been a season its equal in Canadian college basketball. Even the Canadian Football League team in Calgary, the Stampeders, was impressed. They sent Tilleman a letter asking him to come and try out for *their* team.

He said thanks but no thanks, their ball was shaped funny, and he was off to Ottawa, where he went through two weeks of national team tryouts playing the most determined basketball of his life. He liked his chances. He liked the program. He liked Donahue, a coach with credentials of his own. The coach, like Tilleman, was an American transplant. He came from New York City. He once coached at Power Memorial High School in New York City, where his center was a seven-footer named Lew Alcindor (later Kareem Abdul-Jabbar). From there he coached collegiately at Holy Cross, Bob Cousy's alma mater, until the Canadians came calling. In 1976, his first Olympiad, Donahue gave the country hope by not only coaching the National Team to its fourth place finish but also—in the game Tilleman watched on TV—to a spirited battle, albeit a losing one, against a United States team, led by Adrian Dantley, Phil Ford, and Walter Davis, that went on to beat Yugoslavia for the Olympic gold medal.

Because of Canada's boycott of the 1980 Moscow Olympics, the 1984 Los Angeles Olympics were to be Donahue's next Olympic showcase. In the summer of '82, his aim was to line up a roster that would peak in two years. Since Tilleman, just 21 years old, still happened to be peaking himself, he calculated that the conditions were decidedly in his favor.

But when the 12-man national team was picked, Tilleman ranked 13th. For the first time since he started shooting baskets in the driveway in Utah, he was told he wasn't good enough.

Devastated, he walked out of the gym and, for hours, walked the streets of Ottawa, trying to deal with the news he'd been dealt. When he returned to Calgary, he still couldn't quite come to grips with his failure to make the A team. For therapy he drove south across the border, to his grandparents' ranch just outside of Chinook, Montana, where his father was born and raised. There, alone, he brooded, completely unaware that, as with the move from Wisconsin to Alberta, his days as a basketball player were far from over.

★   ★   ★

The disappointment at not making the National Team spurred on a drive in Karl Tilleman to become a more well-rounded player. Returning to the Dinos in 1982–83 for his fourth collegiate season (college players are given five years of eligibility in Canada, compared to the standard four years in the United States), he attacked all facets of the game. Always a shooter — and, more than that, a scorer — Tilleman went to work on his ball-handling, his defense, his court awareness, even his jumping. He was 6-foot-2, 180 pounds, and white, but, still, there was room for more height when he jumped, more pressure when he played defense. He approached basketball that season as if it were a year-round final exam.

The University of Calgary basketball program, and, in particular, head coach Gary Howard, was not ungrateful. In his quest to prove that his 1982 season was no fluke, and that he should be on Canada's national team, Tilleman further entrenched himself as Canada's answer to Pete Maravich, the American college star of the '70s who scored points falling off the bench. Seeing every box-and-one and diamond-and-one defense known to coaching, Tilleman still averaged more than 30 points a game. He led his team again, he led his league, he led his country. He scored 53 points in one game, setting yet another school single-game record, and he didn't play in the final 10 minutes of the game. Mario Toneguzzi, a sports writer at the *Calgary Herald,* gave him a nickname that would stick the rest of his career: King Karl.

King Karl was named the winner of the Mike Moser Award, again, for the second year in a row—a feat never accomplished before (or since). Winning the second Moser trophy may have been the most amazing feat of all. When he won the season before it was startling enough, given that more than half of the universities in Canada are in the East, most of them in Ontario, and that the country's coaches who vote for the award tend to show a traditional bias in favor of the Eastern schools. Winning it from way out in Calgary for a second straight season in 1983 was considered out of the possibility— until Tilleman's encore season exceeded his performance of 1982.

That summer, he was ready again for the tryouts in Ottawa for the National Team—a team that would play in both the Pan American Games in Venezuela and the World University Games in Edmonton, just 180 miles up the freeway from Calgary. He'd have the home-province and home-country advantage.

★   ★   ★

Sitting in the locker room of the Universiade Pavilion in Edmonton, with CANADA written across his jersey, Karl

Above: Karl Tilleman, age six

Above right: In Los Angeles and
 Seoul, Tilleman wore Canada's colors

Right: Karl Tilleman plays defense
in the 1988 Olympic Games

Far right: At the University of Calgary,
Tilleman rewrote all of the school's
scoring records

Tilleman knew that he had finally arrived. At the tryouts in Ottawa he had approached Jack Donahue and told him it was his intent to prove that Team Canada couldn't live without him. Then he proved it. He was put on the A team roster that now, in less than an hour, would play the United States in the semifinal game of the World University Games. The winner would advance to the next night's gold medal game against Yugoslavia.

Earlier in the day, at the dorms on the University of Alberta campus, Tilleman had heard someone open the front door and call his name. He looked up and saw Ed Eyestone, his best friend when they had been classmates at Roosevelt Elementary School in Ogden, Utah. They'd lived on the same street, five doors apart, and were inseparable at 10. After Karl moved they'd lost touch, until now. Eyestone was wearing a U.S. uniform. A distance runner, he was at the World University Games to compete on the track. What were the odds, they said, that two kids from the same street in Ogden, Utah, would both be in this world meet (and what were the odds that they would later appear in the same Olympics?). As he left, the answer hit Eyestone: About the same as the odds that the Canadians would beat the Americans that night in basketball.

This being the year preceding an Olympic Games, the national teams sent to participate in Edmonton were not diluted. The American team included the likes of Charles Barkley, Johnny Dawkins, Karl Malone, Kevin Willis, Ed Pinckney, and Devin Durrant — a team of players that, in less than three years, would be making millions in the National Basketball Association.

But with 12,000 in the Pavilion cheering in top voice — stretching their lungs to decibel levels normally reserved for the Stanley Cup finals — Team Canada won by eight points, 85–77. It was only the second significant international basketball competition between the United States and Canada ever won by the Canadians.

The next night, with the 12,000 still in a hockey brawl mood, Team Canada was on such a roll that beating Yugoslavia seemed almost a foregone conclusion. Tilleman scored 12 points, including eight when the game still had some drama in the first half, and Team Canada won 83–68. The gold medal was theirs.

Tilleman had by now carved a niche as the team's sixth man — the first player off the bench — who had a habit of scoring just after the referee waved him into the game. At the next international meet, the Pan American Games in Caracas, Venezuela, he further cemented his John Havlicek–like role. In the game there against the U.S. — the first rematch between the neighboring nations since Edmonton — he came off the bench early and immediately started filling the basket. The U.S. player assigned to defend him, Leon Wood of Cal State-Fullerton, was summarily benched and replaced by a new player, one the United States hadn't sent to Edmonton — Michael Jordan of the University of North Carolina.

Tilleman and Jordan proceeded to have an offensive showdown that Tilleman won, 28 points to 14. (He still has a picture of Jordan guarding him in that game, enlarged to poster size.)

Nonetheless, the United States avenged its defeat in Edmonton, winning 111–97. The world wasn't ready to lay down for Canadian basketball just yet. Still, the Canadians had them thinking.

Returning for his senior year at the University of Calgary, Tilleman went on his usual early-season rampage and was waging an unarguable campaign for yet another Moser Award. But a knee injury forced him to sit out the middle part of the season. In one-half of a season, he still scored 31.2 points per game. He was denied a third Moser award but was named All-Canadian for the fourth straight year.

For his final game at Red Gym on the University of Calgary campus, the gym his father got him a season pass to as a seventh-grader, the school arranged for Karl Tilleman Night. The plan was for Tilleman's jersey, number 30, to be retired after that night's game against the University of Saskatchewan. His knee fully recovered, Tilleman was coming off a 40-point outing against the University of Alberta two nights before. His wrist was loose, and he was ready for his finale. Little did he realize he wouldn't score a point the night they retired his jersey.

Miffed that a referee from Calgary named Joe Gersline was assigned to officiate the game, Saskatchewan Coach Guy Vetrie protested, saying his team would forfeit. It was no idle threat. When the game officials insisted that Gersline stay, Vetrie turned to his team, said, "Let's walk," and they returned to Saskatchewan.

In the jersey retirement ceremonies that followed, Norm Wagner, the president of the University of Calgary, said, "Karl is the only athlete I know who can draw a sellout without a game being played."

The end of his college career and the retirement of his jersey meant only the beginning of the Olympic year, however. Soon enough, Tilleman and the National Team were in training, preparing for the Olympic Games in Los Angeles to be held in July and August. In the meantime, at the NBA Draft in New York, he was selected in the fourth round by the Denver Nuggets. He was the 79th player taken overall.

★   ★   ★

Playing the United States basketball team in Edmonton in 1983 was one thing. Playing them in the Los Angeles Forum in the 1984 Olympics with Bobby Knight, the perfectionist coach from Indiana, pulling the strings on the sidelines was another. The Forum was filled constantly with flag-waving,

patriotic Americans. All of America's games were being relayed live by network television to a nation anxious for its first
Olympic triumphs in eight years (because of the 1980 boycott
of the Moscow Olympics). Throughout the spring and summer,
the team Knight assembled, led by Michael Jordan, Patrick
Ewing, Chris Mullin, Sam Perkins, Alvin Robertson, and Leon
Wood, worked out relentlessly.

Jack Donahue, the Canadian coach, could feel his second-
round game with the United States slipping away even faster
than he'd feared. He looked down his bench and motioned for
Tilleman to report into the game. Tilleman responded quickly
enough. Seeing the welcome defense of Wood for the first time
since Caracas, he went to work. In the next five minutes he
scored 11 points, making five of seven field goals. But it wasn't
nearly enough. The United States coasted to an 89–68 win.

Canada realistically set its sights on a medal of any color,
and after consecutive wins over Uruguay (95–80, Tilleman had
12) and Italy (78–72), they had their chance at the bronze —
against the team from Yugoslavia.

For Tilleman and the others, it was an opportunity to re-
deem years of working, plotting, and preparing for international verification that Canada basketball was on the rise —
and not only that, but to have an Olympic medal for the rest
of their lives. It will always be curious to them, then, that they
chose this game to play some of the worst basketball they'd
played all season long, in the first half especially.

After trailing badly at intermission, the Canadians came
back strong in the second half, Tilleman coming off the bench
for most of his 13 points. But Yugoslavia hung on to win by
six points, 88–82. The Canadian players were crushed. They
had come within three baskets of a medal. Tilleman walked
the streets of L.A. that night alone, as he had once walked the
streets of Ottawa.

He went to Provo, Utah, after that, to practice against

current and former Brigham Young University players who habitually congregated at the BYU gym during the summer. Danny Ainge, Fred Roberts, and Devin Durrant, among others, were there. They were working on NBA games, and Tilleman wanted to develop one of his own. In just a few weeks he would be in Denver, trying out for the Nuggets, who had already sent him a contract, signed, sealed, and delivered. Now all he had to do was make the team.

With this thought on his mind during a scrimmage, he didn't see Danny Ainge's ankle until he tripped over it. Tilleman went down and didn't get back up. The sprain was barely feeling better two weeks later, when he flew to Denver.

The Nuggets liked their fourth-round draft choice from Canada. They liked him a lot—Dan Issel, especially. The 14-year veteran, who was about to play the final year of a 27,000-point, Hall of Fame–bound career, always asked the already-balding Tilleman to stand next to him at team meetings. He said it made him feel better, having a rookie on the team with less hair than he had.

When the Nuggets released Tilleman on their last cut before the start of the season, head coach Doug Moe made a point of telling him he thought he had a future in the NBA—just not now, at least not now with the Nuggets. He encouraged him to look at Europe—already, Tilleman had received a $50,000 offer from a team in Italy—where he could develop his game and make good money besides.

But the blow of not making the NBA was a tough one. And there was something else bothering the guard with the receding hairline, something he couldn't quite identify. Instead of going directly to Italy and finding out how much lira you got for $50,000, he went instead to the ranch outside Chinook, Montana, to the place he always went when he had to be alone and think.

These were his options as he saw them: Return to school

and get a graduate degree in law. Go to Europe and play professional basketball. Or go on a mission.

It was the last one that was weighing on his mind. He was nearly 23 years old, four years past the age most young men left for missions. He thought perhaps his time had passed. But then it hit him. He'd always been a devout member of the church. He had always told young people that they should serve missions. And he had often prayed for help with his basketball, promising righteous living in return. Serving a mission was the righteous thing to do.

Within two months he was on his way back to California, only this time not as an Olympian; this time as an elder in the Spanish-speaking California-Arcadia Mission of The Church of Jesus Christ of Latter-day Saints.

He surprised himself at how easily he made the transition, how quickly he withdrew from basketball. Soon enough, he had rearranged his goals, with a kind of basketball style to them. "Why are you on a mission," he wrote in his journal not long after he arrived in Arcadia, "if you don't plan on being *unbelievable?*"

★   ★   ★

When Donahue called near the end of his mission, in June of 1986, Tilleman was not in a basketball frame of mind. He had played only sparingly in Arcadia — maybe once every two or three weeks on his day off. He managed to get into one or two games of high quality at a local college, and that was it. But that didn't mean he couldn't come back. And in his mind a new goal germinated — he wanted to be living proof that after a lengthy layoff, a Mormon missionary, with less hair than ever, could return to civilian life and pick up where he left off.

Besides, there was this new three-point shot, a change in the game that Tilleman, like Donahue, knew could be a big help. Barely more than a month returned from California and playing in a pre-season college tournament in Lewiston, Montana, he found out just how much of a help. Playing for a local team from Calgary, the Calgary 88s, against a Montana State team that would win 21 games that season and also win the Big Sky Conference title, Tilleman scored 50 points, 39 of them from beyond the three-point line.

By the summer of 1987 he was back in full stride with the Canadian National Team. And that wasn't all: he was also a married man (he married Holly Walker five months after returning from California), a law student (he was accepted to law school at Brigham Young University), and a Spanish instructor at the Missionary Training Center in Provo. Also, on November 21, 1987, he and Holly had their first son, Karl Benson Tilleman.

In the midst of this rush-hour life-style, he was playing basketball as well as he ever had — maybe better than he ever had. Still Canada's sixth man, he was nonetheless leading the national team in scoring. Every time he stepped in back of the three-point line, he'd smile. Donahue called him the best three-point shooter in the *world*. By the time the Western Hemisphere Olympic qualifications came along in the early spring of 1988, in Uruguay, he was playing less, he was playing loose, and he was playing better.

★   ★   ★

As Karl Tilleman and the rest of Team Canada would soon find out, though, there are easier ways to get to Seoul than through Montevideo, Uruguay. The Canadian basketball team was not being made to feel welcome. Those in the sellout crowd of 12,000 not throwing coins were spitting. The policemen surrounding the court weren't helping matters either; they were joining in.

At stake was a trip to the Olympic basketball tournament in Seoul. Brazil and Puerto Rico had already won Olympic berths in this Western Hemisphere qualifying tournament. The third and final spot would go to the winner of the game about to be played — between Uruguay and Canada.

It had been a long week, and it was getting longer. After losses to both Puerto Rico and Uruguay (by 20 points) in the preliminary round, Canada had to beat Argentina just to get into the round of finalists. Argentina was a lot closer to Uruguay than Canada, by both miles and bloodlines, and the crowd wasn't happy about the Canadians' 112–88 win — a win fueled by Tilleman's 26 off-the-bench points, including three three-pointers in the first half when the lead was going back and forth. They were even unhappier to see the Canadians against their national team in the win-this-or-stay-home third-place game.

In the locker room, Tilleman, now the elder statesman of Team Canada, wrote a letter and pinned it to the bulletin board. In it, he urged his teammates to forget about the rather oppressive conditions — policemen laughing at them, Uruguayans throwing ice and coins, the scorekeeper and the time-keeper both sharing a pregame joke with the coach of the Uruguayan team — and play the game of their lives. "It's us against this whole stinkin' country," he wrote.

The us-against-the-country mood spread. Before game-time, other players pinned up their own notes of inspiration. Thus steeled, the Canadians took the court with an attitude — as mentally prepared as possible to go 12 on 12,000.

Fortunately, a referee from the Big East Conference in America was determined to call the game straight up or be carried from the gym trying, and biased officiating was not to be a factor. Karl Tilleman was. No sooner did he knock down consecutive three-pointers early in the game than Canada managed to take the Uruguayan crowd out of Uruguay. Canada won going away, 87–70. They would live to play in the Seoul Olympics after all.

★   ★   ★

At the Korean Games, Team Canada was every bit as good and as focused as it had been in Los Angeles in 1984. But the Soviets had returned to Olympic competition, after their boycott of the '84 Games. With the Soviets back, nobody said the Olympic competition was going to get easier.

Canada made it to the medal round and placed sixth, behind the Soviets, the Yugoslavs, the Americans, Australia, and Brazil. For Tilleman personally, it was a prolific Olympics. He opened with 29 points against Egypt in a 117–64 romp. Then, after playing only briefly in a 76–70 loss to a United States team coached by John Thompson that had a yen for man defense, Donahue turned him loose, and he scored 37 points in a 94–84 win over Spain, the silver medalists from 1984. Twenty-seven came in the first 15 minutes of the second half, when Tilleman was the only Canadian player to score.

He averaged 11.9 points in eight games while playing just over 20 minutes per game. He wound up as the 23rd top scorer in the '88 Games as well as one of the top percentage shooters, connecting on 13 of 25 two-point field goals and 22 of 45 three-point field goals. Overall, his encore Games surpassed his original.

★   ★   ★

Most of the top 30 scorers from the Seoul Olympics—including number 1 Oscar Schmidt of Brazil, number 4 Drazen Petrovic of Yugoslavia, number 5 Sarunas Marciulinis of the Soviet Union, number 17 David Robinson of the United States, number 18 Jose Ortiz of Puerto Rico, number 22 Vlade Divac of Yugoslavia, and number 26 Danny Manning of the United States—would soon be on their way to professional basketball riches, either in the NBA in America or in the increasingly lucrative professional leagues in Europe.

But approaching his 28th birthday in November, Karl Tilleman did not follow their lead. He returned instead to Provo, where he completed his last two years of law school (and where he was joined by Dave Turcotte, a teammate from the Canadian National Team whom Tilleman recruited to BYU).

Karl and Holly had another son by the time Karl graduated from the J. Reuben Clark Law School in 1990. He finished high enough in his class to clerk for a United States appellate judge in San Francisco, then joined the law firm of Meyer, Hendricks, Victor, Osborn & Maledon in Phoenix. Soon after he moved to Arizona, he also joined three recreational basketball leagues.

ED EYESTONE

BY DOUG ROBINSON

All night long he tossed and turned in his bed, but sleep would not come for Ed Eyestone. He tried staring at the ceiling. He tried relaxation therapy. He tried five or six trips to the bathroom. He tried lying on his back, on his side, on his stomach, and still, maddeningly, he could not sleep. Some rap music that he'd heard in a movie earlier that night kept playing the airwaves of his brain. And then his thoughts would inevitably return to tomorrow, and the adrenaline would start pumping, and the heart would start pounding, and there he was, wide awake again.

In many ways Eyestone's entire life had been building to tomorrow's 1988 U.S. Olympic Marathon Trials, which would be run through Jersey City. All the long miles, the morning runs, the injuries, the dreams, the championship races, the bad races — races in which he had literally crawled to the finish — everything had led him to this moment: making the Olympic team. *I've got to sleep,* he kept telling himself as he lay in his hotel room, but there was no chance. Finally, he resigned himself to fate and decided that if he couldn't sleep then at least he would relax. There was no sense in fighting it.

At 6 A.M. he arose from his bed, dressed, and walked downstairs. The lobby was empty except for Mark Conover, another marathoner.

"Rough night?" asked Eyestone.

"Yeah," said Conover. "I was up going to the bathroom all night."

They waited together for the hotel restaurant to open for breakfast. They shared a table and ordered the same cold cereal, then rode the same bus to the start of the race and warmed up together.

For the first half of the race, which opened a view of the New York skyline and the Statue of Liberty, Eyestone was content to run with the pack, letting others break the stiff headwind they would battle most of the way. Eyestone and Conover, new friends bound by a bad night, urged each other on. At 16 miles, Eyestone, a tall, lanky man with brown wavy hair and a moustache — someone once described him as looking like a gunfighter — surged down a slight hill, feeling out the competition, and opened a 20-yard lead. Just then he saw a TV camera, which was following the race on a motorcycle. Looking directly into the lens of the camera, knowing that the race was being broadcast live on national TV, thinking of family and friends and coaches who were watching him now, thinking of the immensity of leading the Olympic Trials, thinking of all those childhood Olympic dreams, suddenly he had to fight off a lump in his throat. But he caught himself. It was far too early to be sentimental. That much became apparent when a handful of runners, including Conover, closed the gap and caught Eyestone at the 17-mile mark.

This was only the third marathon of Eyestone's life, and his previous attempt had been disastrous. A year earlier he had been running with the leaders 16 miles into the Boston

Marathon when he crumbled. He finished 19th, with a time of 2:19:19. Afterward he told his wife, Lynn, "If I ever want to do this again, talk me out of it." Eyestone had won national championships, earned a good income, and become the nation's top road racer largely by running the 10,000–meter distance, but still he was convinced that the marathon would be his best event. He feared the finishing speed of the Africans and Europeans on the track, and he reasoned that the longer the race, the better his chances. If he failed in the marathon, he could always try the 10,000 at the Olympic track and field trials later in the year.

"Aren't you just hedging your bets?" a reporter had asked Eyestone the previous day at a press conference.

"Yeah, but I think I have a good chance to make the marathon team, too," said Eyestone.

At 17 1/2 miles, Conover surged and Eyestone went with him. No one else followed. Eyestone drafted off Conover for a time, then pulled up to his shoulder. "Run behind me," he told Conover, and for the next few miles they took turns breaking the wind for each other. By 19 miles they had opened a big lead over the rest of the field. They ran in silence until the 25th mile, when Conover looked back at their rivals as they rounded a corner, noted the wide gap between them and the rest of the field, and then turned to Eyestone and smiled.

"We're on the team!" he said.

Eyestone smiled broadly, but a short time later he was rocked by a shooting pain in his right hamstring. *I'm not on the team yet,* he thought. If he pulled a muscle now, he could fail to place among the top three finishers and lose his place on the Olympic team. He ran cautiously, waiting for the verdict of his body, and three more times the electric pain shot through the back of his leg. He backed off the pace to ease the strain on the muscle, letting Conover move ahead. First place was worth $50,000, second place $25,000, but Eyestone wasn't about to risk a spot on the Olympic team for the extra money. Later, Conover would tell Eyestone, "If you hadn't dropped off, I was about ready to ask you for a tie." Eyestone didn't care. He ran carefully to the finish for second place, clocking a time of 2:12:49. He was an Olympian.

★   ★   ★

When Ed Eyestone was in seventh grade, he and his class-mates were required to write letters to themselves, listing their long-term goals. The teacher gathered up the letters and put them away—for five years. Eyestone was a senior at Bonneville High School in Ogden, Utah, when his letter was returned to him. He opened the envelope, recognized the writing as something like his own, and read: "I will be a track star and compete in the Olympic Games." Eyestone shook his head. What na-iveté, he thought. But a track star is precisely what he had become in the intervening years, even if there had been no basis for such ambition when he had written the letter. In seventh grade, Eyestone wasn't even the best runner in his class. He had just taken up the sport, and then only because he had been cut from the baseball team. But he always liked to run. Even when he played little league football, what he liked best was when the team was required to run laps. He liked to run ahead of his teammates, his mouth guard slapping against his face mask.

When he was cut from the baseball team, Eyestone was crushed. Little did he know that it was the best thing that ever happened to him. When he turned himself over to running completely, he attacked it as he did everything else. At night, he got on his knees and asked God to help him become the best runner in the country (a decade later, when he was indeed a national champion, he would joke, "I just wish I had said best in the *world*.") During one family gathering, Eyestone's father went around the room asking each of his five children to state their goals.

"I want to run in the Olympic Games," said Ed.

"That's a good goal, but let's talk about more realistic goals," his father replied.

Later, when Eyestone made the varsity team as a sophomore in high school, his sister Mary Jo casually remarked, "Gee, Ed, if you keep this up, maybe you'll get a scholarship." Eyestone remembers thinking it was a ridiculous understatement. *Of course I will,* he thought to himself. *I'm going to run in the Olympics.*

Then something happened between Eyestone's sophomore and junior years of high school, and he began to look like more than just a dreamer. As a sophomore, he was the fourth or fifth best runner on his team, and no better than 40th in the state meet. A year later, he was the best in the state, and Neville Peterman didn't know what to make of his new prodigy.

Peterman was the cross country coach at Bonneville. Visit Peterman's office these days, and you'll find Eyestone in pictures on the wall, in scrapbooks on the shelves, and somewhere deep in the coach's heart. A small, nervous, devoted man who has officially and unofficially adopted a handful of his athletes, Peterman embarks on lengthy discussions of Eyestone, and his eyes well up with tears. When Eyestone's talent was suddenly revealed early in his junior year, Peterman was surprised and worried. He prides himself in underworking young runners, reasoning that this will give them longer, healthier careers.

"Listen to me," he warned Eyestone. "I don't burn out runners. You must be running too many miles."

But Eyestone was merely running the workouts prescribed by Peterman. He won the state's first big invitational in Provo, and his family and friends were amazed by his sudden improvement. Then Eyestone heard a pop in his foot midway through a race, and his season was finished. A stress fracture.

He was forced to watch the state cross country championships on crutches. It was the beginning of a star-crossed high school career. A year later, Eyestone won the state cross country championships and set a state record, but a few months later, at the height of the track season, he suffered another injury: a broken toe. He watched the state track meet with another cast on his foot.

By then, Eyestone had already made believers out of a number of observers, particularly Pat Shane, who was then a coach at Provo High and would someday coach Eyestone at BYU. During an indoor meet in Idaho earlier in the year, Shane got goose bumps watching Eyestone race. It wasn't so much that he saw Eyestone run away from the field or that he clocked 9:17 for two miles; it was what Shane had felt: goose bumps. Instead of going home, Shane drove straight to the BYU track office to urge the Cougar coaches to recruit Eyestone. "He'll be the best runner you've ever had here," he told them.

The Cougars reached a verbal agreement with Eyestone to award him a scholarship, but when he reported to Provo to sign the papers in the spring he had that cast on his foot. "You probably don't want me now," he told them. He was wrong.

★   ★   ★

Even by Texas standards, the 1980 NCAA Track and Field Championships in Austin were muggy and miserable. At 90 degrees and 58 percent humidity, the conditions were so hot that the start of the 10,000-meter run was postponed five hours, until 10 P.M. Even then, it was hot enough that meet officials had a hose ready to spray the runners. "If you're hot, raise your hand and we'll squirt you," they told them.

Eyestone had tried to prepare for such heat. On training runs in Provo, he wore several layers of sweats to simulate June weather in Texas. From the very start of his collegiate career, he planned to be here. He had set a stiff goal: to become an All-American as a freshman. During training runs, he chanted to himself, "All-A-mer-i-can! All-A-mer-i-can!" in cadence with his stride. Nothing could deter him from that goal, not even if it meant holding a pace set by the great, older African runners.

At the sound of the starting gun, Eyestone sprinted clear of traffic and settled on the heels of the leaders. As the laps rolled by, he continued to maintain contact with the lead pack, but the pace and the heat were taking their toll on everyone. Two runners dropped out ahead of Eyestone, leaving him among the top six, which is where he had to finish to earn All-American honors. With about a mile to go he began to falter, but he didn't know it until someone told him later, and he charged on, raising his hand each lap for the hose. With just two laps remaining in the 25-lap race, he was in fifth place — and in trouble. As he moved down the backstretch, two runners passed him. Eyestone tried to accelerate but fell apart. He staggered and weaved, and then, with a little more than a lap to go, his coaches and teammates rushed out to pull him off the track. With a teammate under each arm, Eyestone walked on the infield for a moment and then passed out. Willard Hirschi, a BYU assistant coach, carried him into the training room. When Eyestone awoke, he was sitting in a tub of ice water, vomiting, and two men in white coats were asking him questions. *"Where are you? What's your name?"*

Late that night, Eyestone was sitting on the edge of a bed in his hotel room, depressed and demoralized after failing to achieve his All-America goal. There was a knock on the door, and Hirschi entered the room.

"Great race," he told Eyestone. "You ran like a horse."

"What?"

Hirschi explained. "You take a mule, and when he gets

tired he stops and he won't go on until he's rested. But a horse will actually run until he dies. That's what you did tonight."

This was to be the hallmark of Eyestone's career. Heart. Guts. Determination. All those things. When it came right down to it, Eyestone really didn't seem to have much else, did he? Speed? None. It was laughable. A beautiful, flowing stride? No way.

In high school, Peterman once filmed his runners during a workout so they could analyze their running technique. When the image of Eyestone flashed on the screen, the room broke up in laughter. The back was hunched, the stride too long, the knees too low, the legs flaring out below the knee, the body wobbling from side to side. Eyestone's technique improved considerably in the coming years, but he would never be a textbook runner. Peterman, and later Coach Sherald James at BYU, tried to correct the form but finally gave up.

"We suddenly realized he was going to succeed regardless," says James. "He was something of an ugly duckling, and he realized it. He just has the strength to overcome it."

"We all think of the picture-perfect runner as someone who flows over the track," says Clarence Robison, who was then BYU's head coach. "Ed isn't one of those kind . . . When I recruited Ed, I saw him as a very competitive, capable distance runner who would be a point-getter always. I didn't see him as a world champion or a national champion. I guess that's because he didn't show great speed and he wasn't a natural runner. But there are so many things you can't see as you look at the outside of athletes. It's hard to know what kind of heart they have, what kind of competitor they'll be. And unless you do some tests, it's impossible to know what kind of a nerve and circulatory system they have. His cardiovascular system has got to be unbelievable. He has that tremendous ability to hold a fast pace for a long time."

Eyestone's most obvious trait was his tenacity, his competitiveness—his heart. Doug Padilla, a BYU teammate and a two-time Olympic distance runner himself, once said of Eyestone, "He wants it so bad. I don't know if I could do what he's done, if I could hurt that bad. He pulls everything out of himself."

Says James, "He just kept pushing the threshold of pain back further and further. He mastered it."

Eyestone has heard all this talk before. "Maybe I do have a higher pain threshold," he says with a shrug. But then he laughs. "But maybe it isn't that I'm so tough at all. Maybe I'm supposed to be able to do that." Eyestone explains:

In 1989, Dave Martin, a renowned coach, exercise physiologist, author, and long-distance running coordinator for the United States Olympic Committee, tested Eyestone's endurance on the treadmill, just as he has done for many world-class runners (including world record holders Sebastian Coe and Arturo Barrios). The results were stunning. Eyestone stayed on the treadmill longer than any other athlete Martin had ever tested. He also recorded the highest max VO2 of any other athlete Martin had ever tested. Max VO2 is short for maximal aerobic capacity, or the maximum amount of oxygen the body can process at a time. It is the essence of endurance. World-class max VO2, measuring milliliters of oxygen per kilogram of blood, measures in the mid-70 range. Eyestone's was off the chart, a mind-boggling 89.

"He's a genetic freak of the very best kind," says Shane. "He's one in a million. That's the highest max VO2 I've ever heard of. He has a talent that most people don't recognize."

"Maybe it's not that I'm tough," Eyestone says again. "Maybe a high VO2 max allows me to run like that."

That might be so, but there's no ignoring Eyestone's toughness and tenacity. He has been known to push himself beyond reason, beyond even the considerable limits of his body. In high school, he won several races while running with a yet-undetected broken bone in his foot. Each morning, when the tender foot was still getting used to the weight of his body again, Eyestone cried in pain as he showered for school, but he still put himself through afternoon training runs.

Perhaps nothing illustrates Eyestone's tenacity better than one 5K race during his freshman season at BYU. Going up against older veterans such as Alberto Salazar and Padilla in a dual meet against the University of Oregon, Eyestone was clearly overmatched, but he insisted on challenging them. They went through the first mile in 4:16, which was already a personal record for Eyestone, and still he wouldn't back off. He matched the lead pack stride for stride, while James watched in disbelief. "You don't take on a lion when you're only a cub," he explains.

I'm either going to run a fast time or die trying, Eyestone thought to himself. He died. Late in the race he began weaving badly, back and forth through two lanes. Coming into the homestretch he fell to the track. His coordination gone, his knees buckling, he got up, staggered a few more steps, and fell again while the crowd urged him on. Eyestone rose again, took a few more steps, and fell once more, some 25 yards from the finish. Then he began *crawling* toward the finish. Robison tried to pull him off the track, but Eyestone pushed him away: "No, Coach, I want to finish." Finally, BYU coaches dragged him off the track, a few yards short of the finish.

"For several meets that season I stationed two track men out on the field," recalls Robison. "They were to watch Ed as he ran, and if he got into difficulty and started weaving and was not able to stay in his lane, they were to go out and physically take him off the track. They were to each grab an arm and pull that arm up over their neck and shoulders and literally carry him off the track. He would not quit, even when he reached a point of collapsing . . . Whenever I see Ed, I think

Above left: Before track, there was baseball

Above right: Eyestone at age 19 in Paris winning
the bronze medal in the World Junior Cross-Country meet

Above: Eyestone in the 1989 World Cross-Country
Championships in Norway—one of many races
in which he has represented the United States

Right: Eyestone was twice named American
Road Runner of the Year

about that great determination. I have relived those words so many times: 'No, Coach, I want to finish.' "

★　　★　　★

Edward Eyestone was born June 10, 1961, in American Samoa, where his father, Bob, managed a Church-owned plantation. When it was time to take the baby home, Bob paid the hospital bill: 75 cents.

The Eyestones eventually returned to their roots in Utah, where their ancestors had settled after migrating from Germany and walking across the American plains with the Mormon pioneers. At the urging of some of their new countrymen, they changed their original name from Augenstein to its literal English translation, Eyestone.

The Eyestones were nothing if not devout, educated, motivated, musical, and industrious. Bob earned a master's degree in psychology, and Virginia a doctorate in education. All five of their children won college scholarships—Suzanne for writing, Janet and Robert for music, Mary Jo for drama, and Ed for running—and all five of them excelled in school and earned master's degrees. They became singers, architects, actors, writers, musicians, beauty queens, athletes.

Virginia wanted Ed, the youngest of the family, to be the next Tommy Dorsey. In junior high and high school he played first-chair trombone in the school band and sang in the choir, and in the summer he played in the marching band. Music and school always came easily to him, as did a dry wit. Eyestone graduated from BYU with a 3.67 grade point average and was one of six scholar-athletes to win a national NCAA post-graduate scholarship. Eventually, he married Lynn Lambert, who was an obvious fit for the Eyestone family. She was a beauty queen (Miss Utah), and she earned a doctorate in clinical psychology.

It isn't difficult to find the origins of Eyestone's running talent. Bob was the only sophomore to make the University of Idaho cross country team in 1941, and he placed fifth in the West Coast AAU Cross Country Championships. But then World War II began, and America asked him to jump out of airplanes in Europe. When he returned from the war three years later, he was no longer interested in running.

Ed picked up where his father left off, and Bob's running experience proved useful. Bob noted his son's lack of speed and explained the facts of life to him: "There are two ways to run a race. You can run along with everyone else and try to kick at the end. Or you can go out hard and take the kick out of them. That's what you're going to have to do."

From then on, Bob stood on the sidelines, yelling to Ed, "Run 'em in the ground, Ed!"

"He did it, too," recalls Bob. "He didn't give the faster runners a chance. He took them out so hard that they were exhausted by the end of the race. He'd push, push, push."

It was a hard way to win a race, but Eyestone had the lungs and the pain threshold to do it.

★   ★   ★

When Eyestone opened his apartment door and saw the police and his bishop standing there, he knew they weren't bringing good news. They asked to come in, and then they gave it to him. His brother Robert had been killed that day in a boating accident. Eyestone was too stunned even to cry. He called his family in Ogden to tell them the news, then helped with the details of the funeral. Eyestone was a senior at BYU, and in two days he was to leave for Austin, Texas, to compete in the 1985 NCAA Track and Field Championships.

At the funeral, well-meaning friends of the family told Ed, "You've got to win the next one for Robert." But Bob, sensing his son's burden, took him aside and told him, "You just run the race as you normally would."

Eyestone drove directly from the cemetery to the airport and flew to Austin, where he was greeted at the airport by the kindly, white-haired Robison. They embraced, and Eyestone broke down, finally.

Already drained, he would have to summon more emotional and physical energy in the coming days. Eyestone was going to attempt to win both the 5,000- and 10,000-meter runs. It is an exacting double under any conditions, demanding three races in as many days, including the trials for the 5,000. In the heat of Texas, Eyestone was the only one who would even dare attempt both races. The irony of it all was not lost on him. Five years earlier, on the same track, in the same heat, in the same meet, he had wilted and fainted.

Eyestone settled near the back of the pack as the 10,000-meter race began, then slowly worked his way up through the field until he was running with the leaders. At three miles, he surged for three laps, taking the pace from 66 to 69 seconds per lap, and opened a 10-meter lead. "Do it again!" Shane yelled from the stands. Eyestone nodded and surged again, this time opening a 30-meter lead. After leading by as much as 70 meters, he backed off the pace, saving himself. After crossing the finish line an easy winner, Eyestone lay partially submerged in the steeplechase water jump pit, using his shoe to pour water over his head.

Less than 24 hours later, he was back on the track for the 5,000. With his lack of speed, he planned to force the pace midway through the race, but when he got there he was still sluggish from the previous night's race and changed his mind. "By then I was just hoping to place," he would say later, but after trading leads with pre-meet favorite Peter Koech, he forged a 20-meter lead with one lap to go. Showing surprising speed, Eyestone blasted the last lap in 58 seconds and won by 5 seconds, becoming only the seventh man in history to win both the 10K and the 5K in the same NCAA meet.

The victories gave Eyestone four NCAA championships and a sweep of the collegiate triple crown. In a single school year he had won the NCAA cross country championships and the 5,000 and 10,000 on the track — not bad for a man who had wondered if his career was finished only a few years earlier.

Following his freshman year, Eyestone gave up running for two years to serve a mission for The Church of Jesus Christ of Latter-day Saints in Barcelona, Spain. A year into his mission he saw a sign advertising a road race. Eyestone saw this as an opportunity to show off for the Church. He imagined the headlines: MORMON MISSIONARY WINS ROAD RACE, THOUSANDS BAPTIZED.

The only running Eyestone had done in the past year was to catch the train, but he was convinced he could run well anyway. *I'm a runner,* he reasoned. And after all, only a year earlier he had placed third in the World Junior Cross Country Championships in Paris. Nearly a dozen missionaries, fully aware of Eyestone's credentials, gathered for the race, ready to pass out Church pamphlets after he won the race and drew attention to their cause. They lined the race course, which covered 8,000 meters, or four laps through the town, to cheer for Eyestone. The suspense didn't last long. Several runners bolted into the lead at the start, but Eyestone was sure they would come back to him. When they didn't, he tried to pick up the pace — and couldn't. By the end of the final lap, he was *walking* up a hill.

"Old ladies and little kids were passing me," recalls Eyestone. "It was humiliating. All the missionaries watched me crumble."

Eyestone laughs now, but it wasn't funny then. He wondered if he'd ever again be the runner he was before his mission. He knew the answer soon enough. Normally it takes returned missionaries at least a year to get their legs back. BYU coaches planned to redshirt Eyestone when he returned to Provo, but they quickly realized it wasn't necessary. Just a few months after returning from Barcelona, he finished eighth in the NCAA Cross Country Championships.

"It's phenomenal," James said at the time. "I have no explanation for it."

During the next three years Eyestone set his sights on winning a national championship, which was a rarity for American distance runners in this day. Foreigners had ruled the collegiate distance events since the early '70s, which is why great American distance runners such as Craig Virgin and Henry Marsh never won an NCAA title. But while other American athletes complained about the presence of the dominating African distance runners, Eyestone did not. He reasoned that if he could beat the Africans, he could beat anyone. As a sophomore he began to challenge them. Late in the races there would be the usual pack of Africans far out in front of the rest of the field, but now there was this one American with them, listening but not understanding as they chattered among themselves in Swahili. Not wanting to be left out, Eyestone memorized some Swahili phrases and from then on, when he felt the urge for comic relief, he "talked" to the Africans in their own language: "What are you saying?" "Run faster." "Slow down." "How's it going?" By the end of his college career he was beating them all.

In 1984, Eyestone became the first American in 12 years to win the 10,000-meter run at the NCAA track championships. The meet was held in—more irony—Eugene, Oregon, the very place he had passed out years earlier. In the process Eyestone ran the second fastest time in meet history (28:05.3), but a year later he ran faster, setting an American collegiate record of 27:41.05 en route to beating a world-class field in the Mt. SAC Relays.

After the NCAA victory, Eyestone celebrated his first NCAA championship with fellow Utah runners Henry Marsh and Farley Gerber. They talked into the wee hours over ice cream and pizza about making the 1984 Olympic team later that summer, but it didn't happen for Eyestone. Still tired from the NCAA meet, he qualified for the finals in the 10,000 at the U.S. Olympic Trials, but he finished 12th. Eyestone lost contact with the leaders with two miles to go, which gave him eight laps to come to grips with his failure.

Well, I've got four more years, he consoled himself. *I have time.*

★   ★   ★

Eyestone was halfway through a 10–mile training run one afternoon when he began to notice pain in his Achilles tendon. The pain continued to worsen until finally he was forced to walk the last mile. After examining the foot, his doctor urged caution. Eyestone took three days off and tried again. The pain was still there, and now panic was setting in. With the U.S. Olympic Marathon Trials just two months away, this was a critical stage in his training. Eyestone returned to the doctor, and this time he was given anti-inflammatory medicine. He took another week off from his training. He cycled and swam and did what he could to maintain some cardiovascular conditioning, but he was getting desperate. If the heel wasn't better by the end of the week, he would have to abandon his plans for the Olympic marathon. When the week was finished and he tried to run again, the pain was still there.

Now he was frightened. He drove immediately to his parents' home and asked for a father's blessing. The following morning, Eyestone went out for a short run and the pain was gone. Two days later he was back to his daily 20–mile regimen, and his Olympic plans were alive again.

"I guess it was meant for me to run well in the trials," says Eyestone. "People can call it a coincidence, but I was there. I know how it felt."

After earning a place on the Olympic team at the trials, Eyestone, a relative newcomer to marathoning, flew to Seoul to meet the best marathoners in the world. His strategy was typically bold: all or nothing. "I'm not here for any other reason but to try to win the gold medal," he told reporters. "I'm not here just to try to finish in the top 10 or 20."

On the day the Olympic marathon was to be held, South Korean soldiers were everywhere, armed with Uzis and clubs. They stood 20 meters apart along the entire length of the course. They were in helicopters overhead. They were riding windsurfing boards on the Han River. Student riots against the South Korean government earlier in the summer and an Olympic boycott by next-door-neighbor North Korea had put the city and the Games on edge for more than two weeks. There were concerns that the violent political mood would spill over into the Olympics. Soldiers used mirrors to check the bottom of buses going in and out of the Olympic villages. Fans were frisked before entering venues. Athletes passed through a couple of metal detectors to return to their quarters.

But for 17 days nothing happened, and only one Olympic event remained — the men's marathon. There had been a pervasive feeling throughout the Games that if anything was going to happen, this would be the event marked for trouble. Certainly it was the most vulnerable. The marathon was to be run through the streets of Seoul, where it couldn't be protected as well as other events. The rumor running through the athletes' village was that the marathon would be canceled or moved. But it wasn't. When the marathoners spilled out of Olympic Stadium, they ran through a solid corridor of soldiers.

By now, Eyestone and the other runners were more concerned with mundane matters, such as water and heat, than the potential for violence. The temperature was 78 degrees, and the humidity 70 percent — hardly ideal marathon conditions. Thanks to American television, the race began in the middle of the afternoon, and there wasn't a cloud in the sky. The women marathoners, who had run their race two weeks earlier, warned the men to drink water at every aid station, but it wasn't that simple. U.S. officials failed to place water bottles for the American runners at the first aid station, which meant they would have to drink from cups. Just as Eyestone was approaching the first aid station three miles into the race, the runner ahead of him grabbed a drink and knocked the remaining cups over. Eyestone got no water, and already he was thirsty. A bad omen, he thought. There was a second omen. As Eyestone approached the second aid station, he sprinted to make sure he got water this time. But in the scramble for position in heavy traffic, a large wooden sign was knocked over and smashed his right foot.

Despite all the pitfalls, Eyestone was one of 15 runners in the lead pack halfway through the race, but it wasn't to last. A short time later he began to cramp and fall off pace. He faded and continued to fade the rest of the race. It was Boston all over again. Perhaps his inexperience at the marathon distance caught up with him. Perhaps the heat. Nine of the 12 male medalists in the four Olympic distance events in Seoul were from humid, warm-weather countries. Eyestone finished in 29th place, in 2:19:09. As promised, he had run an all-or-nothing race, and, as always, he had pushed himself to the limit. He stood at the finish line in the stadium waiting for Conover, but he never arrived. He had dropped out, a victim of the heat.

"I don't look at my Olympic experience as a downer," says Eyestone. "It just whetted my appetite to taste it again and run better. My story isn't finished yet."

★   ★   ★

Since the end of his collegiate career, Eyestone has turned increasingly from the track to road racing because of the better financial rewards. He signed a long-term endorsement contract with the Reebok shoe company, which pays him $50,000 annually. With a regular income, Eyestone doesn't have to over-race to make ends meet with prize money, which would increase the chance for injury and perhaps shorten his career.

Eyestone has become the top American road racer, winning several of the nation's biggest races (the Peachtree Classic in Atlanta, Bay to Breakers in San Francisco, the Boston Milk Run). Three times he has been named Road Racer of the Year. His picture has appeared on magazine covers, calendars, and training logs, and in television commercials. He has also written running-related articles for magazines and newspapers and has done race commentary for TV.

In 1990, Eyestone ran the fastest marathon by an American, 2:10:59, despite tripping and somersaulting to the street, and he set an American record for 25 kilometers. Since the '88 Olympics, he has competed in many of the world's major marathons, finishing fourth and fifth in Chicago, seventh in London, and third in Sapporo. In 1992, he will attempt to make the U.S. Olympic Team in both the marathon and the 10,000.

From his large home in Layton, Utah, Eyestone trains in the morning and again in the afternoon, spending the rest of the day playing with his two children, helping with household chores, and studying guitar. "I could do more, but I want to focus on my running," he says. When Ed climbs out of the family car on a lonely stretch of highway 20 miles from home and watches Lynn drive away, it's no marital spat. It's just the start of another training run.

"I've got at least five years left in me," he says. "I'd like to see two more Olympic Games."

It is certain he will see one more anyway. Eyestone finished a close second again in the 1992 U.S. Olympic Marathon Trials in Columbus, Ohio, to earn another Olympic berth. The Games will be held in Barcelona—site of Eyestone's mission and his most embarrassing race. But that's another story.

OTHER
MORMON OLYMPIANS

Olympian: Anders Hilding Arrhenius
Sport: Track and Field (shot put)
Country: Sweden
Olympics: Munich, 1972
Birth: July 16, 1947; Stockholm,
    Sweden
Education: Brigham Young University;
    Swedish Royal Gymnastics School
Occupation: Coach

As the Swedish shot-put champion five
times, Arrhenius qualified for the 1972
Munich Olympic Games, but he
injured his right wrist before the
competition and was unable to
compete.

"Due to my track ability," Arrhenius
says, "I was able to come to America
and to BYU, and was introduced to
the Church. I joined the Church in
1975."

Olympian: Charles "Wade" Bell
Sport: Track and Field (800-meter
    race)

Country: United States
Olympics: Mexico City, 1968
Birth: January 3, 1945; Ogden, Utah
Education: Ben Lomond High School,
    Utah; University of Oregon
Occupation: Certified Public
    Accountant

Bell was a Pan-American gold-medal
winner in the 800-meters race in 1966
and an NCAA champion at the same
distance in 1967. While competing for
the University of Oregon, he won the
800 meters in the 1968 Olympic Trials.
Sickness kept him from his best
competition in Mexico City.

"In the spring of 1960, a
mathematics teacher at Mount Fort
Junior High School was training for
paratrooping and needed company for
his preparation," Bell says. "We ran a
couple of miles after school each day.

"That summer, Chick Hislop, the
Ben Lomond High School coach at the
time and now the head track coach at
Weber State, came to my home and
literally got me out of bed every
morning to run with him and some
runners from Ben Lomond High
School.

"In the fall of 1960, I was in Mr.
Hislop's home, watching the 1960
Olympic Games. During that viewing,
Chick looked at me and said, 'Wade,
someday you can be in the Olympic
Games. You have the potential to run
with those people.' From that point
on, I had the goal of running the mile
under four minutes and participating
in the Olympic Games."

Olympian: James Hunter Bergeson
Sport: Water Polo
Country: United States
Olympics: Seoul, 1988

Birth: March 21, 1961; Newport Beach, California

Education: Newport Beach Harbor High School, California; Stanford University

Occupation: Self-employed

Bergeson was part of the U.S. water polo team that captured the silver medal in the Seoul Olympics in 1988.

"My highlight was beating the Russians in the semifinals," Bergeson says. "Although the loss to the Yugoslavians in overtime in the final game was upsetting, the Olympics will always be the highlight of my life."

Olympian: Roberto Carmona

Sport: Track and Field (decathlon)

Country: Mexico

Olympics: Mexico City, 1968

Birth: October 21, 1943; Mexico City, Mexico

Education: High School #28, Mexico City, Mexico; National Polytechnic Institute; Brigham Young University

Occupation: Physiotherapist

Carmona won twenty national championships in different track events in Mexico. During competition in the Mexico City Olympic Games in 1968, he was injured on the second day and was unable to continue.

"To compete in the 1968 Olympic Games was a marvelous experience," Carmona says. "I did the best I could, but being injured, I couldn't finish. But, the experience of being there was the best.

"Exactly twenty years later, my son, Roberto Carmona, Jr., qualified and

went to Seoul, Korea, to compete in the 110 [meter] hurdles in the Olympic Games."

Olympian: Kresimir Cosic

Sport: Basketball

Country: Yugoslavia

Olympics: Mexico City, 1968; Munich, 1972; Montreal, 1976; Moscow, 1980

Birth: November 26, 1948; Zagreb, Croatia

Education: Brigham Young University

Occupation: Professional basketball coach

At age twenty, Cosic was a member of the Yugoslavian Olympic team that won the silver medal in Mexico City. Matriculating at Brigham Young University, he became the first non-American to win All-American honors, receiving that recognition in 1972 and 1973.

Cosic went on to win a bronze medal in the Munich Olympic Games in 1972, a silver in 1976, and a gold in 1980 — the only Mormon Olympian to have a set of bronze, silver, and gold medals.

From 1985 to 1987, he coached the Yugoslavian national team and now coaches professionally in Greece.

Olympian: Troy Dalbey

Sport: Swimming

Country: United States

Olympics: Seoul, 1988

Birth: September 19, 1968; St. Louis, Missouri

Education: Gunderson High School, California; Arizona State University

Occupation: Swimmer

After a runner-up performance in the NCAA national competition for Arizona State University in the 200-meter freestyle, Dalbey qualified for the Olympic team in the 200-meter freestyle and two relays. He helped the United States team win gold medals on both relays—the 4x100- and 4x200-meter freestyle events.

Olympian: Michael S. Evans
Sport: Water Polo
Country: United States
Olympics: Seoul, 1988; Barcelona, 1992
Birth: March 26, 1960; Fontana, California
Education: Chaffey High School, California; University of California, Irvine
Occupation: Owner, employee benefits agency

Evans earned a silver medal from his Seoul experience in 1988 and has been selected for the Olympic Games in 1992. His team won the World FINA Cup in 1991 and is seeded fourth going into Barcelona.

"I enjoyed the high level of competition and the energy applied towards a successful performance at the Olympics by the athletes," Evans says. "It's exciting as an athlete to mingle with other athletes, some of whom I'd only seen on TV or in print. Of course, I had to have my picture taken with a few of them while we waited to enter the opening ceremonies in 1988."

Olympian: Bengt Stefan Fernholm
Sport: Track and Field (discus)
Country: Sweden
Olympics: Los Angeles, 1984; Seoul, 1988
Birth: July 2, 1959; Norrkoping, Sweden
Education: Brigham Young University
Occupation: Inventor

Initially, Fernholm was an outstanding shot-putter. Then he switched to the discus in 1983, set an NCAA record, and went on to place eighth in the Los Angeles Olympic Games in 1984. He qualified for Seoul in 1988 but was injured and did not compete.

Olympian: Lelei Alofa Fonoimoana-Moore
Sport: Swimming
Country: United States
Olympics: Montreal, 1976
Birth: November 4, 1958; Sterling, Illinois
Education: Mira Costa High School, California; Brigham Young University; University of California, Los Angeles
Occupation: Shipping clerk, ocean lifeguard, massage therapist

During the Montreal Olympic Games in 1976, Fonoimoana-Moore finished seventh in the 100-meter butterfly competition and swam in the preliminaries to help advance the United States 400-meter medley relay team to the finals, winning a silver medal in that event. Following the Olympics, she won eleven All-

American awards while competing for Brigham Young University.

"I remember swimming in the Olympic Trials at Long Beach in June of 1976," she says. "My high school friends and my family were all there to see me swim in the finals of the 100-meter butterfly. I had to get in the top three to make the Olympic team. I went in with the seventh fastest time but was able to get third place, and I made the team. I remember looking at the clock but not believing it was really true. I waited patiently for an official to give me the news, and I jumped for joy with tears in my eyes. I will never forget that day because years of hard work had finally paid off. I think that I was on a natural high from the day I made the team until I was finished with my competitions. It was the greatest experience of my life, one I will never forget."

Olympian: Mark Albert Fuller
Sport: Greco-Roman Wrestling
Country: United States
Olympics: Moscow, 1980; Los Angeles, 1984; Seoul, 1988; Barcelona, 1992
Birth: March 25, 1961; Roseville, California
Education: Lincoln High School, California; Brigham Young University
Occupation: Entrepreneur

Fuller made an unprecedented fourth Olympic team for 1992. No other U.S. wrestler has achieved that honor. A world junior champion in 1981, Fuller won the Pan-American gold medal in 1991. Unable to go to Moscow in 1980

because of the boycott, he placed eighth at Los Angeles and tenth at Seoul.

"Making my first Olympic team at age nineteen was a terrific experience," Fuller says. "It was a great honor to make the team and a grave disappointment to be a part of the 1980 boycott. My making the Olympic team was a big enough achievement in Lincoln, California. The community passed a resolution for 'Mark Fuller Day.'

"In making the 1992 Olympic team, I will become the first American wrestler to ever make four Olympic teams. But making four Olympic teams is not my ultimate goal. I had a dream as a very young man of being an Olympic champion. It is my belief that with the wonderful support of my wife, Heidi, my Father in Heaven, and others, this may become a reality."

Olympian: Kenth Roland Gardenkrans
Sport: Track and Field (discus)
Country: Sweden
Olympics: Moscow, 1980
Birth: October 2, 1955; Helsingborg, Sweden
Education: Brigham Young University
Occupation: Sales manager

Gardenkrans won an NCAA championship in the discus in 1978 while at Brigham Young University. He reached the Olympic final in the discus at the Moscow Olympic Games and placed twelfth.

Olympian: Richard Lloyd George
Sport: Track and Field (javelin)
Country: United States
Olympics: Montreal, 1976
Birth: May 22, 1953; Fillmore, Utah
Education: Millard High School, Utah;
  Brigham Young University; Harvard
  University
Occupation: Chief executive officer

A great all-around athlete in high
school, George received All-American
honors in football, basketball, and
track in high school. He was the U.S.
national champion in 1975 but did not
make the finals in the Montreal
Olympic Games in 1976.

"One of the highlights for me was to
actually compete against Janis Lusis,
one of the greatest javelin throwers in
history," George says. "When I was a
freshman in high school, I had a
frame-by-frame sequence on my
bedroom wall of Janis Lusis throwing
the javelin. He had won a complete set
of Olympic medals from three
successive Olympic Games. I had no
idea he would still be competing in
Montreal. He was one of the few
Russians who spoke English, so I was
able to get to know him quite well,
which was for me the fulfillment of a
boyhood dream.

"The games were spectacular, and it
was a great honor to represent the
United States. My performance,
however, was not what I would have
liked. In fact, it was one of my poorest
performances over the prior two years.
The disappointment of defeat,
knowing you are capable of far better,
was for me a difficult lesson learned at

the games. But it was also a valuable
insight to the fact that defeat is a
reality, not only of sports, but also of
life. The key is continuing to strive in
the face of defeat."

Olympian: George Howard Greenfield
Sport: Gymnastics
Country: United States
Olympics: Munich, 1972
Birth: May 5, 1948; Altadena,
  California
Education: John Muir High School,
  California; University of California,
  Berkeley; Brigham Young University
Occupation: Manager, aircraft
  electronics firm

After being an All-American at the
University of California at Berkeley
and a national team member from
1969 to 1972, Greenfield helped the
United States gymnastics team to a
tenth-place finish in Munich in 1972.

"At the close of the Mexico City
Olympics in 1968, when the scoreboard
changed to 'Munich 1972,' I made a
commitment to be there!" Greenfield
says.

Olympian: Lorna Joann Griffin
Sport: Track and Field (discus, shot
  put)
Country: United States
Olympics: Moscow, 1980; Los Angeles,
  1984
Birth: June 9, 1956; Hamilton,
  Montana
Education: Seattle Pacific University
Occupation: Massage therapist, track
  coach

Griffin is a former American record holder in the discus. She qualified for two Olympic Games, but did not compete in Moscow because of the boycott. In Los Angeles, she placed ninth in the shot put and thirteenth in the discus.

"My most memorable experience from the 1984 Olympic Games was the overwhelming support that our country showed towards the U.S. athletes," says Griffin. "I have only seen this happen with our country one other time in my life and that was during the Gulf War. Seeing our country gel together to support their athletes and put on a very successful Olympics is comparable to the support and national pride I saw our country give our soldiers in the Gulf War."

Olympian: Bo Gustafsson
Sport: Track and Field (50-kilometer walk)
Country: Sweden
Olympics: Moscow, 1980; Los Angeles, 1984; Seoul, 1988
Birth: September 29, 1954; Skee, Sweden
Education: Stromstad High School, Sweden; Goteborg University
Occupation: Business administration

A three-time Olympian, Gustafsson strolled to a silver medal in Los Angeles in the longest race on the Olympic schedule.

"Preparing for participation in the Olympic Games is a lot like preparing for life," Gustafsson says. "You learn how to meet problems and adapt in order to succeed. You learn how to

prepare yourself for achieving high goals in life."

Olympian: Silo Tansinga Havili
Sport: Boxing
Country: Tonga
Olympics: Los Angeles, 1984
Birth: September 14, 1963; Nua Cualofa, Tonga
Education: Tonga High School, Tonga
Occupation: Contractor

Havili lost his match on a decision to the eventual bronze medalist at Los Angeles. Summing up his perspective on the Olympic experience, he says, "The important thing in the Olympics is not to win but to participate."

Olympian: Walter Creed Haymond
Country: United States
Sport: Track and Field (200-meter dash)
Olympics: Antwerp, 1920
Birth: December 2, 1893; Springville, Utah
Education: Springville High School, Utah; University of Utah; University of Pennsylvania
Occupation: Dentist

Death: March 8, 1983, Salt Lake City, Utah

Besides winning the NCAA championship in the 100- and 200-meter dashes, Haymond set national and world records in the 220-yard dash. He was also the national high school champion in the 100-yard dash while attending high school. Haymond was injured and unable to participate in the Antwerp Olympic Games in 1920.

Olympian: Jackson Stewart Horsley
Sport: Swimming
Country: United States
Olympics: Mexico City, 1968
Birth: September 25, 1951; Salt Lake City, Utah
Education: Indiana University; University of Cincinnati Medical School
Occupation: Physician

In Mexico City in 1968, seventeen-year-old Horsley swam to a bronze medal in the 200-meter backstroke. He was also a world record holder in the 880-yard freestyle and set an American record in the 200-meter backstroke.

"There were several powerful events for me at the 1968 Olympic Games," Horsley says. "The most dramatic was the opening ceremonies. The teams assembled outside the stadium hours before, and each team marched into the stadium through a tunnel at the far end of the stadium. As our team emerged onto the field, I was overcome by the sight of eighty thousand people sitting together in peace. These people came from all over the world. I was seventeen at the time, and the feeling that world peace could be a reality has been in my heart since that day.

"The second event that had a long-lasting effect on my view of the world was meeting Leonid Lychev, one of the Russian swimmers. Before I met Leonid, I pictured Russians as looking like Klingons from *Star Trek.* They embodied all evil in my mind. Leonid was a few years older than I was and very human. The Russian swimmers wore cotton swimsuits and warm-ups. The suits were baggy and ill-fitting, and created much more drag for the swimmer in the water. Their warm-ups were not nearly as sleek as ours. The reason that their suits were cotton was because the Russian government considered nylon an evil, capitalistic substance to be avoided.

"The third event was meeting Mohammed Nassiri, an Iranian weight lifter who was the gold-medal winner in the bantamweight division. This event was on my mind often during the overthrow of the Shah of Iran and the subsequent events in Iran. I have always wondered if he survived the turmoil in his country.

"The fourth event was John Carlos and Tommy Smith holding up their black-gloved hands in silent protest of the treatment of black people in our country. It seemed very petty to send them home before the games were over."

Olympian: Kenneth Robert James

Sport: Basketball
Country: Australia
Olympics: Munich, 1972
Birth: January 19, 1945; Pennsylvania
Education: Evergreen High School,
Washington; Brigham Young
University; University of Washington
Dental School
Occupation: Dentist

A member of the Brigham Young
University basketball team, James
captained the Australian team in
Munich, where they finished eighth.
"Being Australian, we were always
the first team in the Olympic village,
as we came from the opposite
hemisphere and had to adjust to
climatic, hemispheric, and time
changes," James says. "Munich was
the Olympics at which the Israelis
were murdered, and we were all
locked up for two days, as there were
snipers out on the buildings. We were
glad we shared a building with the
Americans, as we figured if we needed
rescuing, the Yanks would do it."

Olympian: Dale Elizabeth McClements
Kephart
Sport: Gymnastics
Country: United States
Olympics: Tokyo, 1964
Birth: December 31, 1944; Winnipeg,
Manitoba, Canada
Education: University of Washington;
University of Nevada at Reno
Occupation: Teacher

Kephart won the 1962 All-Around in
gymnastics at the national
championship and went on to finish

thirty-fourth in the Olympic All-
Around in Tokyo in 1964. She was
chosen to be an Olympic coach in 1976
for the Montreal Games.
"The opening ceremonies were
exciting and made me feel proud to be
an American," says Kephart. "I felt
very patriotic. Meeting athletes from
all over the world, I developed
friendships and an understanding of
other countries. It made me realize
that people are really the same
everywhere.
"Competing was a thrill, and
[because of] the Olympics, I set higher
goals for myself for the future. I
learned from foreign athletes who
were at the top in my sport, and they
inspired me to go back into the gym to
attain higher goals."

Olympian: Canagasabi Kunalan
Sport: Track and Field (100- and 200-
meter dashes)
Country: Singapore
Olympics: Mexico City, 1968
Birth: October 23, 1942; Malaysia
Education: Loughborough University
of Technology, England
Occupation: Lecturer, School of
Physical Education, Nanyang
Technological University

Placing second in the Asian Games in
the 100-meter dash in 1966 and
winning gold medals in the Southeast
Asian Games in the 100- and 200-
meter dashes in 1969 (the same year
he joined the Church) were among the
highlights of Kunalan's career. His
track credentials were good enough to
earn him Singapore's Sportsman of the
Year awards in 1968 and 1969.
Kunalan reached the quarterfinals of
the 100-meter dash in Mexico City in
1968.

Olympian: B. Kenneth Lundmark
Sport: Track and Field (high jump)
Country: Sweden
Olympics: Mexico City, 1968
Birth: March 25, 1946; Skelleftea,
   Sweden
Education: GIH, Sweden; Brigham
   Young University
Occupation: Business management

While at Brigham Young University,
Lundmark won the NCAA
championship and the Swedish and
European championships.
   "We arrived in Mexico City four
weeks prior to the Olympics in order
to acclimate to the higher altitude,"
says Lundmark. "During this time we
trained, and at one of my practice
sessions I cleared 7'4". One of the
Australian coaches measured the bar
and leaked this result to the press.
Consequently, I became the immediate
favorite to win the gold medal.
Unfortunately, our team's early arrival
gave me time to catch the dreaded
'Montezuma's Revenge.' I became very
ill two weeks prior to competition and
did not fully recover until several
months after returning home to
Sweden."

Olympian: Scott Richard Maxwell

Sport: Baseball
Country: Canada
Olympics: Los Angeles, 1984
Birth: August 15, 1964; Lethbridge,
   Alberta, Canada
Education: High School
Occupation: Agent, airlines cargo /
   ramp

Maxwell comes from an athletic family.
His brother Bryan played eleven years
in the National Hockey League and
his brother Marty played three years
of professional baseball. Maxwell hit
.333 on a Canadian team that didn't
make the medal round of the
exhibition sport in Los Angeles.

Olympian: Laman Palma
Sport: Track and Field (marathon)
Country: Mexico
Olympics: Montreal, 1976
Birth: 1954; Chihuahua, Mexico
Education: Brigham Young University
Occupation: Schoolteacher

The first Mormon to participate in the
Olympic marathon, Palma was a top
cross-country runner for Brigham
Young University.

Olympian: Edward Sebastian
   Palubinskas
Sport: Basketball
Country: Australia
Olympics: Munich, 1972; Montreal,
   1976
Birth: September 17, 1950; Canberra,
   Australia
Education: Canberra Narrabundah
   High School, Australia; Ricks

College; Louisiana State University;
Brigham Young University
Occupation: Artist

Palubinskas was an Olympic scoring
machine, setting three records in the
Montreal Games in 1976 with an
average of 33.1 points per game. He
scored the most points in one game —
50 against Mexico — and had the most
points in Olympic tourney history with
269. He led his Australian team to an
eighth-place finish in 1972 and a
seventh-place finish in 1976.

Olympian: Viliami S. Pulu
Sport: Boxing
Country: Tonga
Olympics: Los Angeles, 1984
Birth: May 14, 1960; Kolonga,
Tongatapu, Tonga Island
Education: Liahona High School,
Tonga
Occupation: Truck driver

Pulu was one of the first Tongans to
compete in the Olympic Games. "Even
though I didn't get what I was aiming
for," he says, "I felt so good and
thankful because I did my best. I will
never forget the joy I felt and the
warm feeling I had on the day of the
opening ceremonies."

Olympian: Walter E. "Ed" Red
Sport: Track and Field (javelin)
Country: United States
Olympics: Tokyo, 1964
Birth: March 6, 1942; Kilgore, Texas
Education: Lafayette High School,
Louisiana; Rice University; Arizona
State University
Occupation: University professor

Louisiana's top prep athlete, Red
turned to track and field at Rice
University where he was a three-time
Southwest Conference champion in
the javelin. He qualified for the
Olympic team in Tokyo in 1964, then
qualified for the Olympic finals,
placing eleventh in his event. He is the
brother-in-law of Mormon Olympian
Richard George, track and field
specialist in the javelin.

Olympian: Jon Keith Russell
Sport: Diving
Country: United States
Olympics: Mexico City, 1968
Birth: January 15, 1948; Mesa, Arizona
Education: Brigham Young University
Occupation: Controller

Keith Russell just missed a bronze

medal in Mexico City, placing fourth in the 10-meter platform competition and sixth in the 3-meter event. Subsequent to the Olympic Games, Russell won a bronze medal in the 1973 world championship at the 3-meter event and the silver medal at the 10-meter event.

"To say I made it to the Olympics brings me a lot of satisfaction now as I grow older, because it marks achievement," says Russell. "It wasn't always so, because my goal was an Olympic gold medal. I had no other way of measuring my self-worth (so I thought) other than to become an Olympic champion.

"I dove poorly in the 3-meter diving event, but the 10-meter platform event came next. I dove very well, but missed a dive in the final three that cost me a medal."

Olympian: Timo Pekka Saarelainen
Sport: Basketball
Country: Finland
Olympics: Moscow, 1980; Los Angeles, 1984
Birth: August 23, 1960, Helsinki, Finland
Education: Brigham Young University
Occupation: Sales executive

Saarelainen was the leading scorer on the Finnish national team and the leading scorer during his senior year for the Brigham Young University Cougars. His Finnish Olympic teams were both eliminated in the preliminary rounds.

Olympian: M. Dale Schofield
Sport: Track and Field (400-meter hurdles)
Country: United States
Olympics: Berlin, 1936
Birth: April 14, 1915; Salt Lake City, Utah
Education: Beaver High School, Utah; Brigham Young University; University of Southern California
Occupation: School principal

While attending Brigham Young University, Schofield set a national record for the 200-meter low hurdles. At Berlin, he missed making the final of the 400-meter hurdles in a photo finish.

"Experiencing Germany during a period when Adolph Hitler was at its head was most interesting," says Schofield. "The German people were very friendly toward the Americans. However, the young people of the country were aloof and unfriendly. There was no fraternizing with the German athletes, and the Hitler Youth squads were indoctrinated Nazis of the first order.

"Many German families would come to the Olympic village and make every effort to visit or converse with the American athletes. I had taken two years of German in college so I was able to communicate a bit with a number of people who came to the Olympic village. It seemed to me that the majority of the German people were not anticipating the conflict that exploded in 1939. They appeared to be riding along in a state of happy wariness, pleased with the progressive things that Hitler had done for their country.

"In 1932, I enrolled at BYU with some money that had been left me by my father, who had passed away a year earlier. In the spring of 1933, when President Roosevelt declared a bank holiday, my bank never reopened, and I lost my college money. In the fall of 1933, I planned to stay in Beaver and look for some kind of work. Shortly after the fall term at BYU started, a friend and I had the chance to go to Salt Lake and return to Beaver. We happened to stop in Provo for a short time, and I decided to walk up to the BYU lower campus and say hello to Coach Ott Romney. When I told him why I wasn't in school, he immediately left his office, took me over to a corner lunch counter, and got me a job washing dishes for my board and room. He then escorted me to the registrar's office where he had me sign a note for my tuition. He looked me in the eye and said, 'Now get back to Beaver, pack some clothes, and get up here by tomorrow morning.'

"Since my track letter had been won the previous spring by scoring one point, I was surprised that a coach would take that much interest in me. That was Ott Romney, the greatest man I have ever known. Later, I did latch onto an athletic scholarship, and much, much later, I did get my sophomore tuition notes paid off. But without Ott Romney, there would have been no Olympic experience for me."

Olympian: James Cory Snyder

Sport: Baseball
Country: United States
Olympics: Los Angeles, 1984
Birth: November 11, 1962; Inglewood, California
Education: Canyon High School, California; Brigham Young University
Occupation: Professional baseball player

Snyder won All-American honors at Brigham Young University and has gone on to play with the Cleveland Indians, the Chicago White Sox, the Toronto Blue Jays, and the San Francisco Giants. His U.S. team won the silver medal in the 1984 Olympics when baseball was an exhibition sport.

He recalls some of the highlights of his Olympic experience: "Playing at Dodger Stadium in front of family and friends, running on to the field during the games, and the overwhelming feeling I felt when people chanted, 'USA, USA, USA.' "

Olympian: Usaia Naiteitei Sotutu
Sport: Track and Field (steeplechase, 5,000-meter run)
Country: Fiji
Olympics: Munich, 1972
Birth: September 20, 1948; Nubuyani, Lekutu, Fiji
Education: Bua Central School, Navuso, Agricultural College; Brigham Young University
Occupation: Mechanic, aircraft company

Sotutu, who holds virtually every distance record for Fiji, from the 800-

meter run to the marathon, was named Fiji Sportsman of the Year in 1969.

"I had no idea when I began running that the Lord was preparing me for a marvelous journey to the light of the gospel. Had it not been for my athletic endeavors, I would have never been awarded an athletic scholarship to Brigham Young University. It was at BYU, and through my track coaches and team mates, that I was introduced to the Church and joined in 1971. In 1972, Fiji invited me to participate on their two-man team in the Munich Olympics. I was honored to carry the flag of my country.

"The year 1973 took me back to my native land on a full-time mission. My athletic fame opened many doors, and I was privileged to baptize some of the current Church leaders in Fiji. In 1975, while I was still on my mission, President Spencer W. Kimball allowed me to travel to Guam to participate in the South Pacific Games. When I arrived there and was given the schedule, the preliminary for the race in which I was the record holder (the 1500-meters run) was scheduled for Sunday. I discussed my problem with my coach, who went back to the committee and was able to get the race changed. I subsequently won the gold medal, breaking my old record.

"Although I participated in an individual sport, I have always been cognizant of those I represent, such as the Lord, my country, and my team. This gave me the courage and determination to do what I did."

Olympian: Debbie Lee Stark-Hill

Sport: Gymnastics
Country: United States
Olympics: Munich, 1972
Birth: June 27, 1952; Reno, Nevada
Education: Wheatridge High School, Colorado; Utah Valley Community College; Brigham Young University
Occupation: Assistant teacher

After competing on the United States gymnastic team that won the world championship in 1970, Stark-Hill helped the U.S. women's gymnastics team to a fourth-place finish at the Olympic Games in Munich in 1972.

"I still draw strength and inspiration from my experience in gymnastics," she says.

Olympian: Saimoni Nabiri Tamani
Sport: Track and Field (400-meter race)
Country: Fiji
Olympics: Munich, 1972
Birth: November 17, 1943; Dari, Wainunu, Bua, Fiji Islands
Education: Brigham Young University
Occupation: Worker, paper mill

A bronze-medal winner in the 1970 Commonwealth Games in the 400-meter race, Tamani was inducted into the Fiji Sports Hall of Fame in 1991. He qualified for the Munich Games in 1972 but was injured and unable to compete.

Olympian: Troy Tanner
Sport: Volleyball
Country: United States
Olympics: Seoul, 1988
Birth: October 31, 1963; Whittier,
   California
Education: Los Altos High School,
   California; Pepperdine University
Occupation: Professional volleyball
   player

After leading Pepperdine University to
two NCAA volleyball championships in
1985 and 1986, Tanner became a
member of the 1988 U.S. Olympic
team that went on to win a gold medal
in Seoul.

"Unless you're there, you can't really
appreciate the feeling involved in the
Olympics," he says. "If you could
bottle that and keep it around, that
would be something."

Olympian: Phillip Norman Tollestrup
Sport: Basketball
Country: Canada
Olympics: Montreal, 1976
Birth: October 21, 1949; Raymond,
   Alberta, Canada
Education: Raymond High School,

Alberta, Canada; Brigham Young
University
Occupation: Teacher

Tollestrup had a fine career at
Brigham Young University and went
on to become the third leading scorer
in the Montreal Olympics, making the
All-Olympic team. His Canadian team
placed fourth.

"Just being there and playing against
some of the best players in the world
was the highlight of the Olympics for
me," he says."

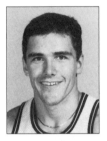

Olympian: David Turcotte
Sport: Basketball
Country: Canada
Olympics: Seoul, 1988; Barcelona, 1992
Birth: July 10, 1965; Ottawa, Canada
Education: Lockerby Composite High
   School, Ontario, Canada; Colorado
   State University; Brigham Young
   University Law School
Occupation: Law student

Turcotte had an outstanding career at
Colorado State University, graduating
as the number three all-time scorer.
He played on the sixth-place Canadian
team in 1988 and is a member of the
1992 team.

"I played in the '88 Olympics in
Seoul, and we placed sixth. I played in
the World Basketball League overseas
and as a free agent with the Indiana
Pacers. After the Pacers cut me, I
went to law school at BYU. While
there, I developed a close relationship
with some very special people who
introduced me to the Church by the
example of their lives. I was not very

approachable to a missionary and would have resented my friends if they had used our friendship as a conversion device. I watched them and reached my own conclusions.

"My interaction with faculty and friends resulted in my intense investigation of the Church. I liked what I found and was baptized by my Olympic team roommate and friend, Karl Tilleman. He was a great example to me—helped me then and helps me now."

Olympian: Tauna Kay Vandeweghe-
  Mullackey
Sport: Swimming, Volleyball
Country: United States
Olympics: Montreal, 1976 (swimming);
  Los Angeles, 1984 (volleyball)
Birth: February 7, 1960; Green Valley,
  California
Education: Pacific Palisades High
  School, California; University of
  California, Los Angeles; University
  of Southern California
Occupation: Sports broadcaster,
  motivational speaker

Vandeweghe is a member of a family of great athletes. Her brother Kiki plays for the New York Knicks in the National Basketball Association; her father, Ernie, played for the Knicks; her mother, Colleen, was a national swimming record holder; and other siblings have been successful athletes as well. She has the distinction of making two Olympic teams in two different sports. As a swimmer, she set an American and Olympic record in the 100-meter backstroke and placed

seventh in the Montreal Games. As a volleyball player, she was part of a team that won the silver medal in Los Angeles in 1984.

"The highlight for me was at the 1976 games," she says. "After setting the American and Olympic record for the 100-meter backstroke, my father, who was an All-American in three sports at Colgate University and an NBA star for the New York Knicks while going through medical school, said to me, 'You've done what I've always dreamed of doing—competing in the Olympics.' That meant more to me than any medal or record."

Olympian: Arnold Vitarbo
Sport: Shooting (free pistol)
Country: United States
Olympics: Mexico City, 1968
Birth: January 31, 1936; Bronx, New
  York
Education: University of Hawaii
Occupation: Custom gun-stock maker,
  Olympic shooting coach

Vitarbo missed a bronze medal in the Mexico City Olympics by a single point in the free-pistol competition. As a member of the United States Air Force, Vitarbo competed for another seventeen years after the Olympics, setting national records in the free pistol. He is now an Olympic shooting coach.

"To compete in this event was a thrill indeed. However, I have been able to remain active in the sport as a competitor, as well as using my experiences to coach the current Olympic shooting aspirants."

"By living here in Colorado Springs, Colorado, and working at the Olympic Training Center, I am constantly amazed at the dedication necessary by not just the shooting team, but by all the athletes who train here. One cannot attain the level of the Olympics without lots of sacrifices in time and money and, in many cases, careers."

Olympian: Daniel L. Vranes
Sport: Basketball
Country: United States
Olympics: Moscow, 1980
Birth: October 29, 1958; Salt Lake City, Utah
Education: Skyline High School, Utah; University of Utah
Occupation: Professional basketball player

Vranes earned All-American honors at the University of Utah, and in 1981 he was the fifth player selected in the National Basketball Association draft. He has played for the Seattle Supersonics, the Philadelphia 76ers, and in Europe. Because of the boycott by the United States, Vranes was deprived of competing in the Moscow Olympics in 1980.

"Nineteen eighty was the year President Jimmy Carter and the U.S. boycotted the summer Olympics," says Vranes. "It was a major disappointment and injustice for all the Olympic athletes — not so much for the basketball team, since most of the members were All-Americans and soon to be NBA first-round draft choices. Our main goals and dreams were to play in the NBA. It was the

other athletes who had trained so hard, and to them the Olympic Games were to be the pinnacle — the epitome of their athletic careers — and it all got flushed down the toilet because of political interference.

"The 1980 U.S. basketball team toured the United States instead of competing in Moscow, and we played six games against NBA All-Star teams. We won five games and lost one.

"Then, the U.S. Olympic Committee gathered all the teams from every sport, [brought them] to Washington, D. C., and basically rolled out the red carpet for each of us and a guest. For one week we were treated like kings. We had dinners at the White House; personal tours of the city and monuments; parties with the president, senators, and congressmen.

"It was all very impressive, but when they had a special ceremony at the end of the week to honor the athletes again, they gave each of us an imitation gold medal. It was then, and even more so as the years go by, that you realize that nothing could replace the opportunity to play in a real Olympics and win a real gold medal."

Olympian: Jack Yerman
Sport: Track and Field (400-meter race)
Country: United States
Olympics: Rome, 1960
Birth: February 5, 1939; Oroville, California
Education: Woodland High School, California; University of California, Berkeley; Stanford University

Occupation: Teacher

The winner of the 1960 Olympic Trials in the 400-meter race, an injured Yerman did not make the finals of the Olympic 400 meters, but came back to run the lead-off leg on the 4x400-meter team that won the gold medal and set a world record in the heats. Yerman also held world records indoors in the 400- and 600-meter races. An outstanding athlete, he also played halfback for the University of California, Berkeley in the 1959 Rose Bowl game.

"There are some things that have a similar high to the feeling at the gold-medal presentation," says Yerman. "It's a combination of what you feel at the birth of your first son, graduation, getting married, and coming home after years of absence.

"I'm sure a Russian or an African has a similar feeling when his flag rises into the air. There is a bond that seems to exist between the crowd and the athlete at the moment the flag goes up and your national anthem is played. This bond is as if everyone, for a brief moment, is a member of the nation of mankind.

"The actual competition of the athlete has to be the most memorable experience. I still have vivid images of the competition, the crowds, and each race. Being in the Olympics brought a lot of us together in a lifelong bond of friendship."

Olympian: Wayne Robert Young
Sport: Gymnastics

Country: United States
Olympics: Montreal, 1976
Birth: March 1, 1952; Westwood, California
Education: Brigham Young University; University of Utah Medical School
Occupation: Physician

Following his NCAA All-Around championship in 1975 while at Brigham Young University, Young captained the Olympic gymnastics team at Montreal where he placed twelfth in the All-Around, the best performance by an American.

Olympian: Walter Ward Zobell, Jr.
Sport: International Trapshooting (clay pigeon)
Country: United States
Olympics: Los Angeles, 1984
Birth: April 21, 1950; Provo, Utah
Education: Dillon High School, Montana; Brigham Young University; Montana State University
Occupation: Rancher

Zobell, a two-time winner of the U.S. Clay Pigeon Shooting Tryouts in 1974 and 1979, was also a part of two world team records, winning four gold medals and one bronze medal in world competition.

"I finished twenty-fifth out of a possible seventy-one," Zobell says. "Perhaps this finish made me feel many times that I really wasn't there. It was an honor to represent my country, but I really feel that I was capable of a better performance than that."

ROSTER OF
MORMON OLYMPIANS

Afele, Uati
Arrhenius, Anders Hilding
Bell, Charles "Wade"
Bergeson, James Hunter
Caceres, Pedro
Carmona, Roberto
Cosic, Kresimir
Cummings, Paul
Dalbey, Troy
Detweiler, Robert
Evans, Michael S.
Eyestone, Edward
Fale, Tualau
Fernholm, Bengt Stefan
Fonoimoana-Moore, Lelei Alofa
Fuller, Mark Albert
Gardenkrans, Kenth Roland
George, Richard Lloyd
Greenfield, George Howard
Griffin, Lorna Joann
Gustafsson, Bo
Havili, Silo Tansinga
Haymond, Walter Creed
Horsley, Jackson Stewart
James, Kenneth Robert
Kephart, Dale Elizabeth McClements
Kunalan, Canagasabi
Lambert, Jay
Lesiva, Viliamu
Lundmark, B. Kenneth
Marsh, Henry
Maxwell, Scott Richard

Naea, Aomua
Padilla, Doug
Palma, Laman
Palubinskas, Edward Sebastian
Pope, Paula Jean Myers
Pulu, Viliami S.
Red, Walter E. "Ed"
Richards, Alma W.
Robison, Clarence
Russell, Jon Keith
Saarelainen, Timo Pekka
Sani, Fime
Schofield, M. Dale
Silvester, L. Jay
Snyder, James Cory
Solovi, Fred
Sotutu, Usaia Naiteitei
Stark-Hill, Debbie Lee
Talia'uli, Sione
Tamani, Saimoni Nabiri
Tanner, Troy
Tilleman, Karl
Tollestrup, Phillip Norman
Turcotte, David
Vaka, Palako
Vandeweghe-Mullackey, Tauna Kay
Vidmar, Peter
Viero, Allesandra
Vitarbo, Arnold
Vranes, Daniel L.
Yerman, Jack
Young, Wayne Robert
Zobell, Walter Ward, Jr.

MORMON OLYMPIC
MEDALISTS AND PARTICIPANTS

OLYMPICS	NAME	GOLD	SILVER	BRONZE
1912	ALMA RICHARDS	1		
1920	CREED HAYMOND			
1936	DALE SCHOFIELD			
1948	JAY LAMBERT CLARENCE ROBISON			
1952	ROBERT DETWEILER PAULA MYERS POPE	1	1	
1956	PAULA MYERS POPE			1
1960	PAULA MYERS POPE JACK YERMAN	1	2	
1964	DALE KEPHART ED RED L. JAY SILVESTER			
1968	WADE BELL ROBERT CARMONA KRESIMER COSIC JACKSON HORSLEY CANAGASABI KUNALON KENNETH LUNDMARK KIETH RUSSELL L. JAY SILVESTER ARNOLD VITARBO		1	1
1972	ANDERS ARRHENIUS KRESIMIR COSIC GEORGE GREENFIELD DEBBIE STARK HILL KENNETH JAMES CANAGASABI KUNALON EDDIE PALUBINSKAS L. JAY SILVESTER USAIA SOTUTU SAIMONI TAMANI		1	1
1976	KRESIMIR COSIC LELEI FONOIMOANA RICHARD GEORGE HENRY MARSH LAMEN PALMA EDDIE PALUBINSKAS		1	

OLYMPICS	NAME	GOLD	SILVER	BRONZE
1976	L. JAY SILVESTER			
	PHIL TOLLESTRUP			
	TAUNA VANDEWEGHE			
	ALLESANDRA VIERO			
	WAYNE YOUNG			
1980	KRESIMIR COSIC	1		
	MARK FULLER			
	KENTH GARDENKRANS			
	HENRY MARSH			
	TIMO SAARELAINEN			
	PETER VIDMAR			
	DANNY VRANES			
1984	PEDRO CACERES			
	PAUL CUMMINGS			
	TEFAN FERNHOLM			
	MARK FULLER			
	LORNA GRIFFIN			
	BO GUSTAFSSON		1	
	SILO HAVILI			
	HENRY MARSH			
	SCOTT MAXWELL			
	DOUG PADILLA			
	VILIAMI PULU			
	TIMO SAARELAINEN			
	FIME SANI			
	CORY SNYDER		1	
	KARL TILLEMAN			
	TAUNA VANDEWEGHE		1	
	PETER VIDMAR	2	1	
	WALT ZOBELL			
1988	UATI AFELE			
	JAMES BERGESON		1	
	TROY DALBEY	2		
	MIKE EVANS		1	
	ED EYSTONE			
	TUALAU FALE			
	MARK FULLER			
	BO GUSTAFSSON			
	VILIAMU LESIVA			
	HENRY MARSH			
	ASOMUA NAEA			
	DOUG PADILLA			
	FRED SOLOVI			
	SIONE TALI'ULI			
	TROY TANNER	1		
	KARL TILLEMAN			
		9	12	3

256

INDEX